Teaching Argument Writing, Grades 6–12

Teaching Argument Writing, Grades 6–12

Supporting Claims with Relevant Evidence and Clear Reasoning

George Hillocks, Jr.

Foreword by Michael W. Smith

HEINEMANN
Portsmouth, NH

Heinemann
361 Hanover Street
Portsmouth, NH 03801–3912
www.heinemann.com

Offices and agents throughout the world

The author and publisher wish to thank those who have generously given permission to reprint borrowed material:

Cartoon from *Crime and Puzzlement 2: More Solve-Them-Yourself Picture Mysteries* by Lawrence Treat, illustrations by Kathleen Borowick. Copyright ©1982 by Lawrence Treat, illustrations by Kathleen Borowick. Reprinted by permission of David R. Godine, Publisher, Inc.

Cartoon from *Crime and Puzzlement: 24 Solve-Them-Yourself Picture Mysteries* by Lawrence Treat, illustrations by Leslie Cabarga. Copyright © 1981 by Lawrence Treat, illustrations by Paul Karasik. Reprinted by permission of David R. Godine, Publisher, Inc.

Cartoon from *The Case of the Dead Musician* puzzle by Marc Furigay. Reprinted by permission of the author.

University of California, Santa Cruz *Banana Slug* logo. Used by permission of the University.

Freeport High School *Pretzels* logo. Used by permission of the Freeport School District, Freeport, Illinois.

"Teaching Argument for Critical Thinking and Writing: An Introduction" by George Hillocks, Jr., originally appeared in the *English Journal*, Vol. 99, No. 6, July 2010. Copyright © 2010 by the National Council of Teachers of English. Used by permission of the publisher.

Library of Congress Cataloging-in-Publication Data
Hillocks, George.
    Teaching argument writing, grades 6–12 : supporting claims with relevant evidence and clear reasoning / George Hillocks, Jr. ; foreword by Michael W. Smith.
        p. cm.
    Includes bibliographical references and index.
    ISBN-13: 978-0-325-01396-1
    ISBN-10: 0-325-01396-9
    1. English language—Rhetoric.   2. English language—Grammar.   3. Persuasion (Rhetoric).   4. Report writing.   I. Title.
    PE1417.H495 2011
    808'.0420712—dc22   2011001313

Editor: Lisa Luedeke
Production editor: Sonja S. Chapman
Typesetter: Cape Cod Compositors, Inc.
Cover and interior designs: Palmer Creative Group
Manufacturing: Steve Bernier

Printed in the United States of America on acid-free paper
15 14 13 12   VP   5

In memory of

Larry R. Johannessen

1947–2009

Excellent student, colleague, and friend

Contents

Foreword by Michael Smith   ix
Acknowledgments   xiii
Preface: Teaching Argument for Critical Thinking   xv
Introduction: Planning for Powerful Learning   1

PART I: Teaching the Basics of Argument Writing   13

1   Whodunit? Solving Mysteries to Teach Simple Arguments of Fact   15

2   What Makes a Good Mascot—or a Good Leader? Teaching Simple Arguments of Judgment   41

3   Solving Problems Kids Care About: Writing Simple Arguments of Policy   67

PART II: Teaching Students to Write More Complex Arguments   99

4   How Are Judgments Made in the Real World?   101

5   Answering Difficult Questions: Learning to Make Judgments Based on Criteria   113

6   What Is Courage? Developing and Supporting Criteria for Arguments of Judgment   144

7   Argument and Interpretation: Teaching Students How to Make Literary Judgments   177

Appendix A: Definitions of Murder in the United States   201
References   209
Study Guide for *Teaching Argument Writing*   215
Index   223

Contents

Foreword

By Michael Smith

LET ME START WITH A CONFESSION. I STARTED WORKING WITH George Hillocks thirty-six years ago. (Yikes!) He has been by far the most powerful influence on my thinking and teaching for all of those years. You know in cartoons sometimes how a character is pictured with a miniature self standing on his or her shoulder and acting as a conscience? I don't have a miniature version of myself standing on my shoulder. No, my teaching conscience has always been George. He's been whispering in my ear the whole time, even when I've wanted him to shut up.

George's genius as a teacher is his ability to create contexts that push his students to do more serious and significant work than they thought possible—and to take pleasure in the doing. I remember how, week after week, after a three-hour seminar my fellow master's students and I would stand in the hall continuing the discussion of a problem George had posed, unwilling to give up our conversation. I've thought long and hard about how he did it. George is not a flashy teacher. He doesn't dress up in costumes and give passionate and eloquent lectures. He doesn't lecture at all. What he does is think about the questions most worth asking, develop activities to encourage his students to grapple with those questions, and then listen hard and respectfully to the results of his students' grappling. I've come to think that that respect is at the heart of George's teaching. He listens to his students harder and better than anyone I know. I've experienced how much of an incentive it is to come up with something worth listening to.

And what's especially amazing is that George's model of instruction works not only with graduate students at the University of Chicago but also with the middle and high school students George continued to teach throughout his entire career as a university professor. We see those kids in this book. We see their deep engagement in high-level thinking. We see the passion that they bring to their writing. We see just how much fun those kids and their teachers (George included) must have had working together on such complex and engaging problems. As I read, I was carried along with George's carefully observed narration of classroom vignettes. As I read, I witnessed the intellectual growth of the students in a way that resembles how I experience the growth of a character in a riveting short story.

Ironically, the strength of the narratives is the cause of my only real worry about the book. I fear that the pull of the stories is so strong that readers may think, "How could it be otherwise?" But the truth is, it is otherwise in most writing classrooms around the country. So I want to highlight what I see as the four central components of George's radical educational agenda, an agenda that I hope will be more fully realized because of the power of this book.

Perhaps most significantly, this book displays the power of what George (1986) has called *environmental* instruction, that is, a kind of instruction in which the students, teacher, and curricular materials are equally important as instructional resources. It seems to me that discussion of literacy education often features critiques of teacher-centered instruction. George himself cites foundational research that demonstrates that in so many classrooms students are bored and apathetic observers of their teachers' activity. What's offered up in its stead is student-centered instruction. George has been a champion for students for his whole career, but as he clearly establishes in this book, simply providing the opportunity for student activity is not enough. Students must be supported in taking on their central role by teachers who systematically analyze their students' needs, who carefully articulate specific goals so students can reflect on their success in achieving them, and who devise engaging and carefully sequenced instructional materials that both teach students crucial procedural knowledge and reward them for employing that knowledge in meaningful social activity.

Another commonplace aspect in contemporary discussions of teaching writing is that the only way for a student to learn to write is to write. And indeed, in the classrooms that George portrays in this book students do plenty of writing. But what those portrayals also make clear is that students can learn to write by talking together while working through problems that provide rehearsals for the kind of thinking they will have to do when they are composing. The importance of this insight is hard to overstate, especially in the urban contexts in which George has done so much of his work. It has always baffled me to read findings of the National Assessment of Educational Progress that say that American adolescents can't argue effectively. Have they ever spent any time with adolescents, I've wondered. They're arguing all the time. What George clearly demonstrates in this book is that that ability to talk can be—no *must* be—a crucially important resource teachers deploy in service of students' academic writing. Over the years I've heard many teachers say, "My kids can't write." I have yet to hear a teacher say, "My kids can't talk." What that means is we have no excuse. If our kids can't write, it's on us, for they bring to our classes their incredibly valuable experience as effective talkers. What we need to do is make good use of it.

If kids are to be engaged in their writing, they have to write what they care about. I think George would agree. The way that this idea most often plays out is through exhortations to let kids choose their topics and through suggestions that personal narratives hold the most promise for fostering interest. If you've read George's latest book (2006), you know how deeply he cares about narratives. I think he'd agree that kids enjoy writing about their lives. But what this book proves is that teachers can create interest. That is, students do not have to be interested in a topic before one begins to teach it. Instead George believes that we can foster students' interest through our teaching. That's important because it allows teachers to engage students in flow experiences in the present even as they are preparing students do the kind of writing they need to do to be successful on future high-stakes tests and academic assignments.

Finally, as I read, I was struck by the length of the engagements students had with a particular kind of argument. When I taught high school, I taught a senior writing class whose curriculum focused on describing a process in week one, writing a personal narrative in week two, writing a comparison/contrast paper in week three, and so on and so on. I don't think that my experience is too far from the norm even today, except in the amount of writing the course required students to do. How many schools require students to do a single research paper, for example? What we see in this book is what happens when students get extended practice in doing particular kinds of thinking and writing. I can't think of a single time in my life when I've learned something complex in a single go-round. I've been playing tennis for nearly fifty years and I still double-fault too darn often.

Remember when I said that George has been standing on my shoulder for the last thirty-six years whispering into my ear? This is what he's been saying: "Have you thought hard enough, Michael, about just what you want your students to do? Have you collected enough data to help you understand them and to reflect on your teaching? Have you written activities that engage them in doing the particular kinds of thinking they'll need to do when they write? Are you listening to them hard enough? Are you having fun together? Have you given them enough practice?'

And this is what I hope: that your reading this book will cause him to whisper in your ear as well.

Acknowledgments

THE IDEAS IN THIS BOOK HAVE BEEN DEVELOPING FOR NEARLY fifty years, since I first tried to teach argument to my seventh and ninth graders in Euclid, Ohio, in 1958. At that point, I concentrated on supporting generalizations with concrete evidence. My classes and I worked out definitions of what we were working on (courage, justice, the hero, satire, comedy, tragedy, and so forth). I worked on helping my students to use these definitions in support of their contentions that a character was not courageous or was indeed just, or that a work was or was not satiric or tragic. At the time, I did not realize how important definitions were in the support of arguments of judgment.

When I moved to the University of Chicago, I worked on putting together sets of data from which students could draw conclusions and the support for them. Some of these were sets of texts or pictures, some were sets of statistics, and some were combinations of all of these. One set, for example, consisted of a set of profiles of murders during a single week in Chicago that included the ages, occupations, and educational status of both killers and victims along with addresses of the murders, the time of day, and the apparent motives. It turned out to be a good tool for helping students learn to examine a set of data about which they were to write before developing the famous thesis statement that so many teachers demand without preparing students for the task. A number of such data sets appear in this book, many of which were brought to my attention by my Master of Arts in Teaching English (MAT) students at the University of Chicago. One of the best of these was brought to my attention by Elizabeth Kahn and Larry Johannessen, "Slip or Trip," which plays a prominent role in Chapter One.

I did not have a good grasp of argument until Michael W. Smith introduced me to Stephen Toulmin's book, *The Uses of Argument* (1958). It was a great fit with what I was already trying to do, and more importantly it filled out several gaps in my little, underdeveloped theory of argument. My work with my MAT students and our mutual work with many high school students enabled me to enrich that theory so that I can bring together Toulmin's theory, Aristotelian theory from *The Art of Rhetoric*, and even the theory of Socratic reasoning into a unified whole, a unification that has made our teaching of argument much more productive and robust.

I owe a very deep debt of gratitude to all of the MAT students who helped in these processes and to all of our middle and high school students who helped us to learn from our mistakes and our successes. Without the latter, we would be no farther ahead in this effort. I am particularly grateful to those who have helped spread the ideas involved in this book: Seth MacLowry, Sherri Koeppen, Thomas McCann, Jenni Roloff, Kiersten Thompson, Sarah Spachman, Marc Furigay, Sarah Ruth Levine, and Tim Pappageorge. In addition, I owe a very special note of thanks to Vera Wallace for her patience and forbearance during the writing of this book, for her help in presenting several workshops based on the material herein, and for her charm and good cheer even when I do not deserve it.

Thanks also to the editors at Heinemann for their help in producing this book, particularly to Lisa Luedeke, who signed the project and helped to shape it from the beginning.

Preface

Teaching Argument for Critical Thinking

> *"Literacy education lies at the center of achieving our stated goals of fostering critical thought, critical dialogue, and a circumspect and vigilant American citizenry . . . [and] has particular value and potential in a culture increasingly unable to distinguish fact from fiction, truth from lies."*
>
> —Alsup et al. 2006, 281

THIS BOOK IS ABOUT THE TEACHING OF ARGUMENT, THE CORE of critical thinking. Argument is not simply a dispute, as when people disagree with one another or yell at each other. Argument is about making a case in support of a claim in everyday affairs—in science, in policy making, in courtrooms, and so forth. As such, this book is intended for teachers at any level who wish to help students become critical thinkers.

The activities in this book, designed for middle and high school students, will help enable students to write strong arguments, but they will also help students *evaluate* the arguments of others, arguments they hear every day—a skill critical to participating in a democratic society. The activities have been used in diverse classrooms, including high-poverty inner-city schools in Chicago, where the students were fully engaged in the process, as demonstrated in the pages of this book. When they are through, students will be able, as the Common Core Anchor Standards ask, to "Delineate and evaluate [an] argument and specific claims . . . including the validity of the reasoning [and] the relevance and sufficiency of the evidence."

Aristotle divides substantive arguments into three kinds: *forensic*, *epideictic*, and *deliberative*. I have found it useful to designate these as arguments of **fact**, **judgment**, and **policy** and approach them in that order, moving students from the simpler to the more complex. If we begin with arguments of fact, as I do in this book, students will be able to use the knowledge they already possess to derive warrants and to use the evidence they perceive to develop basic arguments about the facts of a case. In this way, they will learn the structure of arguments in general and how to draw conclusions that are defensible.

This book deals with simple arguments of **fact** in Chapter One, simple arguments of **judgment** in Chapter Two, and simple arguments of **policy** in Chapter Three. In the various activities, students solve murder mysteries, consider what makes a good leader, and work through the process of trying to solve a school-related problem that matters to them.

In Part Two of the book, we turn to more complex arguments. In Chapter Four, I discuss arguments of judgment and policy in which warrants usually must be defended explicitly. This chapter explains the relationships of warrants and backing in various areas in some detail and gives you the background you will need to teach the chapters that follow.

Chapters Five through Seven deal with how to teach students these more complex arguments. I do this through laying out step-by-step activities that ask students to consider high-interest questions such as, *What is murder?* and *What is courage?* The final chapter lays out teaching students how to make literary judgments.

Because the skills taught in the activities build upon one another, chapter by chapter, I suggest you teach the activities and the chapters in the order in which they are presented.

What Is the Difference between Persuasive Writing and Writing Argument?

The most advanced secondary textbooks for English do not teach students to think critically or to write argument. Rather, they opt for vague discussions of "persuasive writing." One significant text of over 1,100 pages devotes 45 pages to persuasive writing and only 1.5 pages to "logical appeals" (Kinneavy and Warriner 1993), which are the essence of argument. Kinneavy and Warriner tell us that "In a persuasive essay, you can select the most favorable evidence, appeal to emotions, and use style to persuade your readers. Your single purpose is to be convincing" (305). The same might be said of propaganda and advertising. Argument, on the other hand, is mainly about logical appeals and involves claims, evidence, warrants, backing, and rebuttals, terms I'll explain in more detail later. Argument is at the heart of critical thinking and academic discourse; it is the kind of writing students need to know for success in college and in life—the kind of writing that the Common Core State Standards puts first. (See National Governors' Association.)

> *"In a persuasive essay, you can select the most favorable evidence, appeal to emotions, and use style to persuade your readers. Your single purpose is to be convincing. The same might be said of propaganda and advertising."*

What Students Need to Know for Success in College

Those of us who know the needs of college writers and who are familiar with the new ACT and SAT writing samples know that persuasive writing will not suffice. For college and career one needs to know how to make an effective case, to make a good argument. Gerald Graff was recently cited in *Education Week* as giving the following advice to college students: "Recognize that knowing a lot of stuff won't do you much good," he wrote, "unless you can do something with what you know by turning it into an argument."

In 2009, the National Governor's Association Center for Best Practices and the Council of Chief State School Officers put a document on the Internet titled *College and Career Ready: Standards for Reading, Writing, and Communication*. It says this of writing argument:

> The ability to frame and defend an argument is particularly important to students' readiness for college and careers. The goal of making an argument is to convince an audience of the rightness of the claims being made using logical reasoning and relevant

evidence. In some cases, a student will make an argument to gain access to college or to a job, laying out their qualifications or experience. In college, a student might defend an interpretation of a work of literature or of history and, in the workplace, an employee might write to recommend a course of action. Students must frame the debate over a claim, presenting the evidence for the argument and acknowledging and addressing its limitations. This approach allows readers to test the veracity of the claims being made and the reasoning being offered in their defense. (p. 2B)

This statement has been adopted in the Common Core Standards which, at this writing have been adopted by more than 39 states and the District of Columbia. This book is about paying heed to these calls for attending to critical thinking and argument.

What Kind of Logic Can We Teach?

There is currently a widespread notion that we cannot know anything with certainty. Given this, the question we must ask is: What can count as logic in arguments? If argument demands logic, and if we are going to teach it, then we must have an answer.

The kind of logic taught in schools since the time of Aristotle and through the early twentieth century focuses on the syllogism, thought to be the most important, if not the only path to truth (See Aristotle 2007).

"What can count as logic in arguments?"

The syllogism derives a conclusion from a set of statements called premises, which are thought to be true and which have a common term in each. For example,

Major premise:	All men are mortal.
Minor premise:	Socrates is a man.
Conclusion:	Therefore, Socrates is mortal.

In most disciplines (with the exceptions of mathematics and sometimes physics) and in most everyday problems and disputes, we do not have premises that we know to be absolutely true. We have to deal with statements that may be true or that we believe are probably true—but not *absolutely* true.

Even Aristotle recognized that the syllogism was not appropriate for the problems that he saw being debated in the senate and elsewhere. These were arguments of probability, arguments that were not amenable to syllogistic reasoning. His response to that problem was his *Rhetoric* (1991), the work long recognized as one of the most important texts in the subject that deals with arguments of *probability* of three kinds: forensic, epideictic, and deliberative, or, as noted earlier, what I like to call arguments of **fact**, **judgment**, and **policy**.

In the past two or three decades, colleges and universities have turned to a newer treatment of arguments of probability, that by Stephen Toulmin in *The Uses of Argument*.

The Elements of Argument

Toulmin's basic conception of argument includes several elements:

» a **claim**
» based on **evidence** of some sort
» a **warrant** that explains **how the evidence supports the claim**
» **backing** supporting the warrants
» **qualifications** and **rebuttals** or counter arguments that refute competing claims.

Figure P.1 provides a representation of these elements and their relationships.

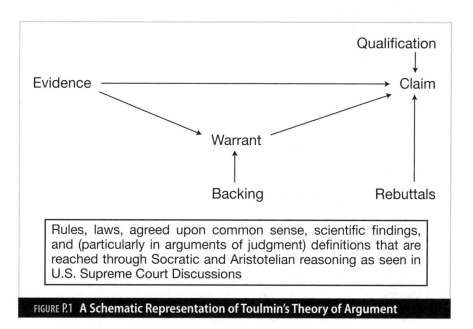

Qualification

Evidence → Claim

Warrant

Backing   Rebuttals

Rules, laws, agreed upon common sense, scientific findings, and (particularly in arguments of judgment) definitions that are reached through Socratic and Aristotelian reasoning as seen in U.S. Supreme Court Discussions

FIGURE P.1 **A Schematic Representation of Toulmin's Theory of Argument**

Claims

Every day we are inundated in electronic and print media with claims about products and what they can do for us, how they can make us happy, healthy, attractive, productive, or popular. Almost without exception, these are never substantiated. Yet we are being asked to spend our earnings to obtain the product purported to make us happy or productive. And people do spend, usually without questioning the claims.

In my experience and in my research, teenagers, including college freshmen, see no reason to question or substantiate claims in any context. In testing situations, the prompts for persuasive essays usually call explicitly for support. For example, the 1993–94 Texas writing assessment offered the following prompt for its "persuasive task":

> Some people believe that all teenagers should be required to perform one year of unpaid service for their community right after they graduate from high school. This community service might include helping to clean up parks, delivering food to the elderly, or working in a hospital.
>
> What is your position concerning this issue? Write a letter to your senator in which you state your position and support it with convincing reasons. Be sure to explain your reasons fully. (Texas Education Agency 1993, G5)

The students had as much time as they wished during a school day to respond.

Here is a response that the scoring guide included as an example of "passing level":

> As a teenager about to graduate from high school, I think it is rather unfair to do these services without being paid for it. Therefore, I believe we shouldn't have to do these services right when we get out of high school.
>
> First of all, when people graduate from high school, a majority of the people will either go to a junior college or college. During the summer break, most of them will get jobs to help pay for college. Another reason is, it takes money to drive around town and do these services.

"In my experience and in my research, teenagers see no reason to question or substantiate claims in any context."

Personally, I think you all should use all of the unemployed people that receive unemployment checks because they're the ones that have nothing to do.

These are the reasons why I think we shouldn't have to do these services. (G14a)

This response is made up entirely of claims. The first and second sentences are the governing claims of the argument. The second paragraph provides two reasons in support of the main claims, but both are sub-claims that remain unsubstantiated. What evidence, for example, is there that a "majority of people will either go to a junior college or college"? The third paragraph states an alternative to the drafting of teenagers, but it too is unsubstantiated.

Here's the scoring guide's commentary on the paper:

This controlled, organized response takes a clear position against requiring community service. The section discussing the necessity of working for pay is somewhat elaborated while the solution adds elaboration by offering a ready alternative (the unemployed) to employing high school graduates. In total, a *minimally sufficient amount of evidence is provided*, and the response demonstrates minimal success with the persuasive task. (G14a, italics added)

This commentary suggests that the test makers do not know what constitutes evidence any more than our youngsters do. In fact, there was no evidence presented at all. (For details on state writing assessments and their impact, see Hillocks 2002.)

Evidence

Although many teachers begin to teach some version of argument with the writing of a thesis statement (a claim), in reality, good argument begins with looking at the *data* that is likely to become the *evidence* in an argument and which gives rise to a thesis statement or major claim. That is, the thesis statement arises from a question, which in turn rises from the examination of information or data of some sort.

This year, I had an opportunity to examine a set of lesson plans that began with the writing of thesis statements. There was no mention of data of any kind. Students were supposed to find problems somewhere and make some claim about them. However, without analysis of any data (verbal and nonverbal texts, materials, surveys and samples), any thesis is likely to be no more than a preconception or assumption or clichéd popular belief that is unwarranted and, at worst, totally indefensible.

For that reason, my graduate students and I have approached the teaching of argument from the examination of data, as a first step. We have tried to find data sets that require some interpretation and give rise to questions. When the data are curious and do not fit preconceptions, they give rise to questions and genuine thinking. Attempts to answer these questions become hypotheses, possible future thesis statements that we may eventually write about after further investigation. That is to say, *the process of working through an argument is the process of inquiry*. At its very beginning is the examination of data, not the invention of a thesis statement in a vacuum.

Data sets do not have to be dry or boring to adolescents. In Chapter Three in this book, students conduct their own research into a schoolwide problem involving chewing gum stuck to school furniture and come up with their own data to support an argument that a school policy be changed. They had chosen the problem to research and were thoroughly engaged in the process of accumulating and examining their data.

Once we have examined data to produce a question and have re-examined the data to try to produce an answer to the question, we may have a claim or thesis worthy of arguing. If the data support our answer to the question, it becomes evidence in support of the claim we make. Laid out step by step, it looks like this:

1. Examine data
2. Ask questions based on data
3. Reexamine data
4. Try to answer the questions
5. Data that supports our answer = Evidence

Evidence, to be useful, must be relevant and verifiable. In some disciplines and fields of work, such as science and criminal justice, special procedures must be followed so that evidence will not be impeached. But basic to any kind of argument is the verifiability of the evidence. A literary critic must cite the works discussed and quote from the texts to prove a claim. A historian must carefully note the artifactual or documentary evidence basic

"In reality, a good argument begins with looking at the data that is likely to become the evidence in an argument."

"When the data are curious and do not fit preconceptions, they give rise to questions and genuine thinking."

to the argument being made. A scientist must explain the nature of observations or experiments, the collection of data, the conditions, so that the study can be replicated.

Occasionally, our readers or listeners are willing to simply accept our data as appropriate support for our answers to the question posed, but, more often, especially in serious arguments, readers will want explanations of *why* the data we produce support the claims we make and are trying to demonstrate. This is the job of the warrant.

"The process of working through an argument is the process of inquiry."

Warrants

Warrants may be simply common sense rules that people accept as generally true, laws, scientific principles or studies, and thoughtfully argued definitions. In contemporary crime scene investigation programs on TV, considerable time is devoted to establishing warrants. Most viewers of such programs are likely to be fully aware, for example, that fingerprints at a crime scene may lead to an arrest of the person to whom those prints belong because any given person's prints are unique, and therefore indicate the presence of that person at the scene.

Similarly, we also know that pistols and rifles leave distinctive markings on bullets fired from them. Thus, a bullet found in a victim or at a crime scene may become the evidence that links a gun owner to the shooting of the gun and the commission of the related crime. The prints and the markings on bullets are the evidence that indicate the identity of perpetrators by way of warrants concerning their uniqueness.

As an activity for teaching Chicago high school students to write argument, Marc Furigay, one of my students at the University of Chicago, invented a problem scenario including a sketch of a dead man's body hanging from a chandelier, his feet dangling a distance above a stool on which the dead man had presumably stood before hanging himself. The sketch is accompanied by a note explaining the man's reasons for committing suicide. Students were encouraged to examine the evidence of the sketch and the note to determine what had occurred.

"In contemporary crime scene investigation programs on TV, considerable time is devoted to establishing warrants."

In Chapter One, I have simplified this scenario a bit. As you will see, when students began their discussion in small groups, they attended to the note and seemed to examine the picture only cursorily. Before long, however, one boy proclaimed to his group that it could not be a case of suicide.

"Look where his feet are," he explained. "If he hanged himself, his feet would've been below the top of the stool. They're not. They're way above it." The young man had hit upon an important warrant. He explained it as follows. "When a person hangs himself, he has to drop from some height so that the noose will tighten and strangle him. See, look where his feet are, a couple of feet above the stool. He couldn't have jumped up, fastened the rope, put the noose around his neck, and hung himself." These were statements of evidence and a warrant that the class could accept.

Backing

Anyone familiar with the criminal investigation programs on TV will know that warrants may be challenged. In Toulmin's terms, the backing is the support for the warrants. In the case of fingerprints and ballistics, there have been many studies that can be cited in the support of the warrants as to the uniqueness of fingerprints and bullet markings. However, in the TV shows themselves, sometimes considerable time is devoted to developing the backing for warrants. One frequently visited kind of backing in one program has to do with studies of the development of beetles in corpses. This is used as the backing for warrants for assertions or claims concerning the length of time a corpse has been dead. Sometimes we see the criminalist studying the development of beetles from larva to adult to establish a time line for the development of the insect through its various stages. This study will be the backing for the warrant for claims about how long a corpse has been deceased.

When serious arguments of **judgment** are challenged, the warrants will likely need to be backed by extended definitions of the abstract qualities involved. For example, my own studies have shown that students have widely diverse ideas of what constitutes courageous action. Boys tend to believe that bank robbers are acting courageously when they try to rob a heavily guarded bank; most girls tend to think they are not. Some believe that just putting on a fireman's uniform and going to a fire is a courageous act; others believe that the determination of courage depends on the dangers a fire presents. The warrant in such arguments will be backed by some criterion based on an extended definition of the nature of courageous action. In Chapter Six, I show how to teach students how to develop this kind of criteria.

Arguments of **policy** involve warrants about what is permissible and appropriate in certain circumstances. These also involve extended definitions as backing. For example, court cases often turn on definitions of the principles underlying the right to freedom of speech or the right to privacy.

In more complex arguments of judgment and policy, the most crucial arguments pertain to the warrants and their backing. Platonic dialogues often deal with the backing for warrants. For example, in the *Euthyphro*, Socrates questions Euthyphro concerning his claim that he is justified in prosecuting his own father for the death of a slave. The United States Supreme Court's discussions of cases are debates about the warrants used in lower court cases that have been appealed. In *Harris v. Scott*, for example, the argument concerns whether a police officer may use lethal force to stop a driver doing on average 90 mph on a two-lane road and crossing the double yellow line even in the face of on-coming traffic. Harris claimed that the officer's ramming of his car was a violation of his Fourth Amendment right protecting him against unjust seizure. Arguments over backing underlie the most important principles of our democracy.

"The United States Supreme Court's debates are about the warrants used in lower court cases."

Qualifications and Counter Arguments

In addition, because these are arguments of probability, two other elements are necessary: qualifications and counter arguments. Simply because we are dealing with statements that cannot be demonstrated to be absolutely true, qualifications are necessary in stating both claims and warrants. For claims, I like to encourage the use of words such as *probably, very likely, almost certainly*, and so forth. Some instructors refer to these as *hedge terms*. But they are not.

Because arguments deal with probabilities, they must be *qualified*. Medical, agricultural, educational, and social science research use statistical procedures to determine the probabilities of a certain claim's being true in fairly precise terms. When statistical procedures are not appropriate or possible, the qualifications take the form of statements such as *probably, in all likelihood, as a rule, beyond reasonable doubt*, and so forth.

"Because arguments deal with probabilities, they must be qualified."

The very idea that we are dealing with arguments of probability suggests that differing claims are likely to exist. For example, for over a hundred years, available evidence has shown that the teaching of traditional school grammar does not contribute to increasing the quality of student writing (see Braddock et al., 1963; Hillocks 1984; and Graham and Perin 2007). Despite what I regard as massive evidence, many teachers and writers continue to argue for the teaching of traditional school grammar, the teaching of the parts of speech, parts of sentences, and concepts of grammar such as gerunds, appositives, and introductory adverbial clauses through the exercises presented in grammar books such as Kinneavy and Warriner (1993). If I wished to make an argument as to the folly of teaching grammar again, I would have to make a counter argument. Because arguments deal with probabilities, they must be *qualified*.

In the course of this book, you will find a series of activities that students find highly engaging, activities that will teach them to understand the elements of argument and how to use them to make effective substantive arguments of their own. In the course of this work, they will also learn to identify a sound argument when they hear one—and how to be thoughtfully skeptical when they hear one that is *not*. These are skills that are essential in college, to be sure, but they are also essential if we are to educate students to become productive citizens in a civil society.

Introduction

Planning for Powerful Learning

THE MOST COMPLEX QUESTION I HAVE EVER TRIED TO ANSWER has been with me for more than fifty years. Since the early sixties, I have been trying to capture in words what I mean by *effective teaching*, the kind of teaching in which students learn to do, with support, what they cannot do or do not already do by themselves, the kind of teaching in which students learn happily, willingly, even enthusiastically.

Under these conditions, when students reach a particular point in their learning, they want to learn more because it is fun and rewarding and makes them feel good about themselves. Learning becomes an adventure, something to look forward to every day. And the teacher looks forward to class, even to reading student work, because it is fun to see what progress students have made. Even when the progress is far less than the teacher hoped—indeed, even when the failure to learn reaches catastrophic proportions—she knows what the goals are and can think about the difficulties students are having and how to overcome them. The difficulties are never insurmountable. They only require some hard thinking, persistent questioning, and creative imagining, perhaps over a period of many hours or even days, before they are solved and learning moves back to its happy state.

Reading over what I have just written, I recognize that I have missed once again. I have described what good teaching feels like to students and teachers, but I have failed to pinpoint its essence. Those reading what I have written will not be able to put such teaching into action, especially with a topic so complex as teaching critical thinking and argument. Worse, many will jump to the conclusion that good teaching is simply a matter of ensuring that students have a good time in the classroom. Perhaps that's preferable to ensuring that they are completely bored out of their skulls, as so many research reports indicate they are most of the time in American schools (Csikszentmihalyi and Larson 1984; Goodlad 1984; Nystrand 1997; Hillocks 1971, 1999). Nevertheless, having a good time does not necessarily result in learning anything meaningful. Kids can have a good time talking about what happened last night.

My notion of a good time in learning is inherent in the joy of learning how to do something successfully and then using those skills to accomplish something new. People take pride in that. When youngsters learn to play a new game, they are usually delighted with themselves. But when the game becomes too easy, they lose interest and move on to other things. A few weeks ago, my fourteen-year-old grandson and I played chess. In each of three games, he checkmated me in seven or eight moves (at least it seemed that few to me). Of his own accord, he showed me his attack, how it worked, and how I should defend against it. Rather than play against me again, he suggested I play against his six-year-old brother. Clearly I was not enough challenge to make the game enjoyable. It's fun to demolish Grandpa once or twice; after that, not so much.

> *"My notion of a good time in learning is inherent in the joy of learning how to do something successfully and then using those skills to accomplish something new."*

Experiencing the Flow

Psychologist Mihaly Csikszentmihalyi (1990) calls the kind of experience I am talking about *flow* or *optimal experience*. Experience like this is based not on simple fleeting pleasure but on more complex enjoyment. Csikszentmihalyi explains that pleasurable experiences such as "sleep, rest, food, and sex provide restorative, *homeostatic* experiences that return consciousness to order after the needs of the body intrude and cause psychic entropy to occur. But they do not produce psychological growth. They do not add complexity to the self" (46). Enjoyable experience, however, is characterized by a sense of moving forward or beyond what one might expect of oneself. "After an enjoyable event we know that we have changed, that our self has grown: in some respect, we have become more complex as a result of it" (46).

Here is Csikszentmihalyi's description of flow experience, which is based on thousands of interviews with and questionnaires completed by people in many widely diverse cultures, in relation to activities ranging from motorcycling to mainstream scientific research to meditation:

> When people reflect on how it feels when their experience is most positive, they mention at least one, and often all, of the following. First, the experience usually occurs when we confront tasks we have a chance of completing. Second, we must be able to concentrate on what we are doing. Third and fourth, the concentration is usually possible because the task undertaken has clear goals and provides immediate feedback. Fifth, one acts with a deep but effortless involvement that removes from awareness the worries and frustrations of everyday life. Sixth, enjoyable experiences allow people to exercise a sense of control over their actions. Seventh, concern for the self disappears, yet paradoxically the sense of self emerges stronger after the flow experience is over. Finally, the sense of the duration of time is altered; hours pass by in minutes, and minutes can stretch out to seem like hours. The combination of all these elements causes a sense of deep enjoyment that is so rewarding people feel that expending a great deal of energy is worthwhile simply to be able to feel it. (49)

In the midst of such experience, one loses track of time and other responsibilities, even certain needs. It is as though everything else disappears from the radar of our conscious state. Most of us have experienced these feelings on at least some occasions.

Flow Among Adolescents

To study flow as it is experienced by adolescents, Csikszentmihalyi and his colleague Larson (1984) conducted research with high school students. In

"Csikszentmihalyi (1990) calls the kind of experience I am talking about flow or optimal experience. Experience like this is based not on simple fleeting pleasure but on more complex enjoyment."

"Enjoyable experience is characterized by a sense of moving forward or beyond what one might expect of oneself."

one study, seventy-five students in the same school carried beepers for a week. During that week, they were beeped randomly, eight to ten times a day. When beeped, they wrote about where they were, what they were doing, and what they were thinking. They also rated their emotional state on semantic differential scales (for example, alert to drowsy, happy to sad, active to passive).

Positive ends of the scales represented flow experience and negative ends indicated the opposite. An examination of over 4,600 student responses revealed that class time in school was largely entropic, time when individuals felt passive, bored, sad, disaffected, and generally wished they were doing something else. In activities such as sports, music, and art, students reported much more often that they felt active, interested, happy, and pleased to be doing what they were doing. The researchers also found relatively high motivation in academic arenas on the few occasions when students were taking part in group work or discussion.

The authors conclude that "schools are essentially machines for providing negative feedback. They are supposed to reduce deviance, to constrain the behavior and the minds of adolescents within straight and narrow channels" (198–99). For the most part schools, especially in academic areas, do not provide flow experience, the kind that results in high levels of pleasure, confidence, and absorption in the tasks at hand. These results are confirmed by the many other studies that show schools to be places in which students are surrounded by deserts of ennui.

Learning and Flow

Is it possible for critical thinking to become an experience students want to engage in and look forward to? Can we plan activities that have flow characteristics? To answer these questions, it helps to separate the characteristics of flow experience into two categories (see Figure I.1). Items 1–4 and 6 in the figure have to do with the circumstances of the experience, its character and nature. The remaining items describe its effects once it is underway. As teachers, we can control items 1–4 and 6 in fairly direct ways, with the hope that if these characteristics are in place, they will create the conditions that generate the remaining three items. For example, a sense of control is the product of appropriate activity, clear objectives, feedback, and the freedom to act, a freedom that only teachers can ensure is present.

FIGURE I.1 **Csikszentmihalyi's Characteristics of Flow Experience**

1. The experience usually occurs when we confront tasks we have a chance of completing.
2. We must be able to concentrate on what we are doing.
3. Concentration is usually possible because the task undertaken has clear goals.
4. Concentration is usually possible because the task provides immediate feedback.
5. We act with a deep but effortless involvement that removes from awareness the worries and frustrations of everyday life.
6. The experience allows us to exercise a sense of control over our actions.
7. Concern for the self disappears, yet paradoxically the sense of self emerges stronger after the flow experience is over.
8. The sense of the duration of time is altered; hours pass by in minutes, and minutes can stretch out to seem like hours.

Planning for Active Engagement and Flow

Below is a list of things we can do to increase the likelihood that students will be actively engaged and experience flow:

1. Choose activities that allow participants to exercise some *control*.
2. Select tasks that have *clear goals* and objectives.
3. Select tasks that students can concentrate on because they are *appropriately complex* for their present abilities. (Problem selection is crucial, and I'll talk more about that later.)
4. Select tasks that *provide clear feedback*.
5. Plan learning experiences around tasks that our students have a chance of completing in the time available.

Following, I will discuss the first four in more detail.

"A sense of control is the product of appropriate activity, clear objectives, feedback, and the freedom to act, a freedom that only teachers can ensure is present."

A Sense of Competence and Control

Study after study has shown that teachers typically constrain their students' freedom to act by talking most of the time available for instruction (Csikszentmihalyi and Larson 1984; Goodlad 1984; Nystrand 1997; Hillocks

1971, 1989, 1999). When teachers talk, student experience is necessarily limited to listening or daydreaming, or simply messing around. Csikszentmihalyi's idea of flow experience is clearly related to far more active experience than the passivity of listening to a teacher talk. The experience for optimal learning and flow must be active, most of the time. Students are not simply engaged in learning information to be recalled on some test or other, they are engaged in learning *how* to do things, *how* to write an essay, *how* to make an analysis, *how* to make an argument, and so forth. When students learn how to *do* something, it provides them a sense of competence and control.

Clarity and Specificity of Goals and Objectives

Clear goals are fundamental to a flow experience. When goals are unclear or very general, too many attempts miss the mark. Too much energy is wasted on unsuccessful moves. Feedback to students is likely to be obscure and unhelpful, perhaps not even to the point. Teachers will be unlikely to rethink their instruction to produce better results. Poorly conceptualized objectives undermine the entire process of teaching and lead to poor learning or nonlearning.

In the community of English education professionals, there is little agreement about the nature and utility of clear objectives. Some renowned writers of books on teaching English virtually ignore objectives, suggest vague objectives, and even warn of the dire consequences of having clear objectives. When objectives do appear, they tend to be general statements of tasks students will do in class. They describe how class time may be spent, not what students will learn how to do.

» Students will write a persuasive essay about a school problem of concern to them.
» Students will explore the imagery of "Stopping by Woods on a Snowy Evening."
» The class will discuss the various conflicts that Trueson faces in *Light in the Forest.*
» Students will study the meanings of twenty vocabulary words.
» Students will write an essay analyzing Mark Antony's funeral speech over Caesar's body.

These objectives are all either assignments or stipulations of how class time will be spent. They do not stipulate what students are to learn.

Furthermore, they do not indicate how the learnings, whatever they are, will be assessed. Consider the final objective, "Students will write an essay analyzing Mark Antony's funeral speech." My guess is that this is either an assignment or a test item for students after they have read the speech alone or in the classroom.

More importantly, we need to ask *what instruction prepared students to make the required analysis of Antony's speech*. If the instruction simply involved some classroom talk about the speech, talk that supplied some analysis, then the objective is merely about recall. Can the students remember what the teacher said about the speech and how it uses irony to undercut Brutus as an "honourable man"? Such objectives are not conducive to flow experience. They offer no opportunity to learn how *to do* something new.

If, on the other hand, the objective is really concerned about how to interpret irony, then it might be phrased differently:

> Given an *unfamiliar passage*, such as Mark Antony's speech at Caesar's funeral, students will write an essay identifying the uses of irony and interpreting its impact on the meaning of the passage.

This objective requires a totally different instructional sequence. The passage that students must analyze for the assessment will be unfamiliar. It cannot be used to prepare students for the assessment. Rather, other passages also employing irony will be used to prepare students for this task. The focus will be not on remembering the teacher's interpretation of a passage but on learning how to interpret irony.

The sequence might begin with cartoons that use irony to make their point. A cartoon that I used many years ago depicted a beach with waves rolling in the background. In the foreground stood a line of rubbish bins stretching into the distance with signs that read "Keep our beaches beautiful." The students had no difficulty recognizing the incongruence of the ugliness of the bins contrasted to their message. From this, we moved to more complex cartoons and then to simple texts using irony to make a point that was not expressly stated (see Booth 1974). The teaching moved from teacher-led discussion in which students learned to recognize contrasts between uses of language that signal ironic intent and speculation on meaning to small-group discussions of more complex texts with reports on their findings to the class to independent reading and analysis.

"These objectives are all either assignments or stipulations of how class time will be spent. They do not stipulate what students are to learn."

"How will what we do
in class today help
students become
more expert in
dealing with specific
tasks tomorrow?"

Shaping objectives in this way demands a reconceptualization of teaching and even the curriculum. Neither can be any longer simply a matter of covering topics or works and making assignments and hoping that some of it rubs off on students. It becomes necessary to ask, *How will what we do in class today help students become more expert in dealing with specific tasks tomorrow?* When students write an essay or a narrative, they use whatever skills they have available to write it. When they read a story or poem, they use whatever skills they have to interpret it. Skill levels do not change by osmosis or magic. Some new learning has to intervene. That new learning is not likely to occur just because the teacher hopes it will. It must be specified and planned.

This book is about how to plan for the learning necessary to write effective arguments independently. Accordingly, the objectives for the sets of lessons will be of the following type. This one is for arguments of fact (Chapter One):

> After independently examining a set of data concerning a certain problem, students will write an argument about what the facts of the matter are. The argument must provide a claim with support including four to five pieces of evidence, warrants explaining how the evidence supports the claim and is relevant, qualifications about the limitations of the claim and warrants, and counter arguments dealing with possible opposing views.

This objective includes criteria for judging what will count as an effective argument and implying what the instruction must include: work on evidence, warrants, qualifications, and so forth.

Appropriate Task Complexity

For us to develop learning activities that may produce the flow experience, we need to have clear goals. At the same time, we need to realize that the goals for neophytes must be simpler than the goals for more experienced writers or the problems to which they are applied must be simpler. Thus, it is simpler to find the evidence in "The Lunchroom Murder" sketch (see Chapter One) than in a complex literary text (see Chapter Seven). However, gaining expertise in any area requires beginning with problems that are manageable for the learner. As neophytes become more and more experienced, we need to raise the complexity of the problems. There are examples of manageable problems with clear goals for students to address in every chapter in this book.

Providing Clear Feedback

I recently observed a teacher who had her inner-city ninth graders write a description of a favorite place. Her goals, she said, were to help students write more elaborately and in greater detail. She showed me their efforts, with her comments written at the top of the first page. Typical comments included "word choice," "sentence structure," "usage," "spelling," and "commas," with no elaboration. The teacher explained that the terms identified the writer's problem areas and were reminders of what they needed to be careful about in their future writing. That these terse lists of words had any beneficial effect on the writing of these inner-city students is highly unlikely. They only reminded students of their lack of competence.

The complexity of the problem, the clarity of the objectives, and the expertise of participants are all related to useful feedback. Experts and experienced participants will understand and respond to feedback better than neophytes still learning what feedback is. The characteristics of flow listed by Csikszentmihalyi are described by people who have experienced flow. By definition, they have some level of expertise ("effortless involvement" and "control over their actions"). In learning situations, if we are working with neophytes, we need to focus our feedback on no more than two or three related dimensions of the task at a time and emphasize what the learners have done well.

Rather than remind our students of their lack of competence, we need to ask them to be experts, even at the beginning of learning something new, reporting their thinking to the class and challenging one another's interpretations and conclusions. Obviously, they are experts on their own thinking. It's never important that our students' interpretations agree with ours, only that they provide evidence and warrants that support their claims. Our feedback should focus on the presence of evidence and warrants, not on the correctness of their interpretation.

Last year, I received an email from a student who had been in my ninth-grade class in 1963 and had recently attended his high school class reunion. He wrote, "When we got together at our fortieth high school reunion

"Gaining expertise in any area requires beginning with problems that are manageable for the learner."

"That these terse lists of words had any beneficial effect on the writing of these inner-city students is highly unlikely. They only reminded students of their lack of competence."

"In learning situations, if we are working with neophytes, we need to focus our feedback on no more than two or three related dimensions of the task at a time and emphasize what the learners have done well."

last month, many of us discovered that the common thread of great experiences seemed to center around our time at Euclid Central Junior High School, and particularly focused on our time with you in ninth grade." I recall that class as delightful. Students were energetic, committed, and willing to engage one another and me in vigorous debate.

I remember one day in particular. Small groups were interpreting *The Old Man and the Sea*, having earlier discussed whether many relatively simple fables, stories, and poems were literal, allegorical, symbolic, or surrealistic. They were the experts. Rick (the young man who wrote me the email) was his group's spokesperson. At the beginning of the hour, he stood confidently before the class and argued articulately that the novel was allegorical. One young man in his audience promptly asked that if the novel were allegorical, what did the beach symbolize? Rick promptly responded that the beach symbolized purgatory. More than forty years later, he recalled that he "thought of that response then and there." The rest of the class had their own ideas about the imagery of the beach, and purgatory was not among them. They peppered him with questions and challenges. But he supported his position with interpretations of specific objects Hemingway includes in the description, the members of his group coming to his aid. The talk was dense, and I hardly said a word. Before I realized it, our seventy-four-minute class had ended.

Although the interpretation was bizarre, the students had met the goals of the class. They made, questioned, and defended interpretations of imagery in a relatively complex literary work. Moreover, they seemed to enjoy it immensely. Arriving at some "correct" interpretation was not important. They were much like the boys Smith and Wilhelm describe in *Going with the Flow* (2006):

> The boys in our study . . . wanted to solve problems, debate, and argue in ways through which they could stake their identity and develop both ideas and functional tools that they could use and immediately share with others. They wanted to develop the competence and capacities of experts. They wanted to be readied to do real work in the world, not just "do school." (57)

Discussion is key to the flow, and that day, the boys and girls in my class were in it. People were listening to what they had to say and responding to their ideas—perhaps the most important feedback for literacy learning.* They were not passive recipients but rather highly engaged participants. Forty years later, Rick recalled those discussions as "exhilarating." I could not ask for more.

*If you want to establish lively discussion in your classroom so that students can experience flow, the best book I know to help you is *Talking in Class* by McCann, Johannessen, Kahn, and Flanagan (2006).

PART 1

○─○─○─○─○─○─○─○─○─○─○─○

Teaching the Basics of Argument Writing

"Flow experience is clearly related to far more active experience than listening to a teacher talk. . . . Students are not simply engaged in learning information to be recalled on some test or other; they are engaged in learning how to do things."

Whodunit?

Solving Mysteries to Teach Simple Arguments of Fact

IT'S CLEAR TO ME FROM OBSERVING STUDENT WRITING IN various contexts that although adolescents may intend to write an argument, they often see no need to present evidence or show why it is relevant; they merely express (usually vague) opinions. Indeed, state writing tests and National Assessment of Educational Progress prompts seem to encourage writing that does not attend to evidence or show how the evidence relates to claims (Hillocks 2002).

However, the Common Core Standards (www.corestandards.org ELA Writing, Grade 6, no page) state that students, beginning in middle school, should be able to "Write arguments to support claims with clear reasons and *relevant evidence*" (emphasis mine). The high school standards expect students to be able to do this as well. I have found that if I use problems, in this case whodunit mysteries, I can encourage students to begin with the evidence and use it to determine what claims they can legitimately make in an argument.

In my inquiry approach to instruction (Hillocks 1984, 1995, 2007), my graduate students and I use the Toulmin model to help students learn to develop arguments from existing data. To do this, we begin with a specific problem—a crime that needs to be solved—that contains data about which claims may be made and for which warrants may be developed. We believe that by starting with a problem, students learn the strategies for making arguments:

» analyzing evidence critically in light of existing knowledge
» interpreting the evidence to explain what it shows
» developing warrants that show why the evidence is relevant
» using the evidence and the explanations to solve the problem

Recently, over a period of seven weeks, I presented a unit on forensic argument to a class of twenty-six ninth graders, six of whom were labeled learning disabled. Twenty-one were Latino/a, four were African American, four were white (one with Polish as her first language), and one was Asian (with Mandarin as her first language). I began with a forensic problem.

Introducing the Problem

It's the first day of real instruction (after a couple of days of pretests to determine what students already know and can do). I distribute the picture in Figure 1.1, which immediately captures the students' interest, and say, "We are investigators trying to determine what really happened at this crime scene." I read the following aloud while they examine the picture.

"Slip or Trip?"

At five-feet-six and a hundred and ten pounds, Queenie Volupides was a sight to behold and to clasp. When she tore out of the house after a tiff with her husband, Arthur, she went to the country club where there was a party going on.

She left the club shortly before one in the morning and invited a few friends to follow her home and have one more drink. They got to the Volupides house about ten minutes after

FIGURE 1.1 **"Slip or Trip?"**

Queenie, who met them at the door and said, "Something terrible happened. Arthur slipped and fell on the stairs. He was coming down for another drink—he still had the glass in his hand—and I think he's dead. Oh, my God—what shall I do?

The autopsy conducted later concluded that Arthur had died from a wound on the head and confirmed that he'd been drunk.

Then I say, "We need to try to determine what happened. Our first question should be, 'Can we believe what Queenie says?' Most of you have learned, from watching various crime shows, that witnesses are not always reliable. What do you think? Is what you see in the picture consistent with what Queenie says? If you have any ideas, raise your hand."

Paper rustles and chairs squeak as students bend over their copy of the picture. Projected on the overhead is a transparency divided into two columns, the left column labeled *evidence*, the right, *rule*. Some kids are whispering to each other, but I can tell it is about the picture because they are pointing to it. After no more than fifteen seconds, Marisol has her hand in the air. I wait for a few more seconds. Soon Jorge and William have their hands in the air as well. Then Isobel and Lucita. I call on Marisol.

"He's still got the glass in his hand. I mean, if you fell, you would drop the glass, wouldn't you?"

"Well, I'm not sure. What do the rest of you think?"

Jorge doesn't wait to be called on. "Yeah, you drop stuff when you fall, except maybe like a football when you get tackled."

Dantonio says, "Yeah, but that a special thing. You drop the ball, everybody hate you. But the glass ain't important. You drop the glass to save you ass." The class laughs. (I let it go. Dantonio is supposedly learning disabled, and I am pleased he's contributed. Besides, I laughed at his comment myself.)

Isobel responds, "It depends on what you're carryin'. I was carryin' my baby sister once, and I tripped, but I dint drop her. I tried to keep her from hittin' the floor."

Dantonio agrees. "That what I sayin'. It depend on how important what you carryin'."

"Okay, how many of you think that the fact that Arthur still has a glass in his hand is important evidence?" Nearly all hands go up. In the left-hand column, under *evidence*, I write, *Arthur still has a glass in his hand*. "Now, can someone explain why that is important?"

Almost immediately, Marisol's hand is up. I point to her. "It's important because if you fall down stairs and die, you're gonna drop the glass. That's obvious." I write Marisol's response under *rule*.

Evidence	Rule
Arthur still has a glass in his hand.	

"Do we only drop glasses?" I ask. "Or does it apply to other things?"

Again, Dantonio jumps in. "If it be important, you hold on, like a football. But if it ain't nothin', you probably drop it to save youself."

"Does everyone agree with that?" Most heads nod in agreement. "Let's see if we can make that into a general rule. We can work with what Marisol said earlier and with what Dantonio just said. Take a minute to think about how to say it and write down a version of the rule." I look around the room. Some students are trying to write something. Some are looking puzzled. A couple of students are staring off into space, perhaps thinking, perhaps not. I wait several more seconds. "Try to write something."

Several students begin to write. I walk about the room, encouraging everyone to write something. I tell Dantonio to use what he just said to the class. I suggest that Maria begin with the word *when* and write a sentence explaining what happens when people fall down the stairs. Most students write a sentence or two, but all of them use second person, as they have done in the preceding discussion. Later I will explain how to make the rule third person so that it is more general.

I call for volunteers.

Barbara raises her hand. "When you fall down the stairs, you drop what you're carrying unless it's really important."

"Very good," I say and write Barbara's sentence on the transparency. I call for other sentences and several students read theirs, all more or less like Barbara's. I add Gladys' and Roberto's sentences to the chart. "Let me summarize what we know so far. Arthur still has a glass in his hand. We know that when people fall down the stairs, they probably drop what they are carrying to save themselves. What can we conclude from that?"

The students are silent. Do they know what I mean by *conclude*? I try again. "What do you make of Queenie's story now?"

Marisol and five more students have their hands up. I call on Victoria.

"I think she's lying."

"What do the rest of you think?"

Dantonio says, "Yeah, she lyin'—probably."

"Why did you add *probably*?"

"'Cause we don't know for sure. But it sure looks like she lyin'."

"That's a very important point. The arguments we will be talking about are all arguments of probability. That simply means that we can be only fairly certain of our claims. That is why we call such statements *claims*—because we are claiming they are true." I know this point will have to come up many times for it to be clear. But Dantonio has put the class on the road to understanding.

Next I point to the statements of rules on the overhead. "Let's look again at these sentences from Barbara, Gladys, and Roberto. These sentences

> **"I suggest that Maria begin with the word when and write a sentence explaining what happens when people fall down the stairs."**

> **"All students use second person, as they have done in the preceding discussion. Later I will explain how to make the rule third person so that it is more general."**

> **"The arguments we will be talking about are all arguments of probability. That simply means that we can be only fairly certain of our claims."**

are important because they explain the evidence and show how it supports our claim that Queenie is probably lying. In writing them, there are a couple of things I would like you to do. First, if I say *you*, to whom does that apply? About whom am I speaking?"

Roscoe, a boy in the back, raises his hand. "You talking to us."

"Right. Now does this general rule apply only to people in this room?" There is a chorus of, "No."

"So how can we make it more general?" Silence.

Just as I decide not to play guessing games, Marisol raises her hand. "You could say, like, um, like we already did, 'When people fall down stairs, they probably drop what they're carrying if it's not important.'"

"Good. That makes the statement a little bit more formal and more generally applicable. Now I want to suggest another way to indicate that this is *probably* the case. What you have stated in that sentence is a general rule that most of us agree with, right? So we can say it that way. *As a rule, when people fall down stairs, they drop what they are carrying to save themselves.*" I write the sentence on the overhead opposite *Arthur still has a glass in his hand.* "I would like us to refer to statements like this as rules or general rules." I underline the *rule* label over the left-hand column on the overhead. "Now, who can put this whole argument together?"

Several hands go up. I call on Roberto, who is so eager he looks as though he might fall out of his seat. "Um, Arthur still has a glass in his hand. As a rule, when people fall down stairs, they drop what they are carrying to save themselves. So I think Queenie is probably lying about him falling down the stairs."

On a clean overhead transparency, I write what Roberto has said, each sentence in a separate column (see Figure 1.2). "Good. What we have here are four basic parts of a simple argument." I label the sentences *evidence*, *rule*, and *conclusion*; I underline *probably* and beneath the line I write *probably = qualification*. "I think you all have the basic idea of argument. But let's try it again. Who has another piece of evidence to talk about? What else do you see that leads you to think Queenie might be lying?"

There are a lot of hands in the air. I call on students who have not contributed already.

Desiree says, "There is something cooking on the stove."

FIGURE 1.2 **Basic Argument**		
Evidence	**Rule**	**Conclusion**
Arthur still has a glass in his hand.	As a rule, when people fall down stairs, they drop what they are carrying to save themselves.	Queenie is <u>probably</u> lying about his falling down the stairs. probably = qualification

I write it down on the overhead, although I will avoid dealing with it. From past experience I know it leads to all kinds of speculations, none of which can be verified. Students usually want to make the case that Arthur was going up the stairs; that Queenie hit Arthur on the head with the frying pan, thus explaining the position of his body; and that she put the pan on the stove to warm hors d'oeuvres and burn off any evidence of skin and hair that could be traced to Arthur. I want to hold off such arguments until we have established that Queenie is lying.

Other hands are still up. Oscar says, "Arthur's clothes are all neat. If you fall down stairs, your clothes get messy."

As I write down Oscar's suggestion, Rebecca says, "He's lying on his back with his face up. If he fell down the stairs, wouldn't he be facedown?"

"Those are all good suggestions, and you'll work with them in your groups in a minute. For now, let's work with Oscar's suggestion. He gave us a first draft of a rule as well as a piece of evidence. So what do you think about that? When people fall down the stairs do their clothes get messy?" All the students seem to agree. "What do you mean by messy? Do you mean dirty?"

The students look back at the picture. Fidel says, "No. Look. His shirt and jacket and tie are all neat. But if he really fell down the stairs probably his clothes would be like twisted around or something."

"There's a word for that," I say, "*disheveled*. It means out of place, in disarray, not neat, out of order. If your clothes are disheveled, your shirt may be pulled out, your trousers may be twisted around, your buttons may be buttoned into the wrong holes. Who can make up a rule using that word?"

Several hands go up. I call on Rebecca, who says, "When people fall down stairs, their clothes get disheveled." I write the statement on the overhead.

"You have two good examples of rules now, so I'd like you, in groups, to work on this assignment."[1] Two students help me distribute the sheets (see Figure 1.3). "Your group assignments are on the board. Find your name and group number. Then look at the diagram of the classroom to see where your group is to meet. For example, group 1 meets in the front of the room by the door. Group 2 meets in the front beside the windows. If you cannot find where you are to go, raise your hand. Students whose names are underlined will be group leaders and are responsible for seeing that the work gets completed and that everyone contributes. I'll visit each group as you work to answer questions. You should each have a worksheet with the labels *evidence* and *rule* at the top. I expect each of you to write down the evidence and the rules that your group develops. You have nearly fifteen minutes until the end of the period. Find as many pieces of evidence and compose as many relevant rules as you can."

I begin to move from group to group. The students in Marisol's group stop talking when I arrive and look up. I ask what evidence they are working with. Marisol says they haven't decided. Oscar says, "There is nothing on the wall messed up." I ask why that is important. Oscar thinks for a minute. "Well, if people fall down stairs, they will be reaching and grabbing stuff to catch themselves. But see, the stuff on the wall is straight and neat." I suggest the group work on that. Before I leave, Rebecca says, "I think the food on the stove is really suspicious, because she wouldn't be cooking that late at night. Would she?"

"Does the food on the stove contradict what Queenie says about how Arthur died?" I ask. The students are silent, puzzled.

Marisol says, "Well, she didn't say anything about cooking. But you don't just start cooking at one in the morning."

"You might if your guests were hungry," says Rebecca.

"Well, I think she is cooking on the pan because she hit Arthur on the head with it. It looks like to me he was going up the stairs and she hit him from behind, and he fell backwards. That's why he's on his back, 'cause that's the way he'd be if he fell backward."

---

[1] Groups developing a piece of writing together need to be heterogeneous. An easy way to do this is to rank-order students' writing ability on previous work. Assuming a class of twenty-eight students, I create seven groups (having more than four students in a group reduces the frequency with which each student can contribute). I place one of the top seven writers in each group; place one of the seven weakest writers in each group; and sprinkle the remaining students equally among the groups. With seventh through ninth graders, it is usually wise to avoid groups with only one boy or one girl, because the contributions of the lone boy or girl are usually minimal.

Your group is an investigative team that must determine what may have happened. You can either agree or disagree with Queenie's version.

1. Do you think Queenie is telling the truth?
2. Find all the evidence you can that indicates whether or not Queenie is telling the truth. Make a list of all the evidence. Evidence includes concrete, observable information; personal testimony; written documents; and material objects and their condition or appearance.
3. Next explain how each piece of evidence supports your claim that Queenie is or is not telling the truth. Each explanation will be a generally accepted rule, which may begin with a phrase such as, "As a rule. . . ." If other members of your team disagree with you, find evidence that will convince them.
4. Be prepared to explain why your evidence supports your case. Eventually you will write a report to convince the others in the class that your analysis makes the most sense.

Oscar says, "That's all maybe, maybe, maybe."

I say, "Marisol, if you can prove that, you can present that to the class. But for now, I want you to stick to what you can prove with the kind of argument we've already made. You have a theory of what may have happened, but you'll need some very direct evidence to prove it. Save those ideas, though. Later we will speculate about the case. Right now, concentrate on whether or not Queenie is lying. Because if she is, we need to ask why she is. I think that is what you're trying to answer."

I look around the room, checking how other groups are doing. They all appear to be discussing the problem. I hear Roberto say, "That's stupid." I approach his group with a smile. "What's up?"

Roberto says, "Anna says he could have twisted around while he's falling and that's why he is on his back. That ain't right. People just don't twist around while they're falling. They fall straight."

Anna says, "Yes, he could have twisted around, and that's why he's on his back looking up."

"What do the rest of you think?" Margaret and Fidel look down at the picture. Roberto and Anna look at me. I wait.

"If you can prove that, you can present that to the class. But for now, I want you to stick to what you can prove with the kind of argument we've already made."

Finally Fidel says, "I don't think he could probably twist around like she says."

"You mean, if he were coming down the stairs and fell forward, you do not think it's likely that he would land on his back?" I ask.

"No, it ain't likely."

"I'm just saying he could have," says Anna.

Roberto says, "Well, would you say that when people fall down stairs, they usually twist around and land on their backs?"

"No, not really."

"Well, okay then. We're just saying that he probably would not for the same reason."

"Keep working. Remember to make your argument based on what you think is most likely. I am going to visit another group." Looking at my watch, I see there are only three minutes left. I visit two more groups before the bell rings. No one packs up before the bell rings, which is a good sign. I ask for the worksheets, telling students to be sure to put their names on the sheets. Immediate inspection of student work is invaluable because:

1. I can verify the observations I have made in class.
2. I can determine specifically who has understood what.
3. I get a clear indication about what to do the following day.

Here are Desiree's evidence and rules:

Evidence	Rule
1. His feet are on the stairs.	*If one falls down the stairs, their feet shouldn't be on the stairs.*
2. Everything is on the wall.	*As a rule, if one falls, they will try to hold on to something to break his fall.*
3. There's food on the stove.	*As a rule, why should the stove be on?*
4. The carpet is neat.	*As a rule, if one falls and lands on the carpet, the carpet will be pushed and unneat.*

In general, she seems to have the idea. The evidence and rules or warrants (rules are referred to as *warrants* in Toulmin logic) for 1, 2, and 4 are fairly well stated and in third person. There are obviously problems with pronoun agreement, but I will model those uses later. Number 2 requires more explanation to connect it more solidly to the evidence. Number 3 is problematic, because all the thinking is not expressed and even if it were, it still wouldn't explain how the fact that the stove is on reveals anything about whether Queenie is telling the truth.

Twelve of the twenty-six students produced work at this level or better, but other groups have not done as well. Ana's worksheet is typical of the weaker work and the kinds of problems some students are having:

Evidence	Rule
1. The stove is on.	[*No rule is provided. Several other students have listed the stove being on as evidence but are unable to explain it.*]
2. She wouldn't had planned on going home ten minutes before her friends.	*She had enough time to kill him.*
3. Everything on the wall was straight.	*Something had to be broken or messed up.*
4. Supposedly he slipped and fell with something.	*If he had slipped something must have been on the stairs.*

Number 2 is difficult to interpret; Ana's thinking isn't clear, and I'll have to ask her. Number 3 comes closest to what I'm hoping for, but it lacks the important clause explaining why something on the wall had to be "messed up." Ana's fourth piece of evidence is hypothetical and unclear. Queenie's statement says nothing about something on the stairs that might have caused Arthur to slip and fall.

Nearly all the students have at least one piece of evidence and have made an attempt to state a warrant or rule, but only about half are able to produce two or more appropriate warrants. I have my work cut out for me. Still, when I first began teaching the Toulmin framework to graduate students at the University of Chicago, the success rate was similar. Understanding and developing warrants is tough.

Reviewing Evidence and Writing General Rules

On day 2, I return the worksheets with brief comments on individual efforts. (For example, I compliment Desiree for her three warrants and the three pieces of evidence she presented.) I ask students to review the rules for the pieces of evidence we worked on the day before: the glass in Arthur's hand and the neatness of his clothes. Everyone seems to know these. But Roberto wants to add another rule about the glass in Arthur's hand. "When you're dead, your muscles relax and you drop what you're holding." I write that on the overhead.

"Good. How can we revise that to make it a general rule?" There is silence for a moment. "Who remembers how to do that?"

Aneta raises her hand. "You have to make it third person, right? So you have to say, like, um, when people die, their muscles relax and they drop what they are holding." I revise the original statement on the overhead, using carets and striking out the second-person pronouns and inserting Aneta's words.

I ask for other evidence. Dantonio says, "The glass in his left hand, but if he drunk, he would hold the banister when he come down the stairs."

"Okay, but what does that have to do with the fact that the glass is in his left hand?"

"Well, if he comin' down stairs, the banister be on the left. He have to have the glass in his right hand to hold on."

"What do the rest of you think about that?"

Most other students nod in agreement. Somebody says, "Wow, I didn't think of that."

"That's very observant isn't it?" There is a murmur of assent. Dantonio smiles and looks down at his paper. I write what Dantonio has said on the overhead and ask what we need to do to make it a general rule. "It cannot refer only to Arthur."

After a few attempts, we have *Drunk people usually hold banisters when they come down stairs. They carry anything in the hand opposite the banister so they can steady themselves with the hand next to the banister.*

I call for other evidence. Marisol says, "He is lying on his back."

"Anything else?" I ask.

Someone adds, "Faceup." Another student says, "His feet are on the stairs."

"Let's see if we can put all of that into one sentence." I know these students do not use absolute modifiers and that I will have to help. But it turns out to be easy. "What shall we call him? *He* or *Arthur*?" There is a chorus of *Arthur*. On the overhead I write, *Arthur is lying on his back.* "How can we add the other information?"

"You could add a comma and say *faceup*," Silvia says. I add that on the overhead.

"How about the feet-on-the-stairs part?" I ask.

Sylvia says, "You could just put another comma and add *feet on the stairs*, couldn't you?"

"Absolutely," I say. "Now, I am coming around to make sure you are all copying what we have written so far on your sheets."

After a moment someone says, "We ain't got no more space. I need a new sheet."

Fortunately, I have extra copies of the worksheet and distribute them. I also say, "If you do not have enough room on the back of the worksheet, use a new sheet of notebook paper. Be sure to put your name on it." I move around the room until I see that most students have written versions of what we have developed on the overhead. Then I ask if anyone has more evidence to talk about.

Marcella raises her hand. "Nobody said nothin' about the glass is still in one piece."

"You're right. What do you make of that?"

"Well, if you fall, and even if you don't drop the glass, wouldn't it break when it hit the floor?"

"That's a good question," I say. "What do the rest of you think?" Several hands are up. "Okay, Roberto first, then Angelina, then Dantonio."

Roberto says, "Well, we already said that when people fall, they usually drop what they're carrying. So it would break."

Angelina says, "But even if you didn't drop it, if you fell down the stairs and if you was holding the glass in your hand, it would probably break when it hit the floor. Wouldn't it?"

I note the tentative quality of these responses and the adverbial conditional clauses and hope the same qualities will appear in the statements they write down.

Dantonio cuts in. "I thinkin' if Arthur hit the floor hard enough to bust his head, that would be hard enough to break the glass, wouldn't it?"

"Okay, you guys have introduced two more conditions. In the first place, we think he probably would have dropped the glass to save himself. But in the second, if he fell hard enough to die from the fall, the glass would have hit the floor with enough force to break it. I like this complex thinking. Let's see if we can write it up." Students propose more or less what I have just suggested, including the transitions.

The final piece of evidence the class suggests is that all the items on the wall along the stairs are straight and neat on the wall. We come up with the following rule, or warrant: "When people are falling down the stairs, they are very likely to reach out for support and, in the process [*my suggestion*], dislodge something on the wall."

I think my students get the idea, but I know it's difficult. We are not simply learning about evidence (which they seldom used on their pretests) and warrants (which were even rarer) but about conditional clauses (especially *if* and *when* clauses). Although the conventions for this kind of writing for the most part exclude the second person, especially in warrants, the students' conversations about rules and warrants is in the second person. I wonder whether using second person avoids the confusion of third person, in which they typically interchange singular and plural (Desiree's "If one falls down the stairs, their feet shouldn't be on the stairs," for example). More likely it is simply a matter of using common vernacular.

I spend so much time on these discussions because I want my students to rehearse these conventions and structures and finally use them on their own. Some teachers feel all the groping around students do is a waste of time, that simply *telling* students what to do is enough. But the students in my education classes and I know that the discussion and the social construction of meaning that go on among our learners jump-start and empower learning. We know that if we don't allow youngsters to explore the problems and make some errors along the way, far less learning takes place. On the initial activities, we work together so that we can provide careful support for difficult thinking.

Writing a Report

After our discussions are over, we write a report that includes the full argument. I begin by asking, "If we were really an investigative team and if this were a real crime, to whom would we have to write a report?" Students suggest the boss, the chief inspector, the district attorney, or the chief of police. We settle on the chief of police. "What would we need to explain to the chief?"

I list their suggestions on the overhead (if they miss any, I ask a leading question: "Should we explain when we arrived on the scene?"):

when we arrived
what we found
what Queenie said

> *"We are not simply learning about evidence (which they seldom used on their pretests) and warrants (which were even rarer) but about conditional clauses (especially if and when clauses)."*

what the autopsy found

whether the evidence supports what Queenie said

our conclusion and/or recommendation

explanation of evidence supporting our conclusion and recommendation

Next, I write on the overhead as the students dictate. With the outline above, organizing the major sections is not a problem. We begin with when we arrived on the scene: *We arrived at the home of Arthur and Queenie Volupides at about 2:15 A.M. on February 6, 2007.* After that, students tend to continue with general statements (for example, the first response to "What did we find?" is often, *We found Arthur dead on the floor*). As a result of my asking a lot of questions to help them clarify their thinking, we finally arrive at:

> We found Arthur Volupides lying at the bottom of the main stairs on his back, faceup, his feet on the third step. He was still holding a glass in the fingertips of his left hand. His clothes were neat. Nothing on the wall beside the stairs was disturbed. The carpet where he lay was undisturbed. Queenie said that Arthur slipped and fell on the stairs. He was coming down for another drink. He still had the glass in his hand.

Next we have to present our thinking about the situation. By this time, students have given up any claim that Queenie is telling the truth. A few questions lead to: *We believe Queenie is not telling the truth. The evidence does not support what she says happened.*

At this point, because students have worked through all the evidence pretty thoroughly, I ask them individually to write out the evidence and the rules (warrants) that allow them to interpret the evidence. They need to include at least five pieces of evidence, each with an appropriate warrant and any necessary explanation. Here is Marisol's presentation of evidence:

> We believe that the evidence does not support her claim. First, the cup is in his hand. When people fall down the stairs, they let go of what they are holding to try and get a grip of something to stop. Second, the way Arthur is facing is weird. When someone falls down the stairs, their body would be facedown. Arthur, though, is faced upwards. Third, she waited to long to call the police or ambulance. She waited for her friends to do anything. When someone sees another person hurt they automatically call the police for help.

The last reason I believe she is lying is because the things on the wall are all straight. They seem like if they hadn't been disturb. If someone falls down the stairs, they will try to hold on to anything. Especially if they you see things in the wall you will try to brake your fall.

Marisol's first language is Spanish. She makes several errors in this passage, but her basic grasp of the syntax of argument is sound. She needs to learn how to punctuate introductory adverbial clauses, but she uses them appropriately. Note also that she slips from third person to second in her final warrant. She needs to learn to proofread for spelling, unnecessary words, and other minor problems. But this essay, written with a good deal of support after only four days of instruction, makes me happy. In teaching any sort of process, when the process is new to learners, it is important to provide as much coaching and modeling as necessary.

Moving Students Toward Independence

When learners reach a level of proficiency, it's time to increase the difficulty of the work and provide less support. How quickly to withdraw support depends on the learners' needs, abilities, and proclivities. Withdraw support too soon and they become frustrated. Maintain support too long and they become bored. It's a judgment call.

In my sequence of activities for developing simple arguments, I use several other forensic-like cases. One for group work is "Peacock's Poser," or as some of my colleagues call it, "What Happened to Winston?" It's adapted from Treat's *The Clue Armchair Detective* (1983) and is a bit more complex, because it is more ambiguous. As with "Slip or Trip," students receive a picture and a narrative. The picture shows a man, Winston Peacock, lying on the floor; the narrative reveals that he is dead, discovered on January 2, when the woman who delivers papers to his house looks through his window. Students must evaluate whether he was murdered or committed suicide. Because the solution cannot be reasonably inferred from the picture, we do not give students the "correct" answer, even though they often demand to know. Our concern is whether they can use evidence to make a case for one or the other possibility. There is evidence on both sides of the problem.

"In teaching any sort of process, when the process is new to learners, it is important to provide as much coaching and modeling as necessary."

For example, when the police arrive at the home, they find the doors and windows locked from the inside. They have to break a window to enter. Winston has a revolver in his right hand, one of a pair of revolvers that had been mounted on his wall (its mate is still there). From this evidence, students deduce that Winston must have committed suicide, because no one else was there. The warrant is that, for a murder to have been committed, there must have been someone else in the room.

On the other hand, Winston is wearing an apron, which suggests he had been doing something in the kitchen, perhaps preparing a New Year's Day dinner. He had also made a list of things to do: "ring" his broker, pay his phone bill. These acts are not in keeping with someone contemplating suicide. The text tells us that everyone in town suspected that Winston had a fortune hidden in his house. The carpet near Winston's body has been rolled back. Students take this as evidence that someone had been searching for the treasure. A suicide intent on ending his life would not bother to roll a rug back.

"The Lunchroom Murder"

Another puzzle is called "The Lunchroom Murder," from Lawrence Treat's *Crime and Puzzlement*. This one is less ambiguous, but it includes several distracting clues. Here's the introduction and the scene:

> On an otherwise uneventful Thursday afternoon police heard a shot inside Ernie's Lunchroom, rushed in, and found the scene shown in Figure 1.4.
>
> They identified the body as that of a prominent racketeer named Fannin. Ernie, who is both the owner and only employee, had only one fact to tell: the murderer had leaned against the wall while firing at point-blank range. The imprint of his hand is in clear view. The cash register has just been rung up at $8.75.
>
> This is a difficult case. Your investigative team must attempt to determine which of the people in the lunchroom killed Fannin. You will have to observe the details carefully. There is enough evidence to help you explain most of what happened. In working out the solution, consider the following questions.

"When learners reach a level of proficiency, it's time to increase the difficulty of the work and provide less support. Withdraw support too soon and they become frustrated. Maintain support too long and they become bored. It's a judgment call."

FIGURE 1.4 "The Lunchroom Murder"

1. With what hand did the shooter fire the gun? What is the evidence? What is the warrant?

2. Did customers B, C, and D know each other? What are the evidence and warrants?

3. How do the three customers differ in their habits or ways of doing things? What is the evidence and what is the warrant?

4. Which set of footprints are Ernie's? What is the evidence? What is the warrant?

5. To whom do the set of footprints marked *X* belong? How do you know?

6. Who killed Fannin? How do you know? Outline all the evidence and all of the warrants necessary to support this claim.

The set of questions originally published with the drawing focused on the footprints, so students also focused on the footprints and failed to notice the placement of customer C's cup and flatware. I believed the students in this class needed the more direct questions above. If you use it, you may want to eliminate question 1 to make the puzzle more challenging. Or you may want to ask directly which customer is left-handed to make it simpler. When students work together on these projects, I sometimes have each group turn in a single piece of writing for which all members receive a grade. Other times, I have individual group members submit their own piece. For the "Lunchroom Murder" puzzle, everyone submitted their own solution based on their own and their group's thinking. Here's Olivia's:

> When I arrived at the lunchroom, the first thing I noticed was the dead body on the floor. Not only that but there were footprints on the floor and a handprint on the wall. Dishes were on the counter and the cash register was open with money still in it. It was hard to figure the question everyone wondered about, "Who killed Fannin?" After long analyzing it hit us. The handprint on the wall was right-handed, because the thumb pointed to the left. Ernie had only one thing to say, the murderer had leaned against the wall while firing at point-blank range. Since it is a right-hand print, the killer must be left-handed.
>
> So knowing that, we looked at where the customers were eating. Customer C is the only left-handed one, because his utencils and cup were on the left side of his plate. So customer C is the killer of Fannin.
>
> Customer A had tiptoed out into the kitchen. We know because of the footprints. They show him going out to the kitchen, and he wouldn't have been able to put his right-hand print onto the wall because the wall was to his left.

Olivia has done well making a tricky argument. Her final paragraph suggests that she was thinking about how to eliminate the other customers. However, she stopped with A. (When I asked, she confirmed this intention but said she wasn't sure how to eliminate customers B and D.) I was pleased with her work because she cited both key pieces of evidence and the warrants governing that evidence.

Most other students also did so. A few omitted one piece of evidence or one warrant. I made comments on the papers about the content that was missing and asked students to revise their paper for a final grade. I corrected misspellings and asked students to add the correctly spelled words to a personal spelling list. Because so many students did so well, I decided to move on to the individual stage.

"The Case of the Dead Musician"

The puzzle I chose was invented by Marc Furigay, a student in the University of Chicago Master of Arts in Teaching English program some years ago. The drawing shows an old man, a musician, hanging from a chandelier, dead. To the right of the hanging body is a grand piano from which several strings have been ripped. (See Figure 1.5.)

FIGURE 1.5 "The Case of the Dead Musician"

Here's a slightly modified version of Marc's narrative:

The Case of the Dead Musician

Anton Karazai had amassed a great fortune in his seventy years as a world-famous pianist, performing for presidents and parliaments, kings and queens, in all the greatest cities' concert halls and children's hospitals. Anyone who watched Mr. Karazai perform understood immediately that he loved his music above and beyond anything else. Music—playing the piano—was his life.

Yesterday evening, May 16, 2006, however, Mr. Karazai's only son and sole heir phoned the police and reported that his father had hanged himself from the chandelier in the piano room at his estate. When the police arrived, they took several pictures of the scene. One of those pictures appears in Figure 1.5. The police noted that Karazai had been hanged by a cord taken from the set of drapes in the corner window of the room and that his feet hung about two feet above the stool beneath him. They also noted that several pieces of steel wire had been ripped from the piano.

The coroner's report confirmed that Mr. Karazai died from asphyxiation. Inspection of his neck revealed a single, thin, skin-breaking line with a small amount of blood across the Adam's apple.

Since it is too small to read in the picture, here is Mr. Karazai's last journal entry in its entirety:

May 16, 2006. Have been sad for weeks now. My strength diminishes every day. It is even difficult for me to play the piano. Sometimes, even piano fails to cheer me. Sometimes my failing ability makes me angry. Yesterday I actually kicked my piano! But my ninety-year-old legs could hardly hurt a little bird. Only my son remains, my only son and the sole heir to all that I have earned and collected over this incredible but lonely life. I wonder if he knows what he will be getting when I die. Perhaps. But perhaps not. I will try to play something simple to cheer me before I retire for the evening—perhaps something form Debussy's "Children's Corner," a wonderful collection of happy, beautiful melodies.

The Assignment

You are the investigator reading the reports above and inspecting the picture of the scene. Mr. Karazai's son claims that his father hanged himself. What do you think is the truth? From the evidence available, make a case for what you think really happened. If you believe that other evidence is necessary, make a recommendation about what other evidence might need to be collected. Before you begin to write your report, list the evidence and warrants you will use in making your case.

Students did this work in class. They had two days to consider the material and write the essay, but on the second day I encouraged them to rethink the case they were making and to revise their papers according to the following checklist:

Checklist for Revisions

1. Have you described what was found at the scene and what the autopsy revealed?
2. Have you incorporated at least three pieces of evidence?
3. Have you provided the rules or warrants that explain why the evidence is important to your claim?
4. Have you made a recommendation about what should happen next or what more evidence is needed?

This is Jorge's second draft:

I have read the police reports and inspected the pictures of the scene. The picture shows Mr. Karazai hanging from the chandelier in the piano room of the house. The grand piano is behind him and to his right. There is a large coffee table in the room to the left of the body. It has a bottle of wine and a glass partly filled. Mr. Karazai's journal is also on the table. The journal was open to the page of the last entry with yesterday's date, May 16, 2006. Mr. Karazai was hanging from the chandelier by a velvet rope, which was apparently the sash for a set of drapes on the corner window of the room. But the coroner's report indicates that Karazai died of asphyxiation and that there is a thin cut on his throat at the Adam's apple.

I believe that Mr. Karazai's son is not telling the truth. There are several pieces of evidence that do not fit with the idea that he hanged himself. First, his journal entry don't seem so depressed that he would kill himself. He says that he will play some happy melodies "to cheer himself up before he retires." People who are going to hang themselves do not decide to play happy melodies. I mean, that would be really weird.

Second, he is hanging from the chandelier by a velvet rope. But the coroner says that there is a thin cut across his Adam's apple. The thin cut would not be made by a thick velvet rope. But piano wire could make a thin cut. I looked at the wires in the music room piano. They are very thin, way thinner than a velvet rope. I think the cut must of been made with the wire used to strangle him. Then somebody, namely the son, hung him from the chandelier with the velvet rope. I am saying that is probably what happened.

But the third piece of evidence is the most important. If you hang yourself, you have to stand high enough to put a rope around your neck and jump off what you are standing on. The stool is too low for Karazai to stand on, put a noose around his neck, and jump off. It is way below his feet. Therefore, he could not of hanged himself as the son said. The son is lying because he wanted to inherit the money.

I recommend that the police should arrest the son immediately and put him to trial. We don't need no more evidence. He is guilty. His father was alone in the house when the son came in. The son pulled wire out of the piano and strangled his father with it. Then he put the rope around his neck and hung him from the chandelier. He did it for the money. In my opinion, that is the worst crime to kill your parent. He should get the death penalty.

Jorge's is one of several good pieces produced by the members of this class. It includes several minor errors in usage and diction, but my instruction was aimed at using evidence and warrants, so I evaluated the paper on that basis. (It is counterproductive, if not unethical, to teach toward one specific target of learning and grade learners on another.) The paper also provides some clues about what kinds of usage instruction might be useful. For example, the warrant for the third piece of evidence is in second person, with which I sympathize, because it is much more difficult—and awkward— in the third person. I need to continue instruction on that syntactic problem. Several other students use *of* for *have*, so I also need to teach the correct usage more deliberately.

> "It is important to realize that this is the way the teaching goes. There is always something more to teach. For me, that has been as true for graduate students as for ninth graders."

It is important to realize that this is the way the teaching goes. There is always something more to teach. For me, that has been as true for graduate students as for ninth graders. I have encountered teachers who have argued that because their students cannot write correctly punctuated sentences, they must spend time with teaching from the grammar book. I firmly believe that such a move destroys learning. It is deadly, wastes time, and does not accomplish the goal of correctly written sentences. But in only a few days of working on the problem above, most of my twenty-six students were using more sophisticated conditional sentences in the expression of warrants. A majority used third person in the warrants instead of the ubiquitous second person. And most presented evidence and linked it to their claims with warrants, which none had done on the pretests of argument writing.

A Note on Pretesting

Before we teach students how to do something new, we need to know what students already know how to do in relationship to the task. In the case of argument, I want to know if students can do the following:

» Look at available data in order to develop a claim.
» Make at least a reasonable claim, if not an insightful one.
» Support it with evidence.
» Supply rules (warrants) tying the evidence to the claim, thus demonstrating that the evidence is relevant.
» Qualify the claim and warrants as necessary.
» Provide backing for warrants when necessary.

To determine if students can do these things, I provide them with a scenario involving a change in the security policy at a high school. The change, according to the scenario, is about to be put in place because of what officials see as an unacceptable rise in the crime rate. The scenario describes both the current and proposed security policies with the proposed policy increasing monitoring of hallways, restrooms, and lounging areas; instituting unannounced locker searches and weapons searches upon students' entering school; and increased penalties of infractions of the school rules. The data sets include statements, in the case of the high school, from the principal, counselors, teachers, concerned parents, and students who have been victims of theft, physical or sexual abuse, and so forth. The data set also includes a chart listing the number of each type of crime over the past ten years and the increase in student population in the same time period.

Students are asked to write a letter to the Board of Education carefully arguing their points of view about the proposed policy change. It is possible to argue against or in favor of the new policy.[2]

[2]An article in the *New York Times* on September 3, 2010 ("U.S. Asks Educators to Reinvent Student Tests, and How They Are Given") states that this kind of performance exam will be part of the new national testing programs being currently developed under the auspices of large government grants. The article explains that "In performance-based tasks, which are increasingly common in tests administered by the military and in other fields, students are given a problem—they could be told, for example, to pretend they are a mayor who needs to reduce a city's pollution—and must sift through a portfolio of tools and write analytically about how they would use them to solve the problem." I believe that this kind of testing will be far superior to what is now available and will demand huge changes in the way teachers teach.

The data permit the argument that there is no need to change the policy because there is no real change in the crime rates. The increase in crime is in proportion to the increase in the population of the school. Our students typically do not make that argument, and in our instruction, we have discovered that most of them cannot deal with proportions or even percentages, an argument pointing to the need for our being more interdisciplinary. In the pretest writing, we find that overwhelmingly students do not bother much with evidence, not even the expert testimony provided. They simply choose to voice their opinions, usually in opposition to any move toward a more restrictive policy. They tend to provide a series of claims about the restrictive policy and why it is evil, writing tantamount to screams of outrage.

It was our findings on this pretest that led to the teaching I described in this chapter.

Advantages of Using Pretests

» You can document what students already know and do not know about what you are planning to teach.
» You can measure progress from a point before instruction to a point after it is complete.
» You can demonstrate to administrators precisely what students have learned and thus defend what you have taught in fairly precise ways.
» You can examine the effectiveness of your teaching in order to make improvements in the future.
» You can use the pretests in combination with later work to help students see what they have learned.
» When you can examine student progress precisely, you will find that your own experience of flow[3] as a teacher will increase.

[3]See Introduction: Planning for Powerful Learning.

What Makes a Good Mascot— or a Good Leader?

Teaching Simple Arguments of Judgment

THE FORENSIC ARGUMENTS ILLUSTRATED IN CHAPTER ONE
are a solid base for introducing the more complex arguments of judgment
and policy. Without instruction in argument of fact, most students use no
criteria for their judgments and opinions. They may think rightly that a policy is unfair, but most students do not articulate the *reasons* that it is unfair;
when they do, they use simplistic criteria.

The Common Core Standards expect students beginning at grade 6 to
be able to write arguments in which they "introduce claim(s) and organize
the reasons and evidence clearly." By ninth grade, they state, students should
"Write arguments to support claims in an analysis of substantive topics,
using valid reasoning and relevant and sufficient evidence."(See Common
Core State Standards, Ninth-Grade Writing.) My graduate students and I
have experienced success in teaching students to support claims with evidence by first helping them understand how to produce sound criteria for

making those claims. We have done so even in inner-city schools populated by many students who are considered "at-risk." First, we introduced them to simple arguments of fact, as we did in Chapter One; then we move on to simple problems of judgment.

Simple Problems of Judgment

When teaching students to use appropriate warrants (rules) or *criteria* in their arguments and to provide *evidence* relevant to those criteria, we found it imperative to begin with simple problems and appropriate scaffolding by the teacher. That is, the problems must fall within the students' zone of proximal development (Vygotsky 1978). When we begin with simple, concrete problems and help students decide the criteria for making judgments, we provide the support they need.

The Proper Mascot

A former student of mine, Thomas McCann, when he was Assistant Superintendent for Curriculum and Instruction in the Elmhurst (Illinois) Public Schools, developed an activity for fifth graders called "The Proper Mascot." The goals of the activity are to:

> » Develop a model for informal reasoning.
> » Use a model for informal reasoning to analyze data and draw logical conclusions.
> » Apply a model for informal reasoning in writing an analysis of a problem that requires the application of criteria in judging the relative merits of a set of proposed school mascots.

What follows is a step-by-step explanation of how you might do this activity with your students.

1. **Introduce the activity.**

   Introducing the activity, you might note something about your own school mascot. For example, my high school teams were known as the "Railroaders," and the school symbol was a locomotive, because the school was only a mile from the New York Central railroad yards on the east side of Cleveland, Ohio. At every reunion, we receive a coffee mug, key chain, or chocolate bar in the shape of a locomotive as a souvenir of our time together. All of us take pride in the school logo.

"When teaching students to use appropriate warrants (rules) or criteria in their arguments and to provide evidence relevant to those criteria, we found it imperative to begin with simple problems and appropriate scaffolding by the teacher. That is, the problems must fall within the students' zone of proximal development."

2 Ask students about their own school mascot and record their answers on the board or on chart paper.

> » How do you feel about it?
> » Do you like it?
> » Why or why not?
> » What comes to mind when you think of it?
> » How was the mascot selected?
> » If you were to select a different mascot, what would it be?
> » Why would you select it?

Tapping into this prior common knowledge becomes the basis for your students' ideas about what makes a good mascot.

"When we begin with simple, concrete problems and help students decide the criteria for making judgments, we provide the support they need."

3 Project images of other school mascots for students to consider.

Project the following images, all of which are real school logos,[1] or several of your own choosing. When we use these, everyone has a good laugh:

The University of California at Santa Cruz
Banana Slugs

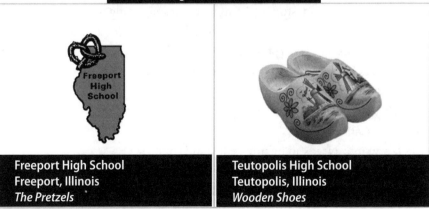

Freeport High School
Freeport, Illinois
The Pretzels

Teutopolis High School
Teutopolis, Illinois
Wooden Shoes

---

[1] You can find a list of offbeat mascots at www.halcyon.com/marcs/mascoths.html and more information about many mascots at www.618football.com/High-School/RokTabs-Frontpage/why-mascots-have-tails. *Why Mascots Have Tales*, a book by Fred Willman, is available from the Illinois High School Association.

4   **Ask students to evaluate the merits of each mascot.**

> » Do you think the mascot is a good one?
> » If you like it, what makes it a good mascot?
> » If you don't like it, what makes it a bad mascot?

Record their thoughts on the board or on chart paper.

5   **Ask students to think about the class discussion they just had and make a list of criteria for what they think makes a good mascot.**

6   **When they have finished their lists, ask students to express their assessments in a whole-class discussion.**

Again, record students' thoughts on the board so that students can refer back to the list later.

7   **Divide students into groups of three or four. Tell them their task is to propose four or five rules, or warrants, a school could use as criteria to guide their selection of a mascot.**

Using as a starting point the criteria the class came up with when they considered other schools' mascots and their own school mascot, students write general rules, or warrants, that state criteria for what a mascot should be. For example, a student might have observed that pretzels are not something that one would take pride in or that pretzels don't suggest a fierce opponent in competitive events. If the group agrees this is important, their warrant might be, *As a rule, a mascot should be something students can take pride in.* Moving from group to group, you can help scaffold students' learning by suggesting some helpful verb phrases: a mascot *needs to be, should be, ought to be,* and so forth.

     Here's an excerpt from the discussion a small group of fifth graders have as they try to formulate their rules:

> *Jacqui:* What about big?
> *Mary Ann:* Maybe like slugs—could be funny?
> *Carl:* Sure!
> *Mary Ann:* Needs to be unusual; stands out.
> *Jimmy:* Interesting.
> *Carl:* It could also be unique.
> *Mary Ann:* Well, that's the same as stands out.
> *Jacqui:* Maybe stands out is too hard.

"Moving from group to group, you can help scaffold students' learning by suggesting some helpful verb phrases: a mascot needs to be, should be, ought to be, and so forth."

> *Jimmy:* Intimidating.
>
> *Carl:* Yeah—that's a good one.
>
> *Jimmy:* Proud.
>
> *Mary Ann:* Has to have something to do with the school.
>
> *Carl:* Representing it!
>
> *Jacqui:* Large instead of tiny.
>
> *Mary Ann:* No! Think about the slugs: they aren't big.
>
> *Jacqui:* Think about the Dukes.
>
> *Carl:* We all like the Dukes!
>
> *Jacqui:* Strong. We like that!
>
> *Jimmy:* Powerful.
>
> *Mary Ann:* That's like strong.
>
> *Jacqui:* What's our school color?
>
> *Jimmy:* Blue and gray.
>
> *Jacqui:* Okay, has something to do with the color.

8 **Call on representatives from each group to report their rules, or criteria in the form of warrants, for selecting a mascot.**

Each group reports back to the class. List their warrants on the board or on chart paper so that students can reference them later.

9 **Through the process of paraphrasing, clarifying, and evaluating these rules, or warrants, the class agrees on a common set of criteria for judging a good mascot.**

These are the criteria one class produced:

> » Mascots have to be strong or tough or fierce (e.g., lions, wildcats, badgers).
>
> » Mascots should have some historical, occupational, or geographic connection to the school or community (e.g., Joliet Ironmen, Wyoming Cowboys, Glenbard West Hilltoppers, Green Bay Packers).
>
> » Mascots should be something that someone would be proud to be (e.g., huskies, dukes, admirals).
>
> » Mascots should have names that fit well (sound good) with the school name (e.g., the Elmhurst Eagles, the Leo Lions, the Hinsdale South Hornets; not the Elmhurst Wagon Wheels or the Hinsdale Green Wave).

After discussing whether *all* the criteria need to be met in order to select a proper mascot (many mascots are chosen for one of the reasons, not all), record the criteria on the overhead projector and ask all the students to copy the final version.

10 **Tell your students they will use the class' criteria to help a new school select a mascot.**

Ask students to imagine that a new school, John L. Lewis Elementary, has just opened in Floodrock, Illinois. The town is in Saline County, in the very southern region of the state. The current enrollment is 315. The area has two major industries: farming and coal mining. Many families in Saline County have some connection to the coal mines. However, since fewer homes and businesses depend on coal as an energy source these days, mine activity has slowed and the coal companies no longer employ many residents. Nevertheless, the citizens of the town of Floodrock associate themselves with the coal industry and have named the school after John L. Lewis, who was the president of the United Mine Workers of America for forty years.

The school has not yet selected a mascot, and the school leaders are running a contest to select one. The mascot's image will appear on the gym floor, on school stationery, on school spirit wear, and on publications. The four possibilities under final consideration are: lowland gorillas, manatees, lemurs, miners. The students have been asked to judge the contest.

11 **Students identify the *attributes* of each finalist.**

> » What features or characteristics do you associate with a *gorilla*?
> » What features or characteristics do you associate with a *miner*?
> » How do these characteristics match the rules or *criteria* you have proposed for selecting a good mascot? (In the class I'm using as an example, students rejected the manatee and lemur, favoring the miner and gorilla.)

12 **Use the mascot of your own school to model the process of composing an argument of judgment.**

In the example that follows, the teacher uses the mascot of the students' school—the bobcat. First, she asks whether students think the school

FIGURE 2.1

manatees

lowland gorillas

miners

lemurs

A new school, John L. Lewis Elementary, has just opened in Floodrock, Illinois. The town is in Saline County, in the very southern region of the state. The current enrollment is 315. The area has two major industries: farming and coal mining. Many families in Saline County have some connection to the coal mines. However, since fewer homes and businesses depend on coal as an energy source these days, mine activity has slowed and the coal companies no longer employ many residents. Nevertheless, the citizens of the town of Floodrock associate themselves with the coal industry and have named the school after John L. Lewis, who was the president of the United Mine Workers of America for forty years.

The school has not yet selected a mascot, and the school leaders are running a contest to select one. The mascot's image will appear on the gym floor, on school stationery, on school spirit wear, and on publications. The four possibilities under final consideration are: lowland gorillas, manatees, lemurs, miners. The students have been asked to judge the contest.

mascot is a good one. Most do. So she asks what characteristics they like about it. The students list speed, aggressiveness, intelligence, and defense of family. Thinking aloud, the teacher, with the help of the class, composes an argument on a projected transparency. The first sentence states that the bobcat is a good mascot; the second, its appealing characteristics; the final two, why those characteristics make the mascot a good one, which is the warrant in this argument:

> The bobcat is a good mascot for Edison School. A bobcat is a very smart animal and is a strong defender of its home and family. A student at Edison can take pride in being represented by an animal that is a smart and strong protector of its family. Although the bobcat can be an aggressive fighter, it attacks to survive and to protect its young, not to be mean.

13 **Students compose their own argument of judgment.**

Tell students they must select one of the finalist mascots and, using the evaluation criteria, the profile of the school and community, and the mascot's attributes, explain in a thorough, logical paragraph why it would be a good mascot for the new school. Remind students to:

> » Keep the evaluation criteria the class came up with (see number 9, above) in mind.
> » Remember the profile of the school and community.
> » Study the details and attributes of the proposed mascots.
> » Use the paragraph the class just composed together as a model.

The following examples are representative of what members of one fifth-grade class wrote:

> The miners are a good mascot for John L. Lewis Elementary School. Everyone in the school can take pride in their past, because their town was a mining town. Another thing, miners have to be strong to get whatever they are mining. These cariseristics are important because kids should be proud about their mascot, and their past.
>
> Hannah, grade 5

The Lowland Gorilla is a good mascot for John L. Lewis school. A Lowland Gorilla is very intimidating, very smart, and is very strong and powerful. The Lowland Gorilla can make the students at John L. Lewis proud. All mascots should be strong and powerful so that the student can be proud and take pride in.

Kristian, grade 5

Though these paragraphs contain only a few sentences and are relatively simple, they both contain the major elements of an argument:

> » a claim
> » evidence
> » a warrant explaining how the evidence supports the claim

Simple arguments of judgment often stem from a single criterion and do not require backing or complete definitions. (More complex judgments to which there is likely to be opposition and whose criteria may be questioned *do* require backing; developing that backing is discussed in Chapter Six.)

"Simple arguments of judgment often stem from a single criterion and do not require backing or complete definitions."

A Picture Is Worth a Thousand Words

My graduate students and I often introduce simple arguments of judgment to older students using a portrait that includes details from which students can infer characteristics of the person depicted. Once, to help a class of seventh graders describe characters in narrative writing, in which judgments may be made but are generally not argued, we used John Gillray's late-eighteenth-century etching of the Prince of Wales (later King George IV). Although I thought it too far removed from their cultural milieu (Hillocks 2007), as soon as the picture (see Figure 2.2) was distributed, it was evident that I had been dead wrong. It was very easy for students to comment on the man, whom they took to be a disgusting person. They listed dozens of details from the picture that they would later use in writing about an imaginary visit to the prince.

With a slight change in focus, my Master of Arts in Teaching English (MAT) students used the same picture for helping ninth-grade students

"More complex judgments to which there is likely to be opposition and whose criteria may be questioned do require backing."

FIGURE 2.2 "A Voluptuary under the horrors of Digestion"

learn to make simple arguments of judgment. Here is how the process looked, which can help guide your own teaching if you choose:

1. Distribute copies of "The Voluptuary" and ask students what they think of the man.

We hand out copies and ask students, "What do you think of this man?" They comment eagerly on his clothing, his belly, the vest he is unable to button, his tight pants, the wine bottles under the table, the corkscrew on his fob, the sneer on his face, his picking his teeth with a fork, and so forth. Soon someone asks about the large pot to his left and slightly behind him (our students usually aren't familiar with chamber pots). When we explain its function and say he may be using it as a *vomitorium* in which to regurgitate previously ingested food in order to be able to eat more, there are always groans of disgust.

The longer students look at the picture, the more details they see: the crossed knife and fork on a plate, suggesting a coat of arms; the pieces of paper under the chamber pot, which are bills from a doctor, a butcher, and a poulterer, all unpaid; a little book on the floor in front of the prince marked "Debts of Honour Unpaid" (we explain that in the eighteenth century, *debts of honor* referred to gambling debts); the small vials on the shelf to the prince's left, which include "Drips for stinking breath," medicines for indigestion, and well-known eighteenth-century quack remedies for venereal diseases (Leake's Pills and Velnos Vegetable Syrup). All these details prompt talk about the kind of person the prince is.

2   **Ask students to define *voluptuary* and write why the man in this picture might be labeled one.**

At this point, we ask what a *voluptuary* is. Students ordinarily don't know. After providing the definition (from the *Oxford English Dictionary*, one who is addicted to sensuous pleasures or given up to indulgence in luxury or the gratification of the senses), we ask one of two questions. The second question is a bit more demanding: (1) What details in the picture indicate that the prince is a voluptuary? (2) What details does Gillray use to portray the prince as a voluptuary?

Answering the first question, students might write, "Several details in the picture indicate that the prince is devoted to pleasure, particularly food and drink. For example, his table is covered with bones and the remainder of what appears to be some sort of animal carcass, and empty wine bottles litter the floor beneath the table. He has adopted a knife and fork crossed on a plate as a coat of arms."

However, an answer to the second question must take into account Gillray's use of detail to make a point about the prince, his agenda in selecting the details he uses to construct the portrait. It might look something like this: "In an effort to portray the Prince of Wales as a greedy degenerate, Gillray has selected details that show him in exactly that light. The prince has apparently eaten to the point of nearly passing out. A mound of food still remains on the table, and the floor beneath the table is littered with empty wine bottles. Gillray suggests that he has chosen a knife and fork crossed on a plate as a coat of arms, an emblem of his gluttony."

If your emphasis is simply on developing an argument of judgment, it seems appropriate to adopt the first kind of question. If the class seems a bit more sophisticated, you may wish to adopt the second. Eventually, students need to learn that every expression, whether in words or visual images, is an intentional construction and implies the creator's attitudes and agendas. This understanding is an important prerequisite for critical thinking. But at early points in teaching argument, it is probably sound practice to go with the easier question.

(3) Ask students, "What makes a 'good king'?" and encourage them to justify their responses. Record their thinking. At the end of your class' discussion, you should have a list of criteria in response to this question.

Since the Prince of Wales is the person in line to become king of England, my MAT students and I often ask a third question: "If Gillray's depiction is accurate, is this man fit to be king?" This naturally leads to the question: "What characteristics are necessary or important in a good king?"

Even in the inner city, students have ideas about what a good king should be. But I recall at least two occasions in which a boy has argued that a good king needs to be tyrannical, greedy, able to cheat people, and so forth. When I asked one of them why, he told me, "That what kings do. They cheat and steal from people. They do what they want."

So I backed up: "You are assuming that kings are evil. Let's assume that a good king rules so that the people prosper and are happy. Now what characteristics must a king have that will help his people to prosper and be happy?"

Responses include a number of ideas:

» A king must be fair to people.
» He must be able to control himself.
» He must be well dressed.
» He must be able to take care of money.

For each response, we ask for justifications. Let's listen in.

Karen, the MAT student in charge for the day, asks, "Why do you think a king must be fair?"

José says, "If he ain't fair, people ain't gonna like him."

"Why does it matter that they like him?"

"If they don't like him, they ain't gonna do what he wants. They might riot or something. But if they think he's fair to them, they might be, you know, more willing to go along with his ideas."

Lakeisha had her hand up. "If people ain't treated fair, they ain't gonna be happy. They're probably gonna revolt or something like that."

"So what if they revolt?" Karen asks.

Lakeisha responds without waiting. "Well, when you got a revolt, people are gettin' killed. They be off their property and maybe out the country. They starvin'. Come on. You see the news with all them—what you call 'em—refugees walkin' down roads like they gonna fall over. You don't want no revolution."

Karen says, "What do the rest of you think of that?" Several students agree with and add to what Lakeisha has said. "Okay, let's see if we can put that all together. You are claiming that a king must be fair to his people, because if he's not, the people will likely rebel. Right?" Students nod affirmatively. Karen writes the statement on a projected transparency. "So tell me what's wrong with a revolution?"

Alan raises his hand. "The problem is that a rebellion brings a lot of death and other suffering to people. Like Lakeisha say, starvation and losing your home, and probably disease because stuff like the water system might be destroyed."

Karen begins writing, "*When people revolt. . . .* What next?"

Alan says, "Revolutions bring about death, starvation and disease."

Karen finishes writing the statement. "Can anyone say why that happens?"

"Eventually, students need to learn that every expression, whether in words or visual images, is an intentional construction and implies the creator's attitudes and agendas. This understanding is an important prerequisite for critical thinking."

"If they don't like him, they ain't gonna do what he wants. They might riot or something. But if they think he's fair to them, they might be, you know, more willing to go along with his ideas."

Lakeisha says, "Because, like, when there's a revolution, the government is fighting the people and not taking care of necessities like water."

"What do the rest of you think of that? Will that do as an explanation?" Students nod, and Karen adds the statement to those on the overhead. Then she says, "It is almost time to stop. But let's talk about one more. Let's see, someone said a king must be well dressed. Why is that? What difference does it make if the king is well dressed?"

Janeefa raises her hand. "If he well dressed, people gonna respect him more than if he look like a slob."

"Kings are supposed to wear fancy clothes and look good in them," says Jerome.

"Who says they're supposed to?" asks Kaneesha. "It's not like somebody tells them they gotta be well dressed. The point is they get more respect if they be well dressed."

Alan raises his hand. "But the main thing is that the king treats the people fair. That's what's important. The respect he might get because he's well dressed is not that important."

Karen says, "Another idea someone suggested is that a king has to know how to take care of money. How important is that?"

Alan immediately says, "It's more important than being well dressed."

"Is it more important than being fair?"

Lakeisha says, "Those are both important. I mean, if you can't take care of money, you can't be fair about it."

"But if you're good at managing money, does that ensure that your kingdom will be happy and successful?" Karen asks.

"Not if you're not fair," says Alan.

"So do you all think that fairness is the most important characteristic for a king to have?" Karen asks. The class nods in agreement. "Okay, then I need to ask what you mean by *fairness*." She pauses, thinking, *too abstract*. "What are some examples of being fair?"

José raises his hand. "Like when we practice for soccer and we take kicks on goal, it's fair for all of us to get the same number of chances to kick."

Maria says, "When my family has a birthday party for one of us, it's fair for everyone to have a piece of cake."

"Instead of what?" asks Karen.

"Instead of one person eating three pieces so that some of us don't get none," says Maria.

"Do you think that that idea applies to anything besides sharing cake or having the same number of turns kicking the soccer ball?"

Alan says, "I saw a TV show last weekend. These guys were talking about money for schools. They said that suburban schools had more money per student than city schools did. Some of them thought that wasn't fair. But another guy thought it was, because he said that the taxpayers of some suburban communities decided to use more money for schools than city people did. Do you know what I mean?"

Karen asks, "Is that the same kind of problem as ensuring that everyone gets a piece of cake or that all players have a turn at kicking the soccer ball?"

Lakeisha says, "It seems like it the same, except money for education seems like more important than cake at a party. Ain't that right?" She looks at Alan.

"Yeah, it's the same," Alan responds. "It's just a matter of scale, I guess you could say. But the principle is the same."

"Do the rest of you agree with Lakeisha and Alan?"

José says, "Yeah, it seem like the same kind of thing to me. Like everybody get an equal turn or amount."

Karen waits to see whether anyone wants to add anything. Then she says, "There's an expression for what you're talking about, *distributive justice*. The basic idea is that people get the same or very similar opportunities or goods or services. This is a right that is protected by the Constitution. But it is a very old idea coming to us from ancient Greece, if not earlier. Sometimes this is called *equity*." She writes the word on the overhead. "People should be treated equitably." She writes the sentence on the overhead. "I would like you to copy this word in the vocabulary section of your notebook. And write down the sentence too. That will help you remember what it means. So what can we say about a good king?"

Janeefa raises her hand. "A good king treats people equitably."

"Good. Another way to say it?"

"So do you all think that fairness is the most important characteristic for a king to have?"

José says, "He treats people with equity."

"Good. Now copy the phrase *distributive justice* into your notebooks as well." Karen waits as they do. "*Distributive justice* implies that there is another kind of justice. If there were only one kind of justice, there would be no need to have an adjective with it. So what do you think is another kind of justice?" When no one responds, she asks, "Are any of you familiar with any of the TV programs like *Law and Order* or *CSI*?" There are several nods. "What are those programs generally about?"

Janeefa raises her hand. "I watch those. They about somebody commits a crime. Then the cops catch 'em and charge 'em with the crime, and take 'em to court. Then they go to jail usually, not always."

"That's a good summary, Janeefa. Now this is for the whole class: what does that have to do with justice? It is not what we just talked about, distributive justice. How would you describe the kind of justice involved in those programs? We are out of time. So let that be your assignment for tonight. Write a paragraph in which you distinguish equity and distributive justice from the kind of justice involved in courts. Everyone understand?" She pauses. "José, what is the homework?"

"Um, we got to write a paragraph about the kind of justice in the court type of TV shows."

"And what else?"

"We should distinguish between distributive justice and the kind of justice in the shows," says Lakeisha.

"Exactly. Anyone have any questions? Do you all know what I mean by *distinguish*? I want you to explain, as best you can, the difference between justice in the criminal system and distributive justice. This is not easy. I expect you all to make an attempt. I am going to collect what you write." The bell rings, and Karen calls good-bye as the students gather up their belongings and head out the door. She knows that homework is a problem at this school. The MAT group has never had everyone turn in even short assignments, even though each assignment receives some credit. But she is confident that Lakeisha and Alan and several others will do the work.

As students file in the next day, Karen has them put their paragraphs on their desks. She tours the room, initialing seventeen papers, more than the usual eleven or twelve. She resists the temptation to give the ten slackers a piece of her mind, knowing it will be counterproductive. Instead, she asks for volunteers to read what they have written. Lakeisha, Alan, Janeefa, and José raise their hands. José ordinarily does not do homework, so she calls on him, reminding him to read loud enough for everyone to hear.

José stands and reads. "Distributive is when people get what they are supposed to in a equity way. People should all get the same stuff or presents or opportunities. That is equity. The TV shows are about when somebody does something bad. The cops catch him and he has to go to court. Usually he gets punished. In a way, that the same kind of justice as the first kind. People get what they deserve."

"Thank you, José. Let's hear a couple of others, and then we will discuss what you all think."

Lakeisha begins reading what she had written. "We said that distributive justice is concerned with equity and treating people equitably. It mean, do they receive goods, services, and opportunities in the same way? Or do some people receive those things more than others? In the TV shows, the justice system is mainly concerned with giving out punishment. Somebody commits a crime, and the cops' and lawyers' job is to punish them for what they done. In distributive justice, the idea is for people to receive what they deserve because they are people like everybody else. But in the court system, the people who commit crime have to receive what they do because they committed a crime. Well that what I thought anyway."

"That is very helpful, Lakeisha. Now, what do the rest of you think? Let me make a little outline on the overhead." Karen writes down two headings, *distributive justice* and *justice in court*. For several minutes, the class discusses the differences between the two. They came to see the essential difference between the two as the difference between what people deserve in the normal course of their lives and what people deserve because they have wronged others. Karen asks whether punishments also have to be equitable, giving the example of a black seventeen-year-old who had been sentenced to ten years in prison for having oral sex with an underage girl. The Supreme Court of Georgia later released him from his sentence after he had served two years. Students conclude that punishments too have to be meted out in an equitable fashion and that the two ideas are therefore intertwined.

Karen now returns to the original problem—what characteristics must a good king have? "We have three," she says. "Can you think of any others?" The class is silent for several moments. Finally, a few hands go up.

Karen calls on Donald. "I think a good king got to be a good leader. You know, like, he got to make people follow his ideas."

"How would he do that?" Karen asks.

Lindsay says, "He got to inspire them by setting a good example."

"What do the rest of you think? Does a good king have to set a good example? Can't he just order people around?"

Donald is adamant. "No, no, no. He can order people around but if he want to get anything done, he got to set a good example. In ROTC we learn that a good leader got to set a good example. If the leader don't do the right thing, why should anybody else do the right thing? You know, if you want other people to put theyselves in danger, you got to be willing to do it youself. If you go hide, everybody else gonna go hide."

"Okay. What do the rest of you think? Is Donald right? Does the king have to set a good example?"

"What do the rest of you think? Does a good king have to set a good example? Can't he just order people around?"

"Yeah, man," Grant says. "If he don't set a good example, why would anyone do different? Say he tell people not to steal. But he go stealing hisself. You think anybody gonna pay attention to what he say? No!"

"No," several students chime in together.

Karen says, "It sounds as though we have good leadership as a criterion for being a good king, but leadership has its own criteria that have to be met before we can decide if a person is a good leader. Right?" She writes *criterion* and *criteria* on the board, briefly explaining that the first word means *one*, and the second word means *more than one*. "One *criterion*, seven *criteria*. Put those words in your vocabulary lists. Okay, then, for one to be a good leader, one must set a good example. Is that right?"

"We studied the Holocaust. Hitler didn't set no good example. But he led the Germans," says Roberto.

Karen says, "Good point. When we say *a good leader*, what do we mean? There are at least two possibilities."

"I think it means is he good at leading people in getting them to do what he wants," says Donald.

"Yeah," Alan agrees. "Do they get results? Like, do they accomplish what they want to?"

"Do you mean that one way to judge leaders is in terms of what they and their followers accomplish?" asks Karen.

"Yes," says Alan, "that is the most important thing, it seem to me."

"Okay, is there any other thing the phrase *good leader* could mean? Any thoughts?" The class is silent. Finally Lakeisha raises her hand, and Alan, and Donald. Karen calls on Donald.

"It could mean, like, um, does he or she do good things. Like, you know, like is he a good guy or not?"

"Good. Who can add to that?"

Lakeisha is waving her hand vigorously. "I was going to say, does he or she do the right thing? You know, does he or she act morally?"

"What do you all think about that idea?" Karen asks. "Is that an important consideration? Do good leaders have to be moral or ethical people? Maybe that brings us back to Hitler, Roberto. Class, do you think that Hitler should be called a good leader?"

Eventually Alan raises his hand. "Didn't we say that there are two, like, meanings for what we mean by good leader, like effective and ethical? Or effective and moral? Because if we did, then we can say he was effective in leading the German people to victory over a bunch of countries. But he was not moral because he did evil stuff."

José adds, "Yeah, like he killed more than six million Jews, and homosexuals, and gypsies."

"So he not moral," says Lakeisha. "Anything *but* moral."

"I don't think he very effective either," Ruthie says. "I mean he lost the war didn't he? He conquered most of Europe, but in a few years he lost it all. And Germany got bombed to pieces. That don't sound effective to me."

"Yeah, and he had to commit suicide to escape," says Ronald.

"That's a good point," Alan says. "Hitler was only effective for a limited time."

"So what does that mean about how we should judge effectiveness?" Karen waits. "That is, how should we judge the effectiveness of a leader?"

> "When we say a good leader, *what do we mean? There are at least two possibilities.*"

She waits again. "Let me try to be more specific. President Bush decided to go to war against Iraq. He thought the invasion was successful. On May 1, 2003, Bush landed a plane on an aircraft carrier, and a sign behind him, as he addressed the nation, said, 'Mission accomplished.' But the vast majority of casualties, both American and Iraqi, came after his statement that the major combat had ended. What do you think of that? Was the invasion effective as Bush said?" There is a chorus of "No" from the class. "So what does that say about judging the effectiveness of a leader?"

José says, "You gotta wait till the thing is done."

"Until what thing is done?"

"It's like, it ain't over till its over," Donald says. "It's like in football. You can't judge which the best team until the game over and you know the final score."

"Okay, and how does that apply to judging the effectiveness of leaders?" Karen asks.

Lakeisha says, "You gotta judge on the whole time he the leader, not just some part. Not just one thing but all the thing he done."

"Do you think that is true for all of our criteria? Including setting a good example, managing money well, being just, acting in a morally responsible way, and even dressing well?"

"Yes," says Lakeisha. "You gotta judge on the basis of everything. Like, he might do one good thing and a million bad things. One good thing ain't gonna make him a moral leader." The class seems to agree.

> "Didn't we say that there are two meanings for what we mean by good leader, effective and ethical? Or effective and moral? Because if we did, then we can say he was effective in leading the German people to victory over a bunch of countries. But he was not moral because he did evil stuff."

(4) **Work with the class to apply one of their criteria to the prince pictured in "The Voluptuary." Record their thinking on a chart under the headings Claim, Evidence, and Warrant.**

"Well," Karen says, "let's apply these criteria to the prince. Do you think he is fit to be king?" There is a chorus of "No." Karen asks, "Why not?"

Donald says, "He not a good money manager."

"Why do you say that? Remember, if you are making a claim, you have to show evidence and explain how the evidence supports your claim."

Donald answers promptly, "He got gambling debts, like we said. Anybody got gambling debts probably not a good manager of money. Because it stupid to gamble."

> "So what does that mean about how we should judge effectiveness? That is, how should we judge the effectiveness of a leader?"

"Can you develop that a bit more? Why is it stupid to gamble?"

"'Cause it be stupid to gamble 'cause you lose you money. Everybody know that. Even gamblers know that."

"Okay, Donald has alluded to evidence. Can we be more specific about that?"

"He got a book on the floor. Says 'Debts of Honor.' You said that mean gambling debts," says Janeefa.

"Good. We have all the elements of an argument. Let's try to put them together more formally. I'm going to write Donald's initial claim on the overhead." Karen writes his statement, replacing the pronoun with a noun and inserting the verb. "*The prince is not a good money manager.* Help me out now. What's the evidence and the explanation of it?"

Janeefa raises her hand. "There a book on the floor called 'Debts of Honor,' which mean gambling debts. That the evidence." Karen writes Janeefa's statement of evidence, correcting the verb. "Now, does that need some explanation?"

Lakeisha says, "Yes, we need to say something like, anyone who has gambling debts is probably not a good manager of money, because spending on gambling result in debt, like Donald said. It stupid to gamble because you lose money. Like he said, everybody know that. Even gamblers know that."

Claim	Evidence	Warrant (Explanation)
The prince is not a good money manager.	There's a book on the floor called "Debts of Honor," which means gambling debts.	Anyone who has gambling debts is probably not a good manager of money because spending on gambling results in debt. It is common knowledge that you lose money in gambling. Everybody knows that, even gamblers.

"There's another way to say that. Do you know the expression *common knowledge*? So we can say it this way." Karen writes, *Anyone who has gambling debts is probably not a good manager of money because spending on gambling results in debt. It is common knowledge that*

"Remember, if you are making a claim, you have to show evidence and explain how the evidence supports your claim."

you lose money in gambling. Everybody knows that, even gamblers. "Is that okay with you?" The class nods. "We have a claim, our evidence, a warrant, and some backing for the warrant." She labels the parts of the argument on the overhead.

5 **Put students in groups of three or four and ask them to work with the remaining criteria established by the class.**

"I would like you to work in your small groups for the next ten minutes. There are five criteria left to deal with: setting a good example; being equitable; being well dressed; being an effective leader; and being a moral leader." She writes these criteria on the overhead. "I would like you to deal with as many as you can in the next ten minutes. But I want to be sure they all are covered. So I am going to put your group number by one criterion. If your group number is beside that criterion, work on that one first and then move to a different one. Here is what I want you to do: (1) Determine whether or not you can use this criterion to come to a judgment about the prince. (2) If you can use the criterion, provide the *evidence*, the *warrant*, and any backing or *explanation* for why the criterion applies. Create a chart like the one we just did together to record your thinking."

Karen stops first at the group nearest her, one without a strong leader, then moves on to others. After ten minutes, she asks, "How many groups need more time?" Hands in every group go up. "All right, take another ten minutes." She continues her rounds, checking that each group has written an argument related to at least one criterion. When she sees that most have worked with at least two, she calls the class to order. "So, group 1, does the criterion of setting a good example apply to the prince?"

"Yeah," says Janeefa. "You can apply it, but he don't set a good example. He eat too much so his clothes bust out. He drink too much. We said all the bottles under the table and on it show that. He gamble and don' pay his debts. And he probly go with some ho' because he got STD. So we don't think he set a good example at all. He set a bad example. We don't think we want a leader of the country like that."

Karen asks, "What do the rest of you think about that?"

Ronald has his hand up. "But he act the way a king act. So he a good example of what a king do."

Janeefa snaps, "But that ain't the kind of king you want to be tellin' everybody what to do. He gonna lead the country on the path to ruin. And you know it. That stupid."

"Janeefa, we agreed earlier that we would not call names," Karen reminds her.

"I din't call him no name. I said what he said was stupid. And it is. We agreed that we were gonna decide what a good king should do, not what a bad king do. Just because that what maybe most kings do, that don't mean we want one of those."

"Ronald, do you want to respond to Janeefa?"

"No, I just sayin' that what most kings do."

"Let's take a minute to talk about this kind of language. You all agreed that we should all respect each other. Right?" Most of the students nod. "Well, when you use words like *stupid*, *dumb*, *silly*, or other slur words, you convey a lack of respect, even if you don't mean to. Now, that doesn't mean you cannot disagree with each other. I would like you to use less nasty language. If you don't agree with someone, you can just say, 'I disagree with that,' and then explain why you disagree. Okay? In the future let's avoid such words." Most students are now looking down at their papers. "Anyone else want to add to what group 1 had to say?"

Afraid that she may have destroyed the class' enthusiasm, Karen moves on, "Okay, let's move to the second criterion. Group 2, what did you have to say about being equitable?"

Lakeisha responds for the group. "We think he probly not equitable because he want everything for hisself. He just take what he want and don't care about nobody. So he probly not equitable."

"Did anyone decide differently?" No responses. "Did any of you explain it differently?"

Alan raises his hand. "We said he indulges himself in every pleasure, food, drink, gambling, and sex. He does all of these to extremes. He appears not to be the least bit interested in others as he looks around the room. In fact, we think he looks down his nose at everyone, like he thinks he's all that. So, he's addicted to pleasure, and he has no concern for anyone else. Because of all that, we think he could not be equitable because he puts himself first in everything. And since he only cares about pleasure, he would not take the time to do justice to others. We think he would see that as beneath him."

"Can you explain a bit more what you mean by *he thinks he's all that*?" Karen asks.

"You know, he looks like he's looking down his nose at everyone. He's picking his teeth with a fork. Isn't that like rude to do in front of people?"

Janeefa raises her hand. "I'd get in big trouble if I did that at the dinner table."

Donald adds, "It be a sign of, what that word we use the other day? Like, um, contempt."

"Yeah," says Alan, "it is a sign of contempt, we think. That's the word for it."

"Well, that is a good word for it, but why is it a sign of contempt?" asks Karen. For a moment the class is silent.

Then Donald says, "My Granny say the reason you show good manners is that it show respect to people with you. When you rude, you disrespect them. And this guy rude. He even vomit at the table. That rude!"

"All right," Karen says. "Do any of you disagree?" No one does.

In the next few minutes, groups report on their ideas about the remaining criteria: being well dressed; being an effective leader; and being a moral leader. The class decides that the prince may have been well dressed at one time but has eaten so much that he is popping his buttons and can no longer be considered well dressed. Students also think that being well dressed is not as important as meeting the other criteria. They think he cannot be an effective leader because he doesn't set a good example and because he doesn't care about anyone and cannot be equitable. They also decide that for similar reasons he cannot be a good moral leader.

(6) **Students write an argument of judgment.**

Karen then asks the students to write an argument of judgment about whether or not the prince would be a good king. She points out that in eighteenth-century England, the kingship was hereditary and that the only way to block an inheritance of the throne was for lords of the realm to mount a coup d'état, which could lead to civil war. Writing arguments to that effect would be regarded as treasonous. In the eighteenth century, people were hanged for treason. Therefore, their arguments that the prince is not fit to be king will have to be powerful. (This could have been a more involved assignment using additional historical documents, but it's appropriate for this class, at this early stage of developing arguments of judgment.)

Karen spends a few minutes asking students what they think would be the best way to organize their arguments. The class settles on beginning with a definition of a good king, applying at least three of the criteria to the Prince of Wales, and presenting evidence for each criterion, along with warrants showing how the evidence supports the judgment of whether or not the prince meets the criterion.

Afterward, the MAT students and I discussed the lesson. We were quite pleased, predicting that at least half the students would complete the assignment. Since the students hadn't been given class time in which to begin their individual pieces, we decided to give them class time the next day to write more and also to edit what they'd written.

Karen collected the papers in the middle of the next class period. There were thirteen papers of three pages or more, seven papers of two pages, and five of about a page—one of the best completion rates we'd ever had. More importantly, all but one paper dealt with at least two criteria and presented evidence and warrants to argue that the prince could not meet the criteria. We were delighted.

"Karen spends a few minutes asking students what they think would be the best way to organize their arguments. The class settles on beginning with a definition of a good king, applying at least three of the criteria to the Prince of Wales, and presenting evidence for each criterion, along with warrants showing how the evidence supports the judgment of whether or not the prince meets the criterion."

Tips on Using Small-Group Discussions

Small-group discussions make for powerful learning environments when they are carefully planned and monitored. We have watched many small groups flounder when the task assigned has not been clearly demonstrated in a whole-class discussion under the direction of the teacher; when the task is too difficult for the present abilities of the students; when the task is ambiguous; or when the teacher fails to visit each group to monitor progress continuously. To avoid small-group failure:

» Demonstrate how to do the task in a whole-class discussion before assigning small-group work on similar tasks
» Be sure that the tasks for small-group work are at the same level of difficulty as the task that you demonstrated with the whole class

» Assign students to groups based on their demonstrated strength as readers or writers so that if there are to be seven groups of four, the top seven students will be assigned one to each group, the seven weakest one to each group, the remainder sprinkled among the groups so that each group has no more than four students

» Avoid allowing students to group with their friends even if they beg you to let them work with their friends

» Teach students how to move into their small groups (I did this by the numbers: One, stand and move to the part of the room where your group will meet; two, find a desk near your group's location; three, move the desk into position with other members of the group, preferably into a square so that you can see one another; four, get to work. Doing this by the numbers once was usually enough in my classes.)

» Visit your weakest group first, then move to the next weakest, saving the strongest until last

» Listen to what the students are saying in their groups only long enough to find out if they are on track

» Keep an eye on all groups, even while concentrating on one group

» Try to find something to praise about the group's work ethic, ideas, or progress

» If groups are off track, give suggestions or hints about how to get back on track

» Move to the next group

You may need to shuffle students in the groups after the first meeting to allow for personal animosities or other problems. Shuffle students among groups when it seems necessary, but I recommend sticking with groupings for the length of a unit of six to eight weeks.

Solving Problems Kids Care About

Writing Simple Arguments of Policy

WHEN MIDDLE AND HIGH SCHOOL TEACHERS ASSIGN RE-
search papers, they often ask for arguments of policy. Arguments of policy
typically make a case to establish, amend, or eliminate rules, procedures,
practices, and projects that are believed to affect people's lives.

For example, a young acquaintance of mine recently wrote a paper on
whether or not the death penalty should be abolished in Illinois. His resources were several newspaper articles and editorials, three magazine articles, and two books. However, there was no real inquiry involved in his
assignment. In his paper, he largely summarized the ideas presented in these
sources. His main problem was figuring out how to organize them.

When I investigated teaching practices related to state assessments in
five states (Hillocks 2002), I interviewed more than three hundred teachers.
Only a handful of them spoke of anything that could be called inquiry. Their
"research paper" assignments were similar to the one completed by my

young friend and focused on policy issues currently in the news: inspecting food products, inspecting toys manufactured in China, restricting handguns, holding dog fights, reducing U.S. armed forces in Iraq, and increasing the cigarette tax.

These weighty, complex questions of policy are relatively easy for students to deal with. The data in the sources they consult have already been digested and are accompanied by summaries, conclusions, and opinions, sometimes supported, sometimes not. As with my young friend, their only problem is how to organize what they find in their secondary sources into a more or less coherent essay. They are not required to collect and interpret any original data.

Such an approach to teaching research, and certainly to teaching critical thinking and logical argument, is pedagogically unsound. Here is why:

> *Students have no way to investigate these problems except through secondary sources.* These provide not raw data but opinions and judgments about data someone else has collected. Indeed, these sources might better be called *tertiary*, for they are reports of reports of the original research. Students don't learn to interpret data for themselves. Rather, they learn how other writers have interpreted data collected and interpreted by other researchers.

> *These problems do not involve real research.* Rather, students review some fragment of the available literature, usually limited to the number of sources the teacher requires (which invariably introduces bias). The goal is to go to the library, find some material related to a problem, take notes, and compile those notes into a more or less coherent essay.

> *Since there are no original data, the only arguments made are warranted by the presumed authority of the writers whose work the student has chosen to quote, summarize, or, in some cases, plagiarize.* This promotes the notion that "if it's in the book, it must be true." In this kind of writing, the student can avoid any pretense of critical thinking. It is an invitation to plagiarism, intentional or not.

> *Students come to school with already learned solutions to the policy questions often favored by teachers (abortion, stem cell research, human cloning, capital punishment, the legality of dog fighting).* Not only have they learned solutions, they have learned the reasons

they offer to support these solutions. Critical thinking is at best undercut, at worst, eliminated.

The Common Core Standards rightly ask middle school students to "conduct short research projects to answer a question" and high school students to "conduct short as well as more sustained research projects to answer a question or solve a problem." But to get students to think about data and their implications, these problems must involve some original research; they must be about students' real concerns and amenable to real investigation. While such real problems may seem trivial to adults, students find them meaningful and are therefore engaged in the research. The first step for teachers is to find researchable problems.

Researchable Problems

Researchable problems can come from many sources. Sometimes parents want to ban a particular book or demand a change in the curriculum (more grammar, for example). And there are nearly always school rules regarding deportment, behavior, and dress that students find unreasonable.

"To get students to think about data and their implications, these problems must involve some original research; they must be about students' real concerns and amenable to real investigation."

When I was teaching junior high, outsiders disrupted a school dance and, as a result, the principal canceled all dances for the rest of the year, a decision not one student condoned. (It would have been a perfect topic for arguments of policy. However, my ninth graders were studying satire, and the incident became grist for that genre.)

Another example: A high school in Chicago reduced the time between classes from five to four minutes. Students had many legitimate complaints, including that they didn't have enough time to get from the second floor of the south wing to the second floor of the north wing, especially when the hallways were jammed, or when they needed to shower and dress after gym class.

It is most useful to work with sets of readily available concrete data when investigating the nature of a problem and deciding what to do about it. Problems like those above, which come from students' immediate lives and surroundings, provide that available data. Further, the best problems for younger students are those in which they have some stake and therefore are more likely to take an interest in collecting and studying the data. Following, you will see an example of one such problem.

Teaching Argument of Policy in Action

"It is most useful to work with sets of readily available concrete data when investigating the nature of a problem and deciding what to do about it."

Mrs. Peterson, a teacher in Texas, knew her eighth graders would be most engaged in their learning if she allowed them to find and present evidence about something they cared about. She helped her class investigate the school ban on chewing gum and prepare letters (arguments of policy) to the principal. I observed her lesson, and the following is an imaginative re-creation (no real names are used).

① Identifying and Clarifying the Problem

Mrs. Peterson wants the students to think about the gum-chewing ban in detail. To that end, the school principal provided a written explanation for her class that identifies the problem:

"The best problems for younger students are those in which they have some stake and therefore are more likely to take an interest in collecting and studying the data."

> Chewing gum is banned at Dickens School because it is very costly to remove gum that students place under their seats and desks. Even with the ban, we have to have the chairs and desks cleaned every year at a cost of thousands of dollars. We can put that money to better use. Further, several parents have complained about gum on the shoes and clothes and in the hair of their children. This occurs because careless and irresponsible students put their gum on the floors and on desks and chairs, perhaps deliberately or perhaps accidentally. In either case, the parents are not happy about the cleaning bills. It is important for the school to have the support of parents. Since the school needs the support of parents and since we have better uses for the money that removing gum takes from our budget, the ban on chewing gum must stay in place.

The students discuss the note. Ronald wonders if there really are gum wads under the seats and desks. Ricardo thinks that if there are, it's because of the ban on gum: Students put gum there to avoid being caught. "Either that or swallow it."

Julie interjects, "You guys ever have gum in your clothes or hair? I don't remember having any in my clothes." Most students agree.

Mrs. Peterson asks, "What questions will we have to ask and answer to deal with this problem?"

Julie raises her hand. "How do we know how expensive it is to remove it? She says it is, but maybe it isn't. And that's her main point."

"Well, how can we find that out?" asks Mrs. Peterson.

"Could we ask to see the bill?" Katrina asks.

"Who does that anyway?" Kenny says, "I bet the custodians do that. How do we know how much time they spend on it?"

"If they do it, there probably isn't a bill," says Ricardo.

"We could ask them," says another student.

Alonzo is skeptical. "They're probably gonna exaggerate, you know, to make them look good."

"Yeah," says Kenny. "We should clean some and see how long it takes. Like how many wads can we get off in an hour?"

With Mrs. Peterson's help, the students develop a short list of questions that will help them learn whether disposing of gum improperly is a serious problem and determine what might be done about it:

1. How many wads of gum are under the seats and desks in a typical classroom?
2. What most students do to discard their used gum?
3. On average, how many times a year do students find gum on their clothes or in their hair?
4. Why do students think that they or others put gum under their chairs or desks?
5. How much does it cost to clean the gum off?

"With Mrs. Peterson's help, the students develop a short list of questions that will help them learn whether disposing of gum improperly is a serious problem and determine what might be done about it."

2. Planning an Investigation

Next, Mrs. Peterson asks what the students can do to answer the questions. The first is easy: They can count the wads of gum they find in their classroom and some others. But how many others?

One girl suggests they need to examine classrooms at every grade level, because more older kids than younger ones chew gum. Mrs. Peterson recommends they make a stratified random sample, examining two classrooms at each grade level, excluding kindergarten and first grade, for a total of fourteen classrooms. She puts all the qualifying room numbers on slips of paper in a bag and mixes them up, and the students pull out fourteen. She briefly explains the importance of anonymity in this kind of research and says she'll reassure the teachers of the rooms chosen that findings for individual rooms won't be reported to the principal. "People are more likely to tell the truth if they know they will not be held accountable."

For questions 2, 3, and 4, students suggest they can just ask other students. Mrs. Peterson tells them that to be most convincing, they need to do this formally. They can make up a set of questions for students to answer, either in an interview or on a questionnaire. They talk about what each method involves and decide a questionnaire will take less time.

Next, Mrs. Peterson has students, in small groups, work on phrasing the questions; she asks them to make sure younger students can understand them. The groups report their ideas, and the class develops the following questionnaire, with Mrs. Peterson's guidance (in particular, she explains the usefulness of finding out frequency in relation to the possible responses):

"Mrs. Peterson tells them that to be convincing, they need to create a formal questionnaire."

1. After you have chewed a piece of gum, how do you usually dispose of it? Circle the frequency that best applies to your getting rid of used gum.
   a. I stick it on the bottom of my seat or desk.
      Always   Usually   Occasionally   Never
   b. I wrap it up in the wrapper and put it in a wastebasket.
      Always   Usually   Occasionally   Never
   c. I throw it on the floor.
      Always   Usually   Occasionally   Never
      I throw it in a wastebasket without wrapping it.
      Always   Usually   Occasionally   Never
2. How many times in the first five months of school did you find gum on your clothes?
3. How many times in the first five months of school did you find gum in your hair?
4. Why do you think students sometimes put gum under their seats or their desks? Circle the letter of all that you think are true.
   a. They are careless and do not think about what they are doing.
   b. They are afraid to get caught chewing gum.
   c. They do it to be mean.

5. How often do you chew gum in school? Circle one.
    Every day   Occasionally   Never

3 **Conducting the Investigation**

The students decide with whom they wish to work, and Mrs. Peterson assigns each pair to one of the randomly selected rooms to check desks and administer the questionnaire. Each pair is also responsible for tabulating the responses to the questionnaire students administer. When the students meet as a class, they discover they have found a total of 13,944 wads of gum. They also tabulate all the questionnaire responses into a single table. (Mrs. Peterson shows them how to use a computer spreadsheet to tabulate the total responses and calculate percentages.)

So the students can find out how long it takes to clean gum from desks, Mrs. Peterson asks for volunteers to clean the desks and seats in her own classroom. Three boys volunteer. Mrs. Peterson suggests that they search the Internet for a good method of cleaning the gum off the surfaces. After investigating, they get solvent and metal scrapers from a hardware store and in sixty minutes clean off forty-five wads of gum, about four minutes per wad for someone working alone.

Next, Mrs. Peterson has the boys use the cleaning rate they have established to calculate the time necessary for one person to clean the gum from all the desks in all the school classrooms (excluding kindergarten and first grade). They discover that it would take over 920 hours to clean the estimated 41,400 wads of gum that forty-two classrooms would be harboring.

Now students need to find out the actual cost. Mrs. Peterson suggests they make an appointment to see the principal some day after school and plan ahead of time exactly what they will say about their project and what they will ask. The boys decide to say they are writing a research paper about the chewing gum problem at the school. (They won't mention the letter the class intends to write.) They'll ask her what it actually costs to clean the gum from the desks and chairs of the classrooms.

During the interview, the principal can't give them an exact amount. She says, "It takes the custodial staff several weeks each summer to clean the gum from the desks." When the boys press her for the

"Each pair of students must check desks for gum in the rooms they are assigned and administer the questionnaire. The students are also responsible for tabulating the responses to the questionnaire they administer."

"They discover that it would take over 920 hours to clean the estimated 41,400 wads of gum that forty-two classrooms would be harboring."

number of days, she tells them to ask Mr. Groat, the head custodian. The boys also ask how much the custodians earn per hour. The principal replies that she's not at liberty to say.

Kenny tells her, "My father says that is supposed to be public knowledge, because you are all public employees. So what do we have to do to find out?" The principal says she doesn't know but they can ask the custodians.

The boys go to see to Mr. Groat. He says that he personally doesn't clean up the gum but assigns it to two or three new hires and that it usually takes them about seven or eight weeks each summer. On average, a new hire is paid $13 an hour.

The three boys report the basic facts to the class: about 41,400 wads of gum, four minutes to clean each wad off, about 920 hours to clean it all, and pay for the custodian at $13 per hour. If the custodian works steadily, that comes to $11,960. According to their estimate, the gum cleaning should take one person about twenty-three weeks, assuming he works forty hours a week. With three workers, it would take about eight weeks. This is a good match with the cost and time Mr. Groat has told them is spent cleaning up the gum.

(4) **Introducing Argument of Policy**

Mrs. Peterson explains that when the students write their letters to the principal, they will want to use their data to make a case about retaining or changing the chewing gum ban. They will need to explain the methods of their research and attach a copy of the questionnaire and, as mentioned above, the table of results.

"We are going to develop this a bit at a time. There is a fairly standard form that is expected in arguments of policy. I'll teach you how to use it now." She puts a transparency on the overhead showing an outline of the components:

Argument of Policy Components

I. Introduction—Describe the nature of the problem to be investigated and explain the major and related questions.

"The three boys report the basic facts to the class: about 41,400 wads of gum, four minutes to clean each wad off, about 920 hours to clean it all, and pay for the custodian at $13 per hour."

II. Research Design and Methods—Explain how you went about investigating the problem and related questions.

    A. Classes and how selected

    B. Counting of wads in classrooms

    C. Questionnaire and tallies

    D. Procedures for estimating time and cost of cleaning desks

III. Results/Findings—Explain what you found relative to each area above as a result of the methods you used.

IV. Interpretation of Results/Findings—Explain what the results mean and why these interpretations are valid.

V. Conclusions and Recommendations—Explain what might reasonably be done in light of the research findings.

Although some teachers might simply present this outline and tell students to write their letters, Mrs. Peterson knows her students will be overwhelmed by that—there are too many difficulties. She needs to structure the tasks and deal with the parts one at a time. In the following pages, you will see Mrs. Peterson working closely with students to create an argument of policy.

(5)   **Writing the Introduction**

"Who remembers why we undertook this study?"

Ricardo responds, "We didn't agree with the rule in the code of student behavior that says you can't chew gum."

"Do you recall why?"

Julie raises her hand. "We didn't think chewing gum was a big deal. I mean it doesn't hurt anybody. It doesn't keep you from doing your work."

"Anyone else?"

Kenneth volunteers, "We did the study to find out if gum was as big a problem as Ms. Langford said it was in her note to us."

"Good, we need to put all of that information in the introduction and state specifically why we undertook the study. I want you to help

"When the students write their letters to the principal, they will want to use their data to make a case about retaining or changing the chewing gum ban."

"Although some teachers might simply present this outline and tell students to write their letters, Mrs. Peterson knows her students will be overwhelmed by that. She needs to structure the tasks and deal with the parts one at a time."

me compose an opening paragraph. I'll write it on the overhead. You all make your own copies. Okay, how will we begin?"

Ricardo says, "We could put what Kenneth just said."

Mrs. Peterson asks Kenneth to repeat what he said, and she writes it on the middle of her transparency: *We did the study to find out if gum was as big a problem as Ms. Langford said it was in her note to us.*

"If readers haven't heard our discussions, will they have any questions about this statement?" Mrs. Peterson asks.

Rosalyn raises her hand. "They won't know what the study is. We should probably say what it is."

"Or say why we did it," Jessica contributes.

"What do we need to explain so readers will understand why we did the study?"

"We should probably say what the rule is and what Ms. Langford wrote," says Patty.

"Okay, how will we say all that?"

Teddy raises his hand. "The Dickens School code of student behavior states, 'Chewing gum is strictly forbidden in the school building.' Then say what Ms. Langford said, like, 'According to Ms. Langford, this ban must remain in place because cleaning the gum from desks is expensive and because parents complain about gum on students' clothing and gum in students' hair.'" Mrs. Peterson writes these two sentences above Kenneth's sentence on the overhead, which now reads:

> The Dickens School code of student behavior states, "Chewing gum is strictly forbidden in the school building." According to Ms. Langford, this ban must remain in place because cleaning the gum from desks is expensive and because parents complain about gum on students' clothing and gum in students' hair. We did the study to find out if gum was as big a problem as Ms. Langford said it was in her note to us.

Mrs. Peterson asks if there are any changes that should be made. Julie immediately suggests saying *a study* instead of *the study*. Mrs. Peterson asks her to explain why.

"We haven't said anything about a study yet. Using *the* makes it sound as though everyone knows what the study is. It's just better to use *a*, until we explain it." Mrs. Peterson adds that *the* is a definite article indicating things that are definitely known, while *a* is indefinite. She asks if anyone has additional changes. When no one does, she suggests that they consider using the word *conducted* instead of *did*. "Researchers generally talk about conducting a study rather than doing a study." The class accepts that suggestion. Then she asks how they can make the study definite by stating its goals more explicitly.

Ricardo responds, "We wanted to find out how much gum was on desks and chairs." Mrs. Peterson writes that on the overhead and asks, "What else did we want to find out?"

Kenny volunteers, "We wanted to estimate the cost of removing the gum." Mrs. Peterson adds that sentence to the paragraph. "What else?"

Melissa raises her hand, "We wanted to see what students said about um . . . uh . . . about how they threw away gum."

Julie adds, "And what they said about other people chewing gum."

"Well," Mrs. Peterson says, "we asked several questions of students, questions related to the chewing of gum. Can any of you think of a more general statement that would refer to all of our questions to students?"

Teddy raises his hand again. "You could say we wanted to find out what students thought and did about the chewing gum problem."

Mrs. Peterson writes on the overhead, *We wanted to find out what students thought and did about the chewing gum problem.* She says, "I think there is a way to put all of these ideas into a single sentence using what are called the *infinitives* in each sentence. An *infinitive* is a verb plus the word *to*, as in *to bring, to sit, to think, to slither.* So in the last three sentences up here, what are the infinitives?"

The class is silent for a moment. Then Ricardo says, "You mean like *to find out*?"

"Yes, precisely."

Kenny offers, "*To estimate.*"

"Yes. You can take the infinitives and the words that follow and use them in what's called a *parallel structure*. You can write it this way:

"There is a way to put all of these ideas into a single sentence using what are called the infinitives in each sentence. An infinitive is a verb plus the word to, as in to bring, to sit, to think, to slither."

We wanted to find out how much gum was on the desks and seats, to esti-mate the cost of removing the gum, and to find out what students thought and did about the chewing gum problem. This sentence removes several words and eliminates repetitive phrases. What do you all think about this sentence?"

Julie says, "It still repeats *find out*."

"Good point. What words can you think of to replace that expres-sion?" The class makes a list of words synonymous with *find out—discover, determine, investigate, reveal, explore, inspect, consider—*and decides to substitute *determine* for the first use of *find out* and *investi-gate* for the second. Mrs. Peterson tells the students that the words syn-onymous with *find out* are important in writing about research and asks students to list the words in their notebooks.

6 **Presenting, Explaining, and Interpreting Findings**

Mrs. Peterson says the introduction is okay for now, and the class be-gins discussing and interpreting the findings so students can clarify the problem and bring related questions into clearer focus.

"What should we tell the principal about checking for gum under seats and desks?"

One boy suggests, "We should tell her that we checked the desks in fourteen classrooms."

"Do you want to say *we checked the desks* or do you want to be more specific?" After a brief discussion, the students decide they should explain that two students looked at every desk and chair in fourteen classrooms, two at each grade level, excluding kindergarten and first grade, and counted the wads of gum they found.

A student adds, "And we should tell her what we found—like there was no gum on about 5 percent of the desks and seats." Other stu-dents eagerly added more specific details about the quantity of gum: "But the rest had an average of thirty-seven wads of gum. That is over seven packs of gum on each."

Mrs. Peterson asks whether they think they should include the total number of gum wads they found. They counted 13,944 wads in fourteen classrooms, and there are forty-two classrooms in the school excluding kindergarten and first grade. In other words, they can estimate that there are likely three times as many as they have counted, probably around 41,382, give or take a few hundred.

Hearing that number, Ricardo complains, "We can't tell the principal that. There'll be a ban on gum forever."

"Well," says Mrs. Peterson, "we should not lie about the findings. If we do, what's likely to happen?" She waits and watches, noticing that some of the students are beginning to squirm. "If you make some claims about something, if you lie, what are people likely to think about you?"

"That you're a liar," Julie says.

"And what will that do to you?" Mrs. Peterson asks.

"It'd probably get you in trouble," says Ricardo.

"What kind of trouble?"

"You know, like go to the principal's office or get detention."

"What do the rest of you think? Would that be all there is to it?"

"I think it would be worse than that," says Julie.

"In what way would it be worse? How do you think people would respond if they found out you had faked the numbers?" Mrs. Peterson waits as the class thinks about this.

Then Ronald raises his hand. "Well, if people think you're a liar, they might not believe when you tell the truth, like in that thing about the wolf."

Jane says, "You mean like in the fable we read, 'The Boy Who Cried Wolf'?"

"Yeah," says Ronald, "he said *wolf, wolf, wolf* just to get attention. Then when a wolf came, the shepherds ignored him."

"It can't get much worse than that," Rosalyn says. "He died."

"No," agrees Mrs. Peterson, "it can't. But that's the problem. Actually there are cases of scientists who fake their findings. They usually get ostracized from the scientific community and lose their jobs. I don't think it's worth it. You all can look that up on the Internet if you're interested. Try looking under *discredited science or scientific hoaxes*. It's not a good idea to falsify results."

Julie raises her hand, "But if we're going to argue against the ban on gum, those numbers are dreadful. I mean, they would convince any adult to keep the ban. I don't think this is a good idea. We're not going to be able to make a case against the ban."

> *"Well," says Mrs. Peterson, "we should not lie about the findings. If we do, what's likely to happen?"*

"Those *are* powerful numbers," Mrs. Peterson agrees. "But can any of you think how we might use other data we collected to make a case?" Again she waits. "Think about the responses to the questionnaire." Slowly Julie, then Ronald, then Ricardo, raise their hands.

Mrs. Peterson calls on Julie. "I am thinking about number 4 on the questionnaire. One response was, 'They are afraid to get caught chewing gum.' Over 95 percent circled that response. That's like nearly unanimous agreement. So maybe that's the reason for so much gum."

Ronald waves his hand vigorously, not waiting to be called on. "Yeah, but on the first question, nobody said they always did that. Only 8 percent said they usually did, 35 percent said they occasionally did, and 47 percent said they never did. So what she said don't make sense. I mean, how can there be so much gum if so many people only put gum on the desks occasionally, and 47 percent say they never do it?"

"Probably people lied," Julie says.

"That's a very good point, Ronald and Julie," said Mrs. Peterson. "We probably need to explain it. I didn't expect to do this kind of thing today, but as long as it's fresh, we'll work on it. You each have a copy of the questionnaire and the summary of results. I want you to think about two questions." She writes the two questions on a transparency. "First, what is the essential difference between the two questions? And second, what are some explanations of the apparent differences in the students' responses to questions 1 and 4? I would like you to work in your small groups of four for ten minutes to figure this out. At the end of ten minutes, be prepared to report your thinking to the whole class."

Students quickly assemble in small groups of four and begin discussing the problem. Mrs. Peterson circulates from group to group, stopping to listen, sometimes asking a question, sometimes murmuring words of approval. After about ten minutes, she asks how many groups need more time. Students in only one group raise their hands. She asks the students to regather as a class and be ready to report their thinking. She points to the first question projected on the transparency: "What is the essential difference between the two questions?" Students from various groups have their hands in the air.

"Those are powerful numbers," Mrs. Peterson agrees. "But can any of you think how we might use other data we collected to make a case?"

She calls on Ricardo, who says, "The first question asks what you do with your own gum."

Julie interrupts, "Like what you *actually* do with it."

Ricardo nods. "Yeah, *actually* do. The second one asks why you think *other* kids do stuff."

"What do you mean by *do stuff*?"

"You know, like why kids put gum on the floor or on desks."

Julie's hand shoots up immediately. "That's not what we said. The question is, 'Why do you think students sometimes put gum under their seats or their desks?' It doesn't say anything about the floor. We said that the second question asks students to think about why they think other students, not themselves, put gum under seats or under desks. That's what our group said."

"Well, thank you, Ricardo and Julie, for your group's report. Now, what do the rest of you think about the differences between the questions?"

Ronald says, "We said pretty much the same thing. But we have an explanation."

"Hold the explanation for now until we see if everyone agrees with Ricardo and Julie's group. Does any group disagree?" Kids shake their heads no. "If you all agree, let's turn to the second question: *What are some explanations of the apparent differences in the students' responses to questions 1 and 4?* Who wants to explain that?"

Ronald already has his hand up. "We thought that kids answering the first question about what they did might want to cover up their own stuff, a little bit. But that when they had to explain what other people did, they would be more honest. You know, like, 'I don't hardly ever do it, but I know that other people do it all the time.' Or like, they think *some* other people do it all the time."

Julie jumps in. "That's what I said before. People lie about their own stuff because they're afraid they'll get in trouble. But if they're talking about someone else, they don't mind telling more of the truth, at least not if they don't have to name them."

Mrs. Peterson turns to Ronald. "Is that what you meant, that people lie in telling what they do in order to avoid trouble?"

"We didn't say they lie. Like that's too harsh. We said they kind of cover it up."

"What do the rest of you think about this? Are students lying about what they do?" Mrs. Peterson asks.

Teddy has his hand up. He doesn't often speak in class but when he does, it's usually insightful. "For both questions, you have to interpret the possible responses. For question 1, the responses are *always, usually, occasionally,* and *never.* Well, *always* and *never* are pretty clear, but what does *occasionally* mean, or *usually?* Those aren't clear. One person might do it six times in two weeks and think that's usually. But another person might think that means occasionally. So it is not like they intended to lie. They just interpret the terms in favor of themselves a little bit. I think it's just natural."

"What do you all think of that idea?"

Julie says, "I think that's still lying."

"I don't think so," Teddy says. "A lie's a deliberate attempt to deceive somebody. Remember when we talked about the woman in that short story? We said she deliberately tried to mislead the police. It was not like an accident. The evidence was right in front of her. And she deliberately lied about it. That is what a lie is. It's deliberate. But if you had to tell cops what you saw, and you left out some details because you forgot them, would that be a lie? I don't think so."

Mrs. Peterson waits, but no one has more to add.

Next, Mrs. Peterson asks students to consider how to report the responses to the questionnaire. She points out that even if they attach a table of the responses, they need to report the major findings in the body of the letter. Students made a number of suggestions: how often kids say they chew gum in school; how they say they dispose of the gum; what they say the reasons are for putting the gum under seats and desks; how many times they report having gum on their clothes or in their hair; and so forth.

(7) **Writing About Research Design and Methods**

Mrs. Peterson suggests that together they write a paragraph about the claims students made about the frequency of their chewing gum in school. She asks what the first sentence of the paragraph should

"For both questions, you have to interpret the possible responses. For question 1, the responses are always, usually, occasionally, *and* never. *Well,* always *and* never *are pretty clear, but what does* occasionally *mean, or* usually?*"*

be. Students begin reciting the percentages for each frequency: everyday, occasionally, never. One student suggests, "Sixty-five percent of the students said they never chewed gum in school." Mrs. Peterson writes that sentence on the overhead in the middle of her transparency. Then she says, "Do you think readers will understand if we begin with this? Do you think they will know what we are talking about?"

The class isn't sure. It's difficult for students to put themselves in place of a reader, especially when working in an unfamiliar genre.

Mrs. Peterson asks, "What do readers need to know about the questionnaire?" Immediately, one student suggests they should explain that a questionnaire was administered in fourteen classrooms. At the top of the transparency, Mrs. Peterson writes, "We administered a questionnaire to fourteen classes. . . ." She stops. "Should we tell how the classes were selected?" The students think they should, and they add the phrases "randomly selected" and "two classes at each grade level from second through eighth."

"Now, what next?" Someone says they can now go on to the sentence already on the overhead. Mrs. Peterson explains that it's a good idea to tell readers how data are obtained before presenting the results. "You have to tell about the questionnaire or question first. Then you tell the results—how students responded." When they finish composing the paragraph, it reads:

> We administered a questionnaire to fourteen classes, two classes at each grade level from second through eighth. One of the questions asked the students how often they chewed gum in school: every day, occasionally, or never. Sixty-five percent of the students said they never chewed gum in school; 29 percent said they chewed gum occasionally; and only 6 percent said they chewed gum every day.

8   Writing About Results and Interpreting Results

Mrs. Peterson then helps the class write the first few sentences of a paragraph about how students who took the questionnaire claimed they disposed of gum:

"Mrs. Peterson asks students to consider how to report the responses to the questionnaire. She points out that even if they attach a table of the responses, they need to report the major findings in the body of the letter."

"It's difficult for students to put themselves in place of a reader, especially when working in an unfamiliar genre."

"What do readers need to know about the questionnaire?"

One question asked students how they disposed of gum when they had finished chewing it. The question provided several options and asked students to circle the frequency with which they used it.

Mrs. Peterson tells students they should name the options and tell the percentage of students selecting each frequency. The students again use semicolons to separate the clauses stating the percentages:

> The first option was, "I stick it to the bottom of my seat or desk." Sixty-three percent said they never did that; 32 percent said they did it occasionally; 5 percent said they usually did; and none said they always did.

Mrs. Peterson suggests a version of the second sentence with fewer words: *Sixty-three percent said they never did that, 32 percent said occasionally, 5 percent said usually, and none said always.* "Which do you like best?" Most like the first version best because it is clearer. Mrs. Petersen tells them they can use either and asks them to write one or the other in their notes as an example.

Next, she asks groups of four to write about the next option using the paragraphs they've already composed as a model. She moves from group to group as they work. When they are finished, Mrs. Peterson asks a representative of each group to read aloud what the group members have written, including the punctuation. The paragraph one group produced is representative of the others:

> The second option for question 1 was "I wrap it up in the wrapper and put it in a wastebasket." Six percent said they always did that; 73 percent said they usually did; 21 percent said they occasionally did; but no one said they never did.

For the remainder of the hour, the students write individually about the third and fourth options for discarding gum. This is a test of whether they understand how to present this kind of data.

The following day, the class finishes writing about the question 1 options and (again individually) moves on to question 4. Mrs. Peterson

"Mrs. Peterson tells students they should name the options and tell the percentage of students selecting each frequency."

reminds them to include the apparent discrepancy in the students' responses to the questionnaire. Ricardo writes:

> The third option for question 1 was "I throw it on the floor." No one said they always or usually did, only 14 percent said they occasionally did and 86 percent said never. The fourth option was "I throw it in a wastebasket without wrapping it." Agin no one said they always or usually did, 27 percent said ocasionally, and 73 percent said never.
>
> Question 4 asked students, "Why do you think students sometimes put gum under their seats or their desks?" The options were
>
> a. They are careless and do not think about what they are doing.
> b. They are afraid to get caught chewing gum.
> c. They do it to be mean.
>
> No one circled c, but 25 percent circled a, and 95 percent circled b.
>
> Our class discussed these results because it was wierd. Nearly everyone thought kids put gum under the desks and seats because they were afraid of being caught, but 63 percent said they never did that themselves. But if they did not do it themselves, why would they think that other kids did? We think they were covering up their own behavior a little bit. Probably because they really do it themselves. They say other kids do it. So we believe that the main reason they put gum under the desks is because they don't want to get caught. That is the main thing the questionnaire told us.

"For the remainder of the hour, the students write individually about the third and fourth options for discarding gum. This is a test of whether they understand how to present this kind of data."

Ricardo has reported the questionnaire results accurately, used appropriate syntactic structures in doing so, interpreted the apparent discrepancies in students' responses, and made a fairly convincing case that what students said about others probably did reflect how most students acted. There are misspellings, somewhat inappropriate diction (e.g., "the main thing the questionnaire told us"), and a sentence fragment (which can easily be corrected by connecting it to the clause that follows). Mrs. Peterson is satisfied.

9　Writing Conclusions and Recommendations

The final part of the project is to develop conclusions (interpretations of the results) and recommendations. As a prompt, Mrs. Petersen rereads the note the principal sent to the class. When she finishes, some class members echo Ricardo's earlier comment that if they reveal how much gum is under the desks and seats, "There'll be a ban on gum forever." Others recall their discussion that they have to be honest in presenting their findings. Some students think it's pointless to write anything.

Teddy raises his hand. "We don't have to ask her to just get rid of the ban on gum. Maybe we should tell her that she's right: there is a lot of gum on the desks and seats, probably more than she thinks. But if kids put their wads there because of the ban, you know, because they're afraid of being caught, then maybe if she ended the ban, there would be less gum on the desks and seats. I mean, that makes sense, doesn't it?"

"What do the rest of you think about that?" A number of hands are raised.

Julie says, "My dad's a doctor. And when I told him about how much gum we found, he was shocked. He said it amounted to a health hazard."

Marielle adds, "My mom's a nurse. She said the same thing."

"That's stupid," says Alonzo, "How can a little bit of gum be a health hazard?"

"Anyone want to comment on that?"

Julie jumps back in. "It is not stupid. We learned that our bodies carry germs of all kinds sometimes. People get colds from talking to other people with colds. Gum has been in a person's mouth. It's gonna have their germs on it. That's clear. If you touch the gum, the germs get on your fingers. And if your fingers touch your mouth, you get the germs. That's why no one wants to pick up someone else's gum."

"Yeah," Kenny agrees. "The janitor told us they wear rubber gloves when they clean the desks. He said it was a disgusting job."

"Well, that might be what he said, but what does that mean? It don't mean it's a health hazard," Alonzo responds.

"Would you want to pry the gum off with your fingers?" Kenny asks. "We can go clean a couple of desks and you can do it with your fingers and see if you get anything!"

Alonzo says, "Kids are in school. They're going to catch germs regardless if someone puts gum under a table or not. And if the kid is touching the gum under the table on purpose, well, then that's just gross."

"Okay," Mrs. Peterson interjects, "maybe we need to do some research to find out what the probability is for contracting disease from gum. How could we do that? Any ideas?"

"We could ask Julie's father for a statement," says Kenny. "Or her mother, the nurse." He points to Marielle. "Or both."

"Other ideas?"

"We could probably find something on the Internet," says Melissa.

Teddy raises his hand. "I already did that. I found one statement that said diseases like colds, chicken pox, and some meningitis are spread through the air by sneezes, coughs, and saliva and snot."

"You mean mucous from the nose or throat," says Mrs. Peterson.

"Right. So that's gum."

"Very good. We should have someone check that for the reference if you don't already have it, Teddy." Teddy says he has bookmarked the site. "I don't think we have to make an argument that disease is communicated through saliva. Everyone is likely to accept that. But we can give the citation, just to indicate that we have checked it out."

Ricardo said, "Boy, that's too much. We got tons of gum and it gives you diseases. How can we argue that the ban should be lifted?"

"That's a good question. But as I recall, you made a suggestion earlier, Ricardo, that perhaps we should consider. Do you remember what you said about why there's so much gum on the desks?"

"Yeah, I think kids put it on the desks so they don't get caught chewing in class."

"And what do we know from our questionnaire that's related to that idea?"

> "Okay," Mrs. Peterson interjects, "maybe we need to do some research to find out what the probability is for contracting disease from gum. How could we do that?"

> "Boy, that's too much. We got tons of gum and it gives you diseases. How can we argue that the ban should be lifted?"

Julie responds at once, "We know that 95 percent of the students we asked said that kids put it on the desks to avoid getting caught."

"Do they know that for certain?" asks Mrs. Peterson. "Or do we?"

Kenny says, "No, not really. That's just what they think and what we think."

"Well, consider this. How can people attribute motives to others even though they haven't interviewed them?" The class is silent. "Let me rephrase that. We know that there is a lot of gum under the desks and seats. How is it that so many students assumed that others put it there to avoid getting caught?"

Melissa says, "Probably because most students do it themselves for that reason. So they assume that others do it for the same reason as them. They know that they are alike in certain ways. And some probably have even told their friends about nearly getting caught. So it's like something everybody knows."

"What we're doing is developing a warrant, a rule that helps us explain why there is so much gum under the desks and seats. But we have to make that into an argument. What do we know for sure?"

Ricardo says, "There's an average of thirty-seven pieces of gum on almost every seat and desk we examined."

"Good." Mrs. Peterson writes this on the transparency. "Now, can we agree or concede that is a problem?" She hesitates. "Do you know that word, *concede*?" A couple of students nod. "Who can tell us what it means?"

Teddy raises his hand. "It means like you give it away, you agree, you like concede somebody's point."

"Good, let's see if we can make up a sentence using the word *concede* that states our agreement with the principal. Anybody? We want to connect this to Ricardo's sentence."

Julie raises her hand. "We could say, 'We concede your point that chewing gum creates a problem in this school.'"

"Good, but we need a phrase or clause connecting this sentence to Ricardo's."

Kenny says, "We could just say like, 'Based on this evidence, we concede that blah, blah, blah.'"

"What we're doing is developing a warrant, a rule that helps us explain why there is so much gum under the desks and seats. But we have to make that into an argument."

Mrs. Peterson says, "That's good for now. There are other ways to say it too, but we have to move along." She adds Kenny's phrase at the beginning of Julie's sentence. The transparency now reads:

> There is an average of thirty-seven pieces of gum on every seat and desk we examined. Based on this evidence, we concede your point that chewing gum creates a problem in this school.

Mrs. Peterson asks, "Do you think it is a good idea to concede this point?" The students think for a moment.

"Probably," says Melissa.

"Why is it important?"

Marielle responds, "It seems so obvious, you gotta admit it."

Kenny says, "Because if we didn't, we'd look stupid."

"Do you think we should let her know that we recognize the kind of problem it is or why it is a problem?"

Melissa says, "I think so, because she needs to know we are serious about it. Like we could say it is a problem in terms of health and cleaning up."

"How should we add that?"

Alicia suggests, "We could just add that to what's there already, like add after *problem*, 'in terms of health and cleaning up.'" Mrs. Peterson follows Alicia's suggestion.

"Now, do we still want to argue for lifting the ban?" The students nod yes. "Then what must we say?"

Bill raises his hand tentatively. "We could just say, 'We want you to lift the ban anyway.'"

"Okay. Bill, do we have any reasons for lifting the ban?"

"Yeah, like we said before." He stops, and Mrs. Peterson looks at him expectantly. "Like we said, um, we said kids put gum under desks and seats so they would not get caught."

"That's what we thought based on the results of the questionnaire. Can we say it straight out like that, as though it's absolutely true?" Mrs. Peterson reinforces Bill's contribution while pushing for amendments to what he said. "Remember, we are making arguments of probability. What in our research indicates that the ban may cause the problem?"

Ricardo repeats his initial contention. "Ninety-five percent said that students put the gum under seats and desks to avoid getting caught."

"That's true. But can we just put that sentence in there like that, or should we prepare for it somehow?"

Julie raises her hand. "We could say 'Even though we agree with your point that there is a problem, we cannot agree with your solution.' Then we could tell about the research and why we think it indicates that the ban is a cause of putting gum where it does not belong."

"What do you think about that?"

"Sounds like a plan to me," says Teddy. Everyone nods in agreement.

During the next fifteen minutes, as students make suggestions and Mrs. Peterson asks for evaluations and elaborations, the class develops the passage below:

> Our research shows that there is an average of thirty-seven pieces of gum on every set of seats and desks we examined. Based on this evidence, we concede your point that chewing gum creates a problem in this school in terms of health and cleaning up.
>
> Even though we agree with your point that there is a problem, we cannot agree with your solution. Our research indicates that there is a very strong probability that the ban may be the reason students are putting gum under desks and seats. In response to our questionnaire item about why students put gum under desks and seats, 95 percent indicated that they did it because they were afraid of being caught chewing gum. When 95 percent agree, it is very probably because each knows what and why he or she does it. They then attribute similar motives to others. It may just be common knowledge among students that one does that to avoid being caught in the act. It is also evident from the research reported above that the ban has not had the desired effect.

The next day, Mrs. Peterson reminds the class how important it is that the students were able to find common ground with the principal by conceding that she was correct about the chewing gum problem. She then asks what they want to propose.

Ricardo says, "Well, if it ain't workin', get rid of it."

"Well, we've agreed that it isn't working and you all want to get rid of it. But do you think just saying that will be convincing?"

"Probably not," Kenny says. The class looks discouraged.

"What was our principal's major concern?" asks Mrs. Peterson.

Julie chimes in, "It's the cost of the cleaning, unless she didn't tell us everything."

"So if the ban were eliminated, what might we expect?"

Bill says, "Probably less gum under the desks."

"And why is that?"

"Because kids wouldn't have to be afraid of getting caught," says Bill.

Pleased, Mrs. Peterson says, "All right. Do you think that taking the ban away would have magical effects? You know, just like that, students would stop putting gum under the desks?"

Alicia responds eagerly, "Maybe we could have an advertising campaign. You know, like have signs about how to throw gum away in paper and not putting it under desks."

"Yeah," Marcella adds, "like you could have a picture of someone putting gum under a desk and have like *censored* across it and have a slogan, like 'Don't be a public menace.'"

Kenny says, "We don't have anything like that now. It's just a rule in the handbook. And the teachers harp about it, but nobody pays attention, because most of the time you can get away with it. So if we had signs up all over, maybe that would really help. I mean, kids would have to think about it more."

"Yeah," Michelle agrees, "maybe kids would develop a conscience about it. I mean once you stop to think about all that gum crap under every desk you use all day, it's pretty disgusting. Most kids don't want to make the school a health hazard."

> *"Mrs. Peterson reminds the class how important it is that the students were able to find common ground with the principal by conceding that she was correct about the chewing gum problem."*

Mrs. Peterson smiles broadly. "Well, it sounds as though you have a concrete proposal to make. Let's get to work on it."

For the next several minutes, the class develops the final paragraphs of the letter. By the end of the period, students have collaboratively written:

> It is also evident from the research reported above that the ban has not had the desired effect. In view of this failure, we respectfully submit the following proposals. First, we propose that the ban be lifted for a period of one year. Second, we propose that an ad campaign be put in place encouraging students not to put gum on the bottoms of their seats and desks, telling them how to get rid of the gum without problems for anyone, and promoting the ideas that those who do not follow this advice are uncool and a menace to other students.
>
> We believe that appropriate signs could be produced by students. We also believe that the project could be developed as a contest, perhaps sponsored by the administration with help from the art department and the English department. Teachers could be the advisors on the production of appropriate signs.
>
> Further, we suggest that the ban be removed after the desks have been cleaned throughout the school. Then, once the ban is removed we can check the desks and seats to determine how much gum there is. At the end of a certain period, the desks can be checked again to determine how much gum has accumulated.
>
> If we put this two-pronged plan into effect, we predict that there will be far less gum left on desks and seats than there is now. The school will save considerable time and money on cleaning up the gum, and the health hazard

caused by so much gum will be greatly reduced. These changes will be of great advantage to the school.

Mrs. Peterson asks each student to produce a complete text of the proposal that the class has worked on collaboratively. They may add to, delete, or change elements of what the class has written, but they have to cover everything the class has discussed.

What's Good About This Series of Lessons

Close Collaboration and Repetition of the Task

Mrs. Peterson supported her students with this close collaboration because it was the first step in learning to deal with a complex writing project. As a next step, she put her class in small groups and each group worked on another problem in which they had a common interest:

» an increase in the cost of student lunches
» too little time between the starting bell and the first class bell
» the number of absences allowed before a grade reduction
» the use of metal detectors at each door of the school
» the length of library loan periods
» removing music and art from the curriculum as a money-saving measure
» removing certain books from the school library
» installing bicycle racks

After these group projects, students completed individual projects using what they had learned in the class and group projects.

These repeated exposures to the process were necessary. Mrs. Peterson said, "One problem I see in the classrooms of this district is that we assume that students learn from *hearing* what to do. I cannot believe that is true. They learn from *doing* things."

What Students Did

Below is a summary of what students accomplished during the three-week chewing gum project:

1. **Used basic strategies of inquiry to clarify and develop the problem they would eventually write about.** Those strategies began

with what Dewey (1938) calls "doubt." Students questioned the advisability of the chewing gum ban. They thought it unreasonable. Therefore, they:

  » asked questions to clarify the problem
  » hypothesized about various aspects of the problem
  » designed an inquiry to test the hypotheses

2. **Developed the three basic types of argument: fact, judgment, and policy.** Each argument led to the next, allowing students to conclude with a fully realized argument of policy:

Arguments of Fact

Claim 1: There are large quantities of gum on school desks and seats throughout second- through eighth-grade classrooms, probably close to 41,382 wads.

Evidence: They had counted 13,944 wads in fourteen classrooms.

Warrant: They had taken a stratified random sample of fourteen of forty-two classrooms, which allowed them to estimate 41,382, give or take a few hundred, for all forty-two classrooms.

Claim 2: Cleaning the gum from desks is no doubt costly, probably over $11,960.

Evidence: A trial cleaning of gum from desks and seats indicated that it takes about four minutes per wad.

Warrant: Arithmetically, that indicates that it would probably take over 920 hours for one person to clean off the estimated 41,382 wads of gum if the cleaning rate remains stable at four minutes per wad. The custodian indicated that a new hire who cleans off the gum receives approximately $13.00 per hour, for a total cost of $11,960.

Arguments of Judgment

Claim 1: The great quantities of gum under desks and seats constitute a health hazard.

Evidence: The argument of fact, claim 1, above, indicates the quantity of gum.

Warrant: The authority of the reference that Teddy found and the statements from Julie's father, a doctor, and Marielle's mother, a nurse.

Claim 2: The large amount of gum (see argument of fact, claim 1, above) is probably due to the ban.

Evidence: On a questionnaire, 95 percent of students in fourteen classrooms indicated that they believed most students put gum under desks and seats to avoid being caught chewing gum.

Warrant: The authors strongly believe that the large number of students probably reflects the real behavior of most students.

Backing: When so many students agree on a response about what others do, it is probably a reflection of what they themselves do or it is simply shared knowledge about how not to get caught chewing gum.

Arguments of Policy

Claim 1: To diminish the quantity of gum on desks and seats, the ban on chewing gum should be rescinded.

Evidence: The large quantity of gum on desks and seats is the result of student fear of being caught. (See argument of judgment, claim 2, above.)

Warrant: If students are not afraid of being punished for chewing gum, they are less likely to hide gum by sticking it to the bottom of desks and seats.

Backing: If people respond to something out of fear, once the threat is removed, they no longer have to respond out of fear.

Claim 2: The school should initiate an advertising campaign aimed at convincing students that they should dispose of gum properly.

Evidence: The school has never conducted such a campaign because it would appear to contradict the no gum policy. Perhaps many students do not know how to dispose of gum. Perhaps they do not understand that disposing of used gum on desks and chairs constitutes a health hazard. At any rate, they are accustomed to sticking it on desks and chairs. (See argument of fact, claim 1, above.)

Warrant: It is well known that advertising campaigns increase knowledge and knowledge is power. The campaign we suggest should increase knowledge that the disposal of gum on desks and seats constitutes a health hazard and that it is easy to throw gum away safely.

These arguments are interrelated. The arguments of judgment build on the arguments of fact, and the arguments of policy build on the arguments of fact and judgment.

3. **In writing their proposal to the principal, the students had used the three major strategies of rhetoric—pathos, ethos, and logos—without even realizing it.**
    1. They aimed the argument directly to the principal's major concern about the expense of removing the gum. They appealed to her by conceding her point that there is indeed a chewing gum problem (*pathos*).
    2. They showed their *ethos* to be one of rationality and concern, likely to win points in any argument.
    3. The strongest appeal is in the *logos*, the arguments outlined above.

Anyone familiar with school administrators' need to maintain their presumed authority will have already guessed that the principal in this particular case rejected the arguments of the students, maintained the ban on chewing gum, and failed to answer the students' arguments. Those of us familiar with the resistance of school administrators to rational argument will not be surprised.

However, if schools develop writing programs that include inquiry, argument, and rhetoric and teach these elements in ways that ensure students learn the related principles, they will have gone a long way in ameliorating the current state of poor thinking and writing in this country. And perhaps, someday, it will even lead to our having more rational school administrators. That is probably wishful thinking, but you never can tell.

Tips on Coauthoring with Students

Collaborative writing with the teacher leading the way is particularly valuable when students are learning a genre that is relatively new to them. At first it may seem to take too much time, but it ensures that students are exposed to the thinking processes involved in creating the form required, and even to the kinds of syntax that students may need to learn. As you do this coauthoring, bear in mind the following:

» When you ask "What should we say?" try to receive several contributions so that students may discuss and evaluate the suggestions.

» Allow the class to sift through the contributions, focusing on the requirements of the point in the writing.

» Try to be alert to what the students know and do not know.

» Allow the class to determine what expressions will work best in terms of the purpose and audience.

» Feel free to make suggestions for students to play with and try on their own, making sure to allow them voice in the final decisions. If the decisions are not good, you can always come back for revision.

» Work slowly and systematically, making certain that students understand the reasons for each decision.

» Suggest and model syntactic structures that may be unfamiliar to students, but try to be certain that your students understand and can write the kind of structure you have in mind.

» The next day, if you think it is necessary, review by revising what you developed.

Eventually in the lesson sequence, students should be doing this in small groups or individually, depending on the sophistication of the students.

PART II

Teaching Students to Write More Complex Arguments

> *"Enjoyable experience is characterized by a sense of moving forward or beyond what one might expect of oneself."*

How Are Judgments Made in the Real World?

THE PRECEDING THREE CHAPTERS PRESENT AN INTRODUC-
tion to teaching relatively simple arguments of fact, judgment, and policy.
They are simple because the contexts and issues do not require extensive defense of warrants and backing. Chapters Five, Six, and Seven will deal with
much more complex arguments, arguments that involve more complicated
judgments.

Before you begin those chapters, it will be useful for you to have some
background information on the real-world role that warrants, backing, and
finely honed definitions play in the making of judgments. In this chapter, I
will describe actual cases that demonstrate this crucial role. An understanding of the complexity of warrants and backing is vital to teaching the more
complex argument that follows in the next three chapters.

Why Do Judgments Matter?

Often, in ordinary conversation, people make complex judgments without much thought. A judgment is the attribution of a quality or characteristic to a person, group, object, or concept. Often no one cares about the judgment. But some judgments make immense differences to the lives and fortunes of all of us. Can education be separate and still be equal for all? Should pay for teachers be partially determined by the effectiveness of their teaching? Does life begin at conception or only after birth? May the government decide questions about who is entitled to what levels of education? Do individuals or groups have the right to decide what books should be eliminated from the school curriculum? Does our government have the right to intern a group of people because they are ethnically or religiously related to a perceived enemy outside the United States?

All such questions involve difficult matters of judgment that must be questioned carefully, and, if they are to become the basis for action, must be defended with appropriate warrants and backing that are sometimes quite complex.

Making Unexamined Assumptions and Judgments

People make judgments all the time without questioning them or thinking them through. Advertisers, for example, rarely support the claims they make about a product, believing that the fewer words used, the better. Several years ago, Revlon promoted a perfume called Scoundrel in an ad showing a beautiful dark-haired woman in a low-cut dress above the words "Scoundrel. Unquestionably female. Undeniably provocative." The perfume is still on the market.

Some advertisers make claims they say are based on fact. For example, a recent Domino's Pizza TV ad claims that in a customer survey comparing the taste of Domino's Pizza to Papa John's, Domino's Pizza was selected as the better tasting. The ad then claims that it is a proven fact that Domino's Pizza tastes better. Obviously, this is not a fact. The fact is that more people chose Domino's as the better tasting in a study conducted by Domino's, a far cry from actually being the better tasting.

Some movie reviewers also see no need to defend their judgments. Mike LaSalle, writing for the *San Francisco Chronicle*, claims that the movie *3:10 to Yuma* "tells a story and, seemingly incidentally—though no movie can be this good by accident—it achieves an elusive mythic quality." LaSalle neither defines nor explains what he means by "mythic quality." Nor does he explain or defend his statement that "no movie can be this good by accident." Roger Ebert, in his review of the same movie, does provide evidence and warrants to back up his claims, but not all reviewers bother.

More seriously, people take to heart and act on judgments based on prejudice and intolerance. Socrates and the Stoic philosophers believed that all people have the capacity for practical reason but tend to lead somnolent lives, accepting traditions, norms, and beliefs learned from infancy without question, without taking charge of their own thinking. This is as true today as it was in the time of Socrates. The 2007 racial crisis in Jena, Louisiana, was precipitated by precisely this tendency to make poor judgments. At least three white students at the predominantly white Jena public high school felt that only whites had the right to sit under a tree in front of the school. As a not very thinly veiled threat, they hung nooses from the branches of the tree. Angered by this threat, six black students beat one white boy. They were arrested and charged with attempted murder. A massive protest ensued.

Think about the judgments involved. Why did the whites conclude that the tree had been somehow reserved for them? Why did the three boys think that putting the nooses, symbols of racial oppression and murder, in the tree was a good idea? What judgments underlay the beating and kicking of the one white boy by six blacks? What judgment underlay the decision of the prosecutor to charge the black boys with attempted murder rather than aggravated battery?

All these actions were no doubt based on unexamined assumptions and judgments. Because of this human tendency to act upon unexamined assumptions and judgments, it is mandatory for us as teachers to help students learn to examine their own judgments and those of others. The Student Practices section of the Common Core Standards states that students should "not simply adopt other points of view as their own but rather evaluate them critically and constructively" (2010). To do this, students need to understand what makes an argument sound. And to do that, it is necessary to understand the nature of judgments and their warrants and backing.

Definitions as Backing for Warrants

Whenever arguments of judgment or policy are likely to be challenged, it is nearly inevitable that the argument will include *definitions of terms* that serve as part of the backing for warrants used in the arguments. The more serious the argument, the more likely definitions will be invoked and defended.

The Case of Karen Quinlan

The Karen Quinlan case involved both an argument of fact and an argument of policy, and both arguments hung on definitions. Ms. Quinlan, after experimenting with drugs, unexpectedly lapsed into a coma and remained on life-support equipment for many months. Doctors believed there was no chance of her regaining sapient life, and her parents requested that she be disconnected from the machines. When the hospital refused, the parents sued, eventually appealing the case to the New Jersey Supreme Court.

The case at that point turned on two definitions: the Harvard Medical School definition of death, which involved a series of tests to be met, and the definition of the right to privacy. The Court found that while Karen Quinlan's cortex did not function (she was in a "chronic, persistent vegetative state"), her autonomic nervous system did function (though not for respiration), and she was therefore, according to the definition of death, not dead. Nevertheless, the Court ruled that her guardian could order that the machines be disconnected, finding that the invasion of her body by the many tubes thought necessary to maintain her life constituted an unjustified invasion of privacy, particularly given the improbability of recovery, thus extending the definition of what constitutes an invasion of privacy by adding a *new criterion* for what counts as an invasion of privacy (see Supreme Court of New Jersey, 1976). Indeed, a major function of appellate courts, and our Supreme Court in particular, has been to modify the definitions of terms used in the backing of warrants, especially by clarifying and adding criteria. This is the kind of thinking that also takes place in Socratic dialogues.

The Case of *Scott v. Harris*

Not long ago the Supreme Court of the United States considered the case of *Scott v. Harris* in which a nineteen-year-old driver, Victor Harris, fled police at speeds that reached over ninety miles per hour. The chase began when

> "Because of this human tendency to act upon unexamined assumptions and judgments, it is mandatory for us as teachers to help students learn to examine their own judgments and those of others."

> "The more serious the argument, the more likely definitions will be invoked and defended."

officer Timothy Scott clocked Harris doing 72 mph in a 55 mph zone. After following Harris' Cadillac for several miles as it sped along a two-lane highway, repeatedly crossing the double yellow line, even in the face of on-coming traffic, and through a red light, the pursuing police officer Scott decided to ram the fleeing car from behind. When he did, Harris lost control of the Cadillac, which crashed into an embankment. Harris was badly in-jured and paralyzed. Harris sued the officer for violating his civil rights by using deadly force to stop his flight. Scott, who had recorded the chase on his dashboard camera, argued that his actions were reasonable and appro-priate and that the suit against him should be dismissed.

The oral arguments before the justices of the Supreme Court focus on the use of deadly versus reasonable force. In other words, how can we define *reasonable force* in such a case? Under what circumstances is it reasonable to ram a vehicle posing such a threat to the public?

Lawyers for Harris argue that it is not reasonable to use deadly force against their client because the danger of harm to the public must be bal-anced against the possible harm to a speeding driver if deadly force (the ramming) is used.

Justice Scalia immediately challenges that idea. "I don't know that I agree with that. I mean, if this fellow driving 90 miles an hour is responsible for endangering people, you're proposing a rule that says if there's a 50 per-cent chance that he'll hurt some innocent person and a 50 percent chance that he'll get hurt if you try to stop him, you shouldn't do anything. I don't agree with that. . . . I'd stop him. I mean, he's the fellow that's causing the . . . endangerment, isn't he?"

Justice Stevens shifts the focus to the danger to the fleeing Harris: "Isn't it a fairly high probability that if you hit someone at that speed that there will be something, either death or serious injury as a result?"

Justice Scalia counters, "Well, I suppose there is also a high probability where you're going 90 miles an hour . . . crossing over the double yellow line, with oncoming traffic, that you're going to hurt somebody else. . . . I mean, the more you increase the speed the more likely he's going to be hurt. But also the more likely if you let him go somebody else is going to be hurt."

Mr. Savrin, an attorney for Scott, adds, "Yes, Your Honor. And to put it in a more complete perspective, 90 miles an hour is mathematically equiva-lent to over 130 feet per second."

The discussion moves through a sequence of related issues about the dangers arising from speeding, the dangers likely to result from ramming the speeding car, and the probability that discontinuing the chase might have led to the fleeing driver returning to safer speeds. At one point Justice Alito asks, "When someone is fleeing and creating a grave danger, let's just assume that that's the case, creating a very [great] danger for other drivers on the road, when in your view is it reasonable for the police to use deadly force to stop that, as opposed to breaking off the chase? What is the test?" (*Scott v. Harris*.)

In other words, he is asking, "What is the criterion for making a decision about the use of deadly force?"

Eventually, an attorney for Harris argues that "the facts are that he was driving fast but he was under control. He only crossed the center line to pass and when he passed, he used his turn signal when he passed."

In response, Justice Kennedy comments, "He used the turn signal. That's like the strangler who observes the no smoking sign." There is laughter in the court.

But the attorney for Harris continues, "As the tape indicates, Mr. Harris didn't run anybody off the road. He didn't ram anybody. He didn't try to ram anybody. He was just driving away. . . ."

Several Justices argue that Harris was creating "a tremendous risk [to] drivers on that road." Justice Souter asks, "The question was whether he was creating a substantial risk doing that. . . . And my question is how could a jury find otherwise? Your answer up to this point is that well, he used signal lights and his reflexes were good, and they sure were. But the question is whether he was creating a substantial risk of death or serious bodily harm to others. And my question is—assuming that his reflexes were good and he knew how to use the signal lights, how could the jury fail to find that he was creating such a risk?"(*Scott v. Harris*).

The lawyer for Harris admits that Harris was creating a risk but argues that the risk did not include other factors that needed to be present to justify the use of deadly force. In an earlier case, *Tennessee v. Garner*, a case concerning a fleeing felon who posed no immediate threat but whom the pursuing officer shot to death, the Supreme Court found that deadly force could be used only if a law enforcement officer pursuing a fleeing suspect had rea-

"In other words, he is asking, 'What is the criterion for making a decision about the use of deadly force?'"

son to believe that the suspect posed a threat of serious bodily harm or death to the officer or others.

In light of the precedent, the attorney for Harris argues, "This was simply a person who was driving fast. This was not a person who was driving assaultively. He wasn't driving violently. He wasn't a threat to anyone that would authorize the use of deadly force against him." He continues, "This is the issue. If what this person is doing is driving, say driving unsafely, but they are not driving violently, they are not driving aggressively, they are not menacing anyone on the road. They are simply driving fast trying to get away, that in and of itself, is that going to be justification for the use of deadly force or is something more going to be required?"

The Justices do not agree that the driving they saw on the tape recording made from the officer's dashboard camera was not aggressive or menacing. Justice Scalia argues, "You say—that he maintained control over his vehicle. Well, that doesn't prove he's not endangering anybody. [You say] that he used his turn signals—wonderful—[*Laughter.*] 'and did not endanger any particular motorist on the road.' I think that's true. In that scary chase he didn't come close to hitting any particular car, but I don't think that's . . . a finding that he was not endangering anybody, 'any particular motorist,' but he was endangering the public at large."

Mr. Jones responds, "Well, this is my point. . . . If the hazard caused by driving in and of itself is the only threat here, does that rise to a level of immanency and immediacy that justifies the use of deadly force? If it does, then any officer who perceives that someone is driving unsafely and that they may cause an accident to someone who may or may not be down the road if not stopped, would be justified in using deadly force, to literally take out anyone who is speeding."

The court does not accept this argument. As Justice Scalia points out, "It depends on how fast the car is going, whether it's a two-lane road or four-lane divided highway. All those factors come . . . into account. And it doesn't seem to me that we have to adopt a rule . . . that will discourage police officers. There's enough disincentive to engage in this kind of activity in the fact that the police officer may hurt himself. It's pretty risky to conduct this kind of a maneuver, don't you think? I wouldn't have done it if I was Scott."

The Supreme Court ruled eight to one in favor of Officer Scott, holding that Harris was driving recklessly and posing a high probability of harm to innocent bystanders by his reckless driving and speeding. The opinion, written by Justice Scalia, relied heavily on the video of the chase, which he argued clearly contradicted Harris' claim that he was driving "responsibly" and "not . . . assaultively."

The majority opinion said, "It is clear from the videotape that [Harris] posed an actual and imminent threat to the lives of any pedestrians who might have been present, to other civilian motorists, and to the officers involved in the chase." The opinion said there was a need to consider the harm that Harris might have caused by his recklessness against the probability that Harris himself might be harmed. It also pointed out Harris' culpability in starting the chase in the first place. The Court, in short, ruled that it was reasonable to use deadly force to stop a driver who posed a threat to others by his speeding and reckless driving to the point of serious injury or death. (*Scott v. Harris*)

This entire discussion has focused on what counts as posing a threat of bodily harm or death to the public that will warrant the use of deadly force to end that threat. It has elaborated the *definition of* "threat of bodily harm or death" in very concrete terms and has clarified the circumstances under which an officer may use deadly force. The Supreme Court has clarified the backing for the warrant used to justify Officer Scott's ramming the speeding car by essentially adding a criterion by which to make the judgment.

> "This entire discussion has focused on what counts as posing a threat of bodily harm or death to the public that will warrant the use of deadly force to end that threat. It has elaborated the definition of "threat of bodily harm or death" in very concrete terms."

Backing for Warrants: Why Humpty Dumpty Won't Do

"When I use a word," Humpty Dumpty said in rather a scornful tone,
"it means just what I choose it to mean—neither more nor less."

Lewis Carroll, *Through the Looking Glass*

Teaching students how to construct—and recognize—a sound argument is our responsibility. Not long ago, in a workshop that Vera Wallace and I ran in Denver, we asked teachers for examples of units that they might develop involving arguments of judgment. One teacher talked about her unit on "the hero." The hero, she said, could be anyone the students proposed. Further, the warrants could be "whatever the students came up with"—there were no criteria that had to be agreed upon. "Everyone has a hero, and we do not have to agree on the reasons." Does that mean, I wondered to myself, that students could say someone is a hero because she bites her fingernails, enjoys watching comedy shows on TV, sings out of tune, or does rude or crude things in public? If so, then this assignment could not prepare students for the rigors of making a serious case in any field. Words cannot have whatever meanings our whims propose, as Humpty Dumpty suggests in *Through the Looking Glass*. Further, when the reasons for calling someone a hero are challenged, they must be defended. For serious argument, the Humpty Dumpty school of thought will not do.

If one sets out to demonstrate that a character is heroic, that an act is courageous, that a story is mythic, that an act is one of terrorism, that a play is tragic, or that a poem is satiric, a warrant is almost mandatory, and a warrant nearly always must be defined and defended. This is particularly true in competent academic writing, where a critical audience is expected. The easiest way to attack claims of judgment is to attack the warrant and the definition underlying it. If writers do not wish to be attacked, they must present the warrants and argue the definitions (backing) that underlie the warrants by providing the criteria used to make the judgments.

As demonstrated in the Supreme Court cases discussed earlier in this chapter, one or more of the following may be used to build an argument in support of a warrant:

» extended definitions
» references to laws
» explanations and justifications of rules

Warrants and Backing Through Invention

Often, writers, lawmakers, researchers, and others find it necessary to devise definitions to guide policy and research or simply to make a case.

In the eighties, the United States found itself under attack in various locations around the world. For example, in 1983, more than fifty people, many of them Americans, were killed in a bombing attack on the United States embassy in Beirut, Lebanon. A fanatical pro-Iranian, anti-American group made up of Shiite Muslims claimed responsibility for the bombing. Although the American media called the assault *terrorism*, others, including countries sympathetic to the Muslim cause, referred to the attackers as revo-

"The Supreme Court has clarified the backing for the warrant by essentially adding a criterion by which to make the judgment."

"Teaching students how to construct—and recognize—a sound argument is our responsibility."

"If one sets out to demonstrate that a character is heroic, that an act is courageous, that a story is mythic, that an act is one of terrorism, that a play is tragic, or that a poem is satiric, a warrant is almost mandatory, and a warrant nearly always must be defined and defended."

lutionaries resisting unlawful occupation by a foreign military force. Was this attack terrorism or an act of war?

The situation was alarming enough that President Reagan asked Vice President Bush to chair a task force on terrorism. One of the first chores of that task force was to define *terrorism*. The work of that group illustrates the *major components of extended definitions.*

After examining several existing definitions, the task force formulated the following short definition:

> Terrorism is the unlawful use or threat of violence against persons or property to further political or social objectives. It is generally intended to intimidate or coerce a government, individuals, or groups to modify their behavior or policies. (U.S. Government Printing Office 1986, 1)

This brief definition is much like a dictionary definition. It places *terrorism* in the class of "use or threat of violence." Then by providing some essential characteristics of terrorism, it distinguishes terrorism from other members of the same class. For example, laws provide for the use of violence under certain specified conditions in apprehending armed criminals. Other threats or uses of violence do not have social or political objectives. Robbers and kidnappers typically use and threaten violence, but their goals are usually selfish. Brief definitions that place the term to be defined in a class are called *analytic definitions* because they provide a basis for making distinctions.

The short definition of terrorism above, however, does not provide all the essential characteristics necessary to distinguish terrorism from, say, some criminal acts or acts of war. Therefore, the task force added several *criteria* to make the distinctions between terrorism and other similar actions clear:

1. The targets of terrorism are governments and civilian populations. Terrorism involves an official, deliberate policy of hurting civilians.
2. Terrorism involves the deliberate attempt to create intense fear in order to coerce the wider target (including the public at large) into giving in to what the terrorist wants.
3. The goal of terrorism is ideological (or political) rather than personal.
4. Terrorism involves an audience. Common crime usually involves only two parties (the criminal and the victim), whereas terrorism,

which seeks to amplify and spread fear, has three: the victim, the criminal, and the audience, usually reached through the news media.

According to these criteria, the 1983 bombing of the U.S. embassy in Beirut is an act of terrorism. First, the target was government officials and civilians working in or dealing with the embassy. Second, it involves an attempt to create fear in order to coerce the wider target, the United States and other governments, to stop "interfering" in Middle Eastern affairs. Third, the goal is ideological (or political)—to focus worldwide attention on the Shiite Muslim cause. Finally, although the attacker remains unknown for certain, ten minutes after the blast, an anonymous caller warned the French press that the strike was "part of the Iranian revolution's campaign against imperialist targets throughout the world." Therefore, this incident fulfills each of the criteria established by the task force.

Writers typically use examples in extended definitions to illustrate the criteria and differentiate the term from other closely related concepts. For example, the following text illustrates the use of examples to clarify a criterion.

The targets of terrorism are governments and civilian populations. Whereas acts of war may result in the accidental killing of civilians, terrorism involves harming civilians on purpose.	CRITERION
The 1983 bombing of the U.S. embassy in Beirut, Lebanon, is an example of a terrorist act. The targets were ambassadors, government officials, and civilians working in the embassy. For the attackers, the embassy was a symbol of the enemy—the U.S. government.	EXAMPLE that fulfills the criterion
On the other hand, if civilians are killed by guerrilla fighters in the process of bombing enemy soldiers launching offensive operations, the action cannot be labeled *terrorism*. In this case, the killing of civilians is accidental; the target is the enemy soldiers.	CONTRASTING EXAMPLE that is close to the term defined but does *not* fulfill the criterion
Unlike an act of war that may result in the accidental killing of civilians, terrorism involves an official, deliberate policy of hurting civilians.	RESTATEMENT of the criterion

This text incorporates two kinds of examples to clarify the criterion:

1. **An example that *fulfills* the criterion.** Its purpose is to give the reader a concrete illustration of what is meant by the criterion.
2. **A *contrasting example*.** Its purpose is to help distinguish the term defined from other similar terms or to set the limits of the definition by explaining what the term does not include.

Often the contrasting example involves a specific incident that someone might mistakenly think fits the definition. In the example text, the incident with the guerrilla fighters shares some of the criteria for terrorism. The bombing was probably at least in part intended to create fear and to coerce the enemy into withdrawing. The guerrillas may have been fighting for political gain, perhaps for a certain form of government. Also, civilians were hurt in the bombing. Yet, the incident does *not* fulfill all the criteria for terrorism because, although they were harmed in the incident, the civilians were not the primary target.

Definitions are important in research. They provide criteria allowing us to test what we know and to generate new concepts. For example, in the seventeenth century, people did not know that air was a mixture of several gases. They knew that men and animals needed it to live and that fires needed it to burn. Scientists did more and more experiments with combustion and breathing using a bell jar to trap air above a liquid. One experiment involved burning a candle under a bell jar. They found that as the candle burned, water or other liquid rose inside the jar. This indicated that the volume of air inside the jar had decreased. They also found that when a certain proportion of the air was gone, the candles went out. These proportions were always the same. These findings helped to establish the first defining characteristics or criteria for oxygen. Continued work on defining oxygen led to understanding breathing processes and chemistry.

Although most textbooks dealing with writing argument do not connect definition with the writing of arguments, definitions clearly provide the warrants and their backing for arguments of judgment and for many arguments of policy. The criteria developed in extended definitions are the warrants for arguments in nearly all fields of endeavor—medicine, law, literary criticism, philosophy. Ignoring definition is a serious mistake in the teaching of argument.

The following chapters deal with methods of helping students become more skilled in developing warrants and their backing, and particularly in developing the criteria to be used in the definitions so important for backing of warrants in arguments of judgment.

Answering Difficult Questions

Learning to Make Judgments Based on Criteria

WHEN STUDENTS ARE FIRST LEARNING TO USE A NUMBER OF criteria to make judgments, they often focus on a single criterion and ignore others that are perhaps more important. I begin criteria work by giving students a definition and several criteria, along with cases to which to apply them.

The Giraffe Award Activity

The Giraffe Project, a small foundation in Washington State, applies several criteria to identify individuals or groups of individuals who "stick their necks out for the common good," who do something "to make the world a better place," and gives these individuals or groups Giraffe Awards (see www.giraffe.org/).

The immediate goal of the activity is to ask students to apply the criteria provided and to defend their decisions about who should receive the

Giraffe Awards. Similarly, decisions about who does not receive the award must be defended by showing how the candidate does *not* fulfill the criteria.

The long-term goal of the activity is for students to learn how to independently apply and defend a set of criteria in making various kinds of decisions, from buying a new camera to voting for president, from granting admission to college applicants to deciding on the best policy to stop global warming.

(1) Introducing the Activity

First, I hand out the page in Figure 5.1 describing the Giraffe Awards and the criteria for their selection. I ask students to underline or color-code the criteria on their copies while we read the paragraphs aloud.

The students and I then make a list of the criteria, which I record on the board or a projected transparency. Then I ask a few questions about how Mr. Flowers meets the criteria.

> » What risk does he take?
> » What sacrifice does he make?
> » How is what he does healing?

Students can answer these literal questions without making any inferences, but doing so helps establish the criteria they will use in discussing other Giraffe Award cases.

(2) Applying the Criteria to Giraffe Award Candidates

The best way for students to learn how to apply criteria is to engage in doing it. If I take students through at least one specific case, allowing them to make the judgments about whether or not the award candidate meets each of the criteria, they do better, more thorough work when they evaluate candidates in small groups. If we just discuss a number of candidates, students do not become competent at applying the criteria on their own.

The candidates I present to my classes (see Figure 5.2) are adapted from an article in *Newsweek* (Annin et al. 1995).

"The long-term goal of the activity is for students to learn how to independently apply and defend a set of criteria in making various kinds of decisions."

"The best way for students to learn how to apply criteria is to engage in doing it."

FIGURE 5.1 **The Giraffe Project**

The Giraffe Project, a small foundation in Washington State, applies several criteria to identify individuals or groups of individuals who "stick their necks out for the common good," who do something "to make the world a better place." The foundation publicizes these "Giraffes" and their good deeds on over five hundred radio stations. To qualify for the Giraffe award, one must meet several criteria.

According to the foundation, "A Giraffe must be taking on significant personal risks, either physical, financial, or social. Giraffes act out of caring. They may well rock the boat, but they do it to make things better, not just more exciting; their activities are ultimately healing, not divisive. . . . Giraffes act above and beyond the call of duty. People doing jobs they're trained and paid to do may be brave and caring, but they're only Giraffes when they go beyond their job descriptions."

Ralph Flowers worked for the Washington Forest Protection Association. Part of his job was to shoot black bears that were ripping the bark from trees in order to eat the sapwood beneath. Flowers decided he had to disobey the Association's orders because he did not want to kill the bears. Instead he spent $12,000 of his own money developing a special feed for them made of sugar beet pulp, which he set out in troughs for the bears to eat. As soon as the bears began to chow down on the sugar beet pulp, they gave up stripping the bark from trees. The Forest Protection Association and the timber companies now support this project.

Mr. Flowers was chosen to be a Giraffe because what he had done met the Giraffe Project's criteria. First, he undertook the project himself. Second, he risked losing his job when he rejected the policy of shooting the bears. Third, he made a personal sacrifice. The project cost him $12,000 of his own money. Fourth, Mr. Flowers undertook his project out of caring. He had no expectation of personal gain. Fifth, his work was healing in the sense that it united the Forest Protection Association and the timber companies in an effort to conserve wildlife. Finally, what he did went beyond his job description. He did far more than he was trained or paid to do.

FIGURE 5.2 **Giraffe Award Worksheet**

Giraffe Award Worksheet

Read over the following cases and decide which persons, if any, could receive the Giraffe Award. Be prepared to defend your decisions based on the foundation's criteria. That is, if you decide that one or more cases should not receive the award, be prepared to explain what criteria are not met. If you decide someone should receive the award, explain how that person meets all the criteria.

CASE A

Joseph Nicholas and David Francis Sr. have worked very hard to reinvigorate the language of Maine's Passamaquoddy Indian tribe. Passamaquoddy is New England's last living Indian language, and fewer and fewer people speak it every year. This native language has great competition from mass media, local businesses, schools, and other institutions that use English. To reverse this trend, Nicholas and Francis create and distribute bilingual booklets and videotapes and teach classes in the Passamaquoddy language. The two men also encourage tribal members to pass along their many skills such as woodcraft, making birch-bark canoes, building fires without matches, and basket weaving. Francis is seventy years old. This former clam digger, woodchopper, and blueberry picker is gathering words and phrases for a second edition of the Passamaquoddy dictionary. He says, "If we lose our language, we lose our identity. It is the last thing Indians have." Nicholas, sixty-one, a former tribal councilor and state representative, says, "Indians are always the lazy, bad guys in the history books. Our own kids had no sense of who we really were." The two believe that such attitudes are in great need of change.

FIGURE 5.2 **Giraffe Award Worksheet** *(continued)*

CASE B

The Columbia Point area of Boston is beset with problems, including rampant drugs, guns, and poverty. It is a difficult place to live because of the guns and drugs. Betty Washington can watch the guns and drug commerce from her second-floor window in the housing project. She is forty-seven and has raised eleven children by herself. She has worked full time to support them. One summer, she decided to try to stop the drug traffic. She organized the Columbia Point Antidrug Committee. With other community groups, she held an antidrug rally in a parking lot frequently visited by drug dealers. She demanded that police be more vigilant and set up a hotline to collect anonymous tips on drug dealer activities. In the first few months of her work, there were six arrests for drug dealing (in the preceding eighteen months, there had been none). She is determined to make the area safer for kids and adults who live there.

FIGURE 5.2 **Giraffe Award Worksheet** (continued)

CASE C

Jerry Foster, a TV helicopter pilot, is paid to look for news stories for Phoenix (Arizona) station KPNX. In the course of his work, he has saved dozens of lives, from mountain climbers who became lost or stranded to desert hikers who ran out of water. Sometimes he gets so involved in his rescuing efforts that he forgets to load the camera for his TV feeds. He doesn't care. "I'm no *bleeping* journalist," he says. It doesn't bother his bosses either, because he has become a star. During some of his rescues, he has violated Federal Aviation Administration safety regulations. As a result, he was grounded for a while. While appealing this decision, he continued to fly. "I love saving lives. . . . Nobody has it better than I do."

FIGURE 5.2 **Giraffe Award Worksheet** (continued)

CASE D

Every day, just before noon, Sister Beth Dadio drives a van to the Omaha (Nebraska) Central Park Mall to deliver sandwiches, chips, and fruit juice drinks to large groups of homeless who live on the streets of Omaha. She and her colleagues once operated a daytime shelter where the indigent and homeless could find shelter and food. However, the shelter drew many complaints from area businessmen, which prompted the building's owner to cancel the shelter's lease. So Sister Beth began taking food and drink to the Central Park Mall, a location chosen to bring attention to Omaha's homeless problem. Not unexpectedly, the city fathers tried to prevent these public displays of feeding the poor. But city officials lost the battle and even promised to open a new shelter.

FIGURE 5.2 **Giraffe Award Worksheet** *(continued)*

CASE E

In 1980, Fidel Castro allowed almost 125,000 Cubans to leave for the United States. In so doing, he managed to rid Cuba of a host of criminals, mentally ill people, and other undesirable folks. As a result, the people of Miami have been wary of all immigrants from Mariel. But not all the Marielitos were socially undesirable. Many were honest, hard workers who were seeking a better life for themselves and their children. Esteban Torres and his family were among the honest group. Esteban, now eighteen, remembers, "I know they had some crazy guys come over from Mariel, but I don't like it when people try to put me down." He had to work hard to overcome the stereotype. To do so, he took extra classes to learn English, earned mostly As, and became editor of his junior high school paper. During his senior year in high school, he took science courses at a nearby college and helped teach physics at his own school. Recently graduated, he plans to attend MIT.

FIGURE 5.2 **Giraffe Award Worksheet** *(continued)*

CASE F

A little over fifty years ago, Chester A. and Mary Ruth Blackburn became homesteaders on a bleak plain in northwestern Wyoming near Heart Mountain. They lived in a barracks that had been home to 11,000 Japanese-Americans interned there during World War II after the sneak attack on Pearl Harbor by Japanese naval and air forces. As the Blackburn couple farmed the land, they developed a bond with the former residents of the barracks, partly because of the living conditions. "There's no *insulation* in those barracks," explained Chester. But they also realized that the camp symbolized "one of the greatest violations of Civil Rights laws in the United States." In 1972, the Blackburns retired, sold their farm, and began transforming the barracks into a memorial for the victims of the internment. They created two memorials at the camp, got the place declared a national historic site, and saved documents about its past. The Blackburns were honored at two reunions of Japanese Americans who had once lived at the Heart Mountain barracks.

FIGURE 5.2 **Giraffe Award Worksheet** *(continued)*

CASE G

Some people call Ray Proffitt "the river vigilante" because he has decided to do his best to protect the Delaware River and its tributaries. He makes regular cruises along the Delaware and its tributaries, sometimes in a plane and sometimes in an amphibious vehicle. He looks for any sign of trouble—sewage spilling in through drain pipes from towns; chemical spills and industrial waste dumps; dumped debris such as asphalt, garbage, and even furniture. He attempts to trace the pollution to its source and confront those responsible with his log notes and photographs. If they don't agree to stop polluting and clean up what they have done, he takes them to court under the Clean Water Act. He has sued "land developers, corporations, towns, and EPA officials," including the EPA Administrator and the U.S. Attorney General. He charged the latter two with failure to enforce environmental regulations. No attorney was willing to represent him against the nation's chief attorney, so Proffitt filed the suit himself. Usually his lawsuits cause the defendants to scurry to change their ways. When the cases do go to trial, the polluters often receive heavy fines and sanctions that require their compliance with the environmental laws. Sometimes the case settlement provides reimbursement for the money Proffitt has advanced to lawyers. But all other costs—vehicles and their maintenance, photography, and so forth—come out of his personal funds. "I don't do this for money," he says. "I do this for the river."

To introduce students to applying criteria, I use case B, about Betty Washington. After they read the case, I ask, "Do you think we can argue that she should receive the award?"

Some students say yes; others say no. I ask, "Which criteria does Betty Washington fulfill?"

A student says, "All of them."

"Let's be specific," I say. "Who can say one criterion she fulfills?"

Rodney: She take a risk. Big one.

Teacher: What risk does she take?

Mariellen: Those drug guys could kill her she busts up their business. They don' like that.

Teacher: What do the rest of you think? Do you agree that she is taking a risk?

Wesley: It don't say nothin' 'bout no risk.

Takiesha: It do too. What the matter with you? You can't read? It say, "a difficult place to live because of the guns and drugs." Right here it say it. She take a risk all the time.

Wesley: You could say we all takin' risks every day just coming to this school. We could be killed by a car or some crazy gang-banger. If you livin' the risk, you ain't takin' it. You hear what I'm sayin'?

Henry: I think Wesley's right. This award is for a person that takes a extraordinary risk—you know, one outside what he usually gets just because he lives in a place.

Takiesha: But Ms. Washington, she takin' a extra risk cause she confrontin' the drug dealers. She don't gotta do that. She doin' that to get rid of them. They gonna shoot her, or beat her, or somethin'. She takin' a big risk.

Rodney: Takiesha right. She takin' a big risk, tryin' to stop drug dealers.

Wesley: Well, she din't sacrifice nothin'. Nothin' at all. So she don't get the award.

Rodney: She poor. She ain't got nothin' to sacrifice.

Mariellen: She sacrifice her time and her energy. It take time to organize and do all that stuff she done.

Wesley: But it ain't no sacrifice like the guy in the example. Like he gave twelve thousand bucks.

Takiesha: She had to spend a lot of time. That be time she can't do other stuff like watch TV or go to the mall. You can sacrifice things that ain't money.

Wesley: Spendin' time ain't no real sacrifice. It don't cost you nothin'.

Teacher: The problem is, what counts as a sacrifice? Let me put it this way. If you give up something for the sake of something else, how valuable does what you give up have to be before it's a sacrifice? [*I wait for a response.*] No? Let me try again. I have a pile of good magazines like *National Geographic* and the *Smithsonian* sitting in my study, and I have to get rid of them because they are taking up too much room. If I give them to a nursing home, is that gift a sacrifice?

Rodney: No, that ain't no sacrifice.

Teacher: Why not?

Rodney: Because you had to get rid of them.

Teacher: Is there any condition in which that would be a sacrifice?

Priscilla: I think you would have to really like them and want them for yourself but be willing to give them up so that people in the home could enjoy them. If they just garbage or a nuisance, giving them away ain't a sacrifice.

Teacher: Okay. So how can we define sacrifice to reflect what Priscilla says?

Priscilla: It has to have some real value to the person making the sacrifice.

Teacher: Good. That's a start. Can anyone give an example of that?

Priscilla: My Aunt Celia had these friends that lost everything in a fire. She gave them a thousand dollars to help them get through the worst times after the fire. She did not have a lot of money. That a real sacrifice 'cause she had to scrimp for a couple of months.

Teacher: Bill Gates is supposed to have a fortune of several billion dollars. If he gave a thousand dollars to those people, would that be a sacrifice for him?

Rodney: A thousand? He wouldn't even notice it be gone.

Teacher: Given what we have been saying, how can we define what we mean by sacrifice?

Takiesha: We could say, "A sacrifice has to be something of real value to the person giving it." [*I write this on the overhead.*]

Teacher: Who can add anything to that? You have to explain what *real value* means.

Wesley: You could use Priscilla's example. Like you could say, "For example, when a person give money to a family who lost everything, but the person don't got a lot herself, that a sacrifice."

Teacher: [*writing on the overhead*] "For example, when a person gives money to a family in need even though she cannot afford it, that giving is a sacrifice." Anything else? No? So what do you think about Ms. Washington in light of this definition?

Wesley: That the thing. She don't give nothin' of real value. She only give her time and effort. She got nothin' else to do. She don't have a job.

Takiesha: She do got a job. It say so right here. "She has worked full time to support her children."

Wesley: That don't mean she still workin'. It sound like she used to work but don't work no more.

Teacher: Actually that verb, *has worked*, implies she worked in the past and is still working. She did not stop working.

Wesley: That still don't mean she is sacrificing anything. I think what gets sacrificed has to be something specific.

Priscilla: Time and effort are specific. You can count hours worked. It takes a lot of effort to get people to cooperate.

Wesley: It ain't specific like money is specific.

Teacher: I think the word Wesley wants is *tangible* rather than specific. When something is tangible, you can see it and touch it. You can do something with it. So time is specific, but not tangible like a coin is.

Priscilla: I don't think a sacrifice has to be tangible. You could sacrifice a lot of time to a project. And all that time is tangible in your life anyway. You would know you used it up. There lots of things you maybe could have done with the time.

"Given what we have been saying, how can we define what we mean by sacrifice?"

Teacher: Maybe we can't reach an agreement on this. How many of you agree with Priscilla? Let's see your hands. Looks like most of the class agrees with Priscilla. How many agree with Wesley? Four of you. That's okay. One thing I want you to realize is that people will have slightly different definitions of the words they use as warrants and in backing. The result is that in making an argument, it is nearly always best to define the terms and explain how you are using them to make your judgment.

$\textbf{3}$ **Students Apply Criteria in Small Groups**

Judgments of Murder

$\textbf{1}$ **What Is Murder?**

Perhaps because of the many crime shows on television, most students seem very interested in cases of murder and believe they know a good deal about it. I ordinarily begin by asking them what they think murder is and asking for examples. I have a number of examples of my own to use if necessary.

One discussion with a class of juniors went as follows:

Teacher: We have been talking about warrants and backing. In some fields, those are already worked out and codified. For example, there are laws that tell us what our government says murder is. Do you know what murder is?

Steve: Sure. It's like when you kill somebody.

Teacher: Everybody agree with that? [*No response.*] Do you agree with that, Marilyn?

Marilyn: Yeah, I suppose, I mean, isn't that what it is?

Teacher: What about the rest of you? Do you agree? [*There are murmurs of dissent.*] Cecily, what do you think?

Cecily: It's not that simple. Like you can kill somebody by accident. We don't call that murder. Or if you kill in a war, that's not murder either. At least we don't call it murder.

Teacher: So what's the difference exactly? When do we call murder *murder* and when don't we?

> *"One thing I want you to realize is that people will have slightly different definitions of the words they use as warrants and in backing. In making an argument, it is nearly always best to define the terms and explain how you are using them to make your judgment."*

Carolyn: For it to be murder, it has to be intentional. I'm pretty sure. I mean, the murderer has to want to kill and it's not justified, like, like in self-defense.

Teri: Right. In murder, somebody kills somebody else without a good reason.

Cecily: I think you gotta say more than that. It's not just "without a good reason." Like if you break into my house and point a gun at me, I could shoot you, and it would be justified, I think. But you could break into my house, and then the next day I see you on the street, I can't be justified in shooting you then, I don't think.

Jorgé: Right, right. You can't because you aren't threatened anymore, because the guy doesn't have a gun pointing at you anymore.

Cecily: Jorgé's right. The threat has to be immediate, I mean, right there. It can't be yesterday. Can it?

Teacher: Okay. I think we are in agreement that self-defense has to be in the presence of an immediate threat of bodily harm. But let's go back to the word *intentional*. How do we know that a killing is intentional? Ordinarily murderers don't go about announcing that they intend to kill someone. So how do we know?

Jorgé: If someone shoots you, that is pretty certain intentional.

Teacher: Is only shooting with a gun intentional? Does it have to be a gun?

Jorgé: No, you could attack someone with a knife, a baseball bat, anything that could kill you.

Carolyn: It could be like anything that you know is going to kill a person. Like a rope or a big hammer or a tub of water, if you hold someone's head under the water. Remember, Richard the Third killed his brother by having him drowned in a butt of Malmsey. So that would be a deadly weapon.

Teacher: Can anyone provide a definition that will fit what we have been saying about what a deadly weapon is?

Cecily: It could be anything that, if you use it right, could kill another person.

Steve: That's pretty vague, Cecily. You need something more specific, like *tool* or *instrument.*

Cecily: No. We said poison could be a deadly weapon but we don't call poison a *tool* or instrument. It could be water, fire, or a pile of gravel. Those things are not tools or instruments. It depends on how you use the thing.

Sam: I think you can say that poison is instrumental in bringing about a death. So, in a general sense it's an instrument. You know, I mean, poison is an instrument in a sense. So I think you could say anything instrumental in bringing about a person's death is a deadly weapon.

Teacher: I think that is pretty strong. Let's put that up on the overhead. Sam, dictate your definition to me. [*I write it down as he does.*]

Sam: "Anything used in such a way as to be instrumental in bringing about another person's death is a deadly weapon."

Teacher: Good, Sam. Class, you've done a nice job in thinking this through. That is a strong definition of a complex notion. It will certainly do for now. We can always revise it later if we need to.

2 Introducing a Specific Case

Once students have come up with a strong working definition of murder, I introduce them to a specific case to which they can apply their definition. In the course of classroom discussion, students practice clarifying and modifying their thinking.

Teacher: Let me complicate this a bit. I read a case about a relatively young woman married to a man over seventy who was sick with a bad cold. One night, in the winter, the woman opened a window in the man's bedroom. The open window let a freezing draft in on the man. He developed some hypothermia as a result of the open window. His health failed, and he died. Would you charge her with murder?

Marilyn: Doesn't it depend on whether she opened the window on purpose to let the draft in on her husband?

Tom: It has to be on purpose to be murder. If it is by accident, then it's not.

Marilyn: How could anyone open a window by accident? "Oh, I pushed the window up when I wasn't thinking?" That doesn't make any sense.

Jorgé: Yeah, opening a window has to be intentional unless the person is wacko. But leaving it open is another matter. I mean, people forget to close windows all the time. So it depends on how long the window was open, doesn't it?

Marilyn: The main thing is the wife opened the window and made her husband more sick. That's what matters. I think it is murder.

Teacher: How could a defense lawyer defend her?

Marilyn: Did she know her husband was in the room? Because, then, there is no defense. If she knew he was in the room, and if she knew he had a bad cold or something, then she should have known not to let a cold draft on him. I mean, that's just common sense.

Jorgé: Marilyn's gonna be a prosecutor. You better not let her get on your case.

Teacher: He became much more sick after she opened the window.

Marilyn: Well, she knew he had a bad cold. You do not let really cold air on someone with a really bad cold. Especially not a wife.

Teacher: Why do you say that about the wife, Marilyn?

Marilyn: Well, it seems like a wife has like a responsibility to her husband to act to protect him and not harm him. I don't know if that's the law, but it seems reasonable from the wedding vows and all.

Teacher: Actually, it is in the law. It is called *duty to act*. Some people have a duty to act to help or protect others: parents have a duty to protect their children, police have a duty to protect and help the public, teachers have a duty to protect and help their students, and so forth. Did any of you ever hear about that? No? Well, for example, let's say that I see one of my students lying on the floor of my classroom bleeding from cuts on the wrist. Do I have to do anything?

Loretta: You better call an ambulance or something.

Teacher: Do you mean I should call an ambulance or I have to?

Loretta: You should do something to help the student.

> *Teacher:* Do you mean I do not have to do anything?
>
> *James:* I think you have to. But it doesn't seem fair. I heard about this on the radio. A teacher was saying that they have to act to keep students safe even when the kids endanger themselves. It's still the responsibility of the teacher. The teacher said that he could be sued if something bad happened to one of his students in his presence or even in his classroom and he wasn't there. That doesn't seem fair. If the student is doing something stupid, the teacher shouldn't be responsible.
>
> *Cecily:* It's still the responsibility of the teacher even if the kid is doing something stupid, because a teacher has a responsibility for his students.
>
> *Teacher:* Teachers have a duty to act; so do babysitters, grandparents left to care for children, policemen, and so forth. If people in positions to be responsible do not take the responsibility, they can be charged. On the other hand, a passerby who sees a teenager on the street with bleeding wrists can keep on walking.
>
> *Loretta:* That isn't right. The person should help or call an ambulance or police or do something.
>
> *Teacher:* Well, perhaps they should do something. But they will not be charged if they do nothing. In the eyes of the law, a passerby has no duty to act.

A teacher-led discussion like this introduces most of the concepts involved in analyzing different levels of culpability in the death of another. Students always know a little bit about the issues, and examples like the wife who opens a window in her sick husband's bedroom get them thinking. Misconceptions are rampant. But discussion and contrasting examples help students clarify and modify their thinking. Needless to say, teachers should know the material well and be able to draw on many examples.

"Discussion and contrasting examples help students clarify and modify their thinking."

Cases for Discussion

I usually set up groups to discuss a number of criminal cases (see Figure 5.3) and deal with the questions. Each group prepares to present and argue their findings to the class. The key focus should be the criteria used to

FIGURE 5.3 **Homicide Cases for Analysis**

Directions: For each of the following cases, decide what charge to bring and explain what evidence you will need to make the case. Be prepared to explain why the other possible charges are inappropriate.

CASE 1

On the night of January 14, Stanley Kowalski was walking home from work. He took the same route he always did. As Stanley approached the alley that ran beside Second National Bank, a man appeared from the shadows of the alley and fired a pistol point blank at Stanley. Stanley fell dead. The culprit disappeared. The medical examiner said the bullet had come for a .38 caliber pistol.

1. What charge should you bring against the culprit?

2. Why? Explain your use of the definitions.

CASE 2

Charles Cankerson waited outside for customers to leave Jimmy's Bar and Grill. Ralph Lando came through the door and headed for a Mercedes. When Ralph opened his car door, Charles ran up, pulled a pistol from his coat pocket, pointed it at Lando's chest, and said, "Give me your wallet, Hotshot. Give it to me now." Ralph swung at his attacker, and Charles fired his weapon once, killing Ralph.

1. With what will you charge Charles?

2. Why? Explain what criteria you would bring to bear on the case.

FIGURE 5.3 **Homicide Cases for Analysis** *(continued)*

3. Assume that you discovered that Cankerson's real motive in shooting Lando was his discovery that Lando had cuckolded him many times over. How would that influence the charges brought? Explain why.

4. What might Lando's defense attorney argue? Why?

5. Would a "heat of passion" defense work? Why or why not?

CASE 3

Two college boys, Jake and Jimbo, wanted to get even with a theater manager. A week earlier, when the boys were singing dirty songs very loudly during a movie, the manager caught them with two cans of beer each and with four empty cans under each of their seats. He had the theater guards forcibly remove the boys and shove them out into the parking lot. So the following Friday night, when they knew it would be crowded, the boys returned and found seats at the front of the theater. At the point of highest suspense, they lit a rolled-up newspaper and waved it over their heads. "Fire," they screamed, "Fire. Fire. Fire!" Everyone in the theater saw the blazing paper and heard them scream. There was instant panic. People stood and began pushing over others to get out of the theater. Several audience members were pushed to the floor and trampled. When order was restored, police and aid workers found three people dead and four badly injured. Jake and Jimbo were apprehended.

Their defense attorney argued that they were only playing a prank, that they did not intend to kill anyone, and that the deaths were attributable to the panic of those in the theater. The deaths were accidental. They could not have killed anyone with a roll of burning newspaper.

1. With what should Jake and Jimbo be charged?

2. What are the reasons for the charges you bring against the boys?

FIGURE 5.3 **Homicide Cases for Analysis** *(continued)*

3. What evidence will you need to justify your charges?

4. What would you argue in opposition to the defense attorney?

CASE 4

Matthew and Mary Winkler appeared to be the ideal couple, married for ten years, with three beautiful little girls, the oldest of whom was eight. They'd met at a Church of Christ college. Matthew had been pastor of the Church of Christ in Selmer, Tennessee, since January of 2005. On Wednesday, March 22, 2006, Matthew failed to appear for the evening prayer meeting at the church. The parishioners waited for a long time, and when Matthew did not show up, a group of them went to the parsonage, entered, and found Matthew dead on the floor of the couple's bedroom. Mary Winkler and the girls were not at home. The car was gone.

Police located Mary and the girls at a motel at Orange Beach, Alabama, on the Gulf coast. She did not try to escape but kept the girls close to her. Later she told police that she had risen at 6:15 A.M. when her alarm went off. She retrieved her husband's shotgun from the closet and was holding it while in a kind of delirium. She said, "The next thing I remember was hearing a loud boom. I heard the boom, and he rolled out of the bed onto the floor." She claimed that she did not mean to kill him, that the shotgun had just gone off.

Matthew Winkler was not yet dead, but seventy-seven birdshot pellets had broken his spine and punctured several organs. He lay on the floor and asked one question, "Why?" She testified that she had wiped the blood bubbles from his mouth. She said, "I told him that I was sorry and that I loved him."

She testified that her husband had been abusive, physically, sexually, and psychologically. He had forced her to engage in sexual practices that she considered unnatural. She said he had insisted that she view Internet porn as a prelude to sex and dress up "slutty" in a black "Afro wig," miniskirts, and platform shoes with eight-inch heels. (These articles were found

FIGURE 5.3 **Homicide Cases for Analysis** *(continued)*

in a closet in the Winkler home.) She also claimed that he had punched her and kicked her. Other witnesses testified that they had noticed that she wore makeup to cover bruises on her face and elsewhere.

Police investigators also discovered that several months before, Mary had been duped by a Nigerian Internet scam in which people receive emails saying they have just been awarded some large amount of money (usually several million dollars). Supposedly all they have to do to receive the money is send a small handling fee of a few hundred dollars along with other information such as their social security number, bank account number, and so forth. Once people get caught up in the scheme, it is difficult for them to get out. Mary had deposited two fraudulent checks for $17,500 in the family account, then shifted some of the money to a different bank, then withdrew $500. Matthew was angry about Mary's involvement in this scheme. However, he had neglected the family accounts and let his wife worry about the money.

1. What charges would you bring against Mary? Explain why you think they are justified.

2. If you were the defense attorney, how would you defend Mary against these charges?

3. What evidence would you need to find her innocent?

4. What evidence would you need to find her guilty?

decide the charges to be brought: first-degree murder, second-degree murder, voluntary manslaughter, or involuntary manslaughter. (See Appendix A for definitions.)

Small-Group Discussions

If students have been taught how to work in small groups, they will be able to monitor their behavior and complete this complex task, especially if they've previously worked on simpler problems like those in Chapters Two, Three, and Four. Nevertheless, since these discussions need to be productive if students are to experience the "flow" of learning, they need to be monitored for off-task behavior, points that may need to be clarified, and conflicts among students that become too lively.

I move from group to group, always trying to remain alert to what is happening elsewhere in the room. During thirty minutes of discussion, I can visit each of six groups at least twice, sometimes more often. (It's not necessary to spend equal amounts of time with all groups.) I focus on what group members are saying about the problem. If it's on target, I move immediately to the next group. My goal is to troubleshoot problems. If I stop to listen to a group that is going well, I may miss problems another group is having.

The first two cases are fairly straightforward. The last two are more ambiguous and therefore more difficult. Below a group is discussing case 4, the Winkler case:

> *Jorgé:* Man! This is crazy. She just got out of bed, got the shotgun, and plugged the guy.
>
> *Peter:* A shotgun don't exactly plug you.
>
> *Jorgé:* Well, maybe not plug. At close range a shotgun could tear a hole in you.
>
> *Cecily:* You mean, it's that big a bullet?
>
> *Peter:* A shotgun doesn't have bullets. It's got these little pellets, maybe hundreds in a shell. They come out with a lot of force, and when it's close range they are concentrated in one pretty small spot. The farther away, the more spread out they are. The more concentrated they are the more damage they do.
>
> *Nancy:* Oh. I didn't know that.

Peter: Yeah. Once we fired a shotgun at close range at a piece of three-quarter-inch plywood. It put a hole about six inches wide in it.

Cecily: So a shotgun shot is worse than a pistol shot?

Peter: I think it depends on how close you are. You know, if the target is far away, the pellets of a shotgun blast spread out and probably cause less damage. But a bullet from a pistol can kill you from fifty or a hundred yards.

Cecily: So she, Mary, had to know that her husband was hurt, because it would leave a big wound?

Jorgé: Yeah. There would be a lot of blood and you could probably see the wound, like clothes wouldn't cover it up. From pictures I seen, it would be really obvious.

Nancy: And then she said, "I love you." That's hard to believe. Like he must be sayin', "I don't need you to love me, honey. Keep away from me. Give your love to somebody else."

Cecily: Well, so what do you guys think? What should we charge her with?

Peter: First degree. She wanted to kill him and she must have planned it. You know, "Get up early while he's still sleepin' and kill him while the girls are still in the sack." Boy, that's cold.

Jorgé: There's no evidence that he did anything to her. Just what she says. At least, what we have does not give any evidence. She is probably making it all up to make herself look innocent.

Nancy: Making what up? What do you mean? What is she making up?

Jorgé: All that stuff about abuse. She could have made it up. There is no evidence that he actually made her do anything weird. Only her word. Nothing more. She's one of those, what do you call it, you know, the spider that kills her mate after mating.

Nancy: The black widow.

Jorgé: Yeah, yeah. The black widow. That's what this is.

Nancy: I don't agree. She's probably telling the truth. He probably is an abuser. He's in a great position to do it. He's a respected member of the community, as they say. He's a preacher, for God's sake! Everyone believes the preacher. And she's got the evidence, the high heels, the wig. She is a little woman, and a fundamentalist Christian. She is not gonna buy that stuff or be caught with it. She's just not likely to do that unless her husband demands it. And she's such a mess, she probably thinks it's her Christian duty to please her husband. That's what those fundamentalist people preach, you know. So that's why she went along with his perversions. She thought she had to. Then, something changed her mind. Something changed her, somehow. And she shot him. I think it's a crime of passion and she should be charged with second-degree murder.

Peter: Oh, come on! She set the alarm, got up after a sound sleep apparently. She needed it so she could drive from Tennessee to Orange Beach on the Gulf coast. She went directly to the closet to get the shotgun. That was not sleepwalking, you know. She knew exactly what she was doing every step of the way. She had to remove the gun from its case. Then she had to aim the gun, and she hit him in the spine. It says the shot broke the spine. It had to be a direct hit. That don't happen by accident. She planned this and carried it out. What a cold bitch.

Hazel: How do you know that she's not telling the truth? What evidence is there? She says that she was in a delirium. That means she did not know what she was doing. It is possible that she could have walked to the closet, found the gun, taken it out of its case, loaded it even, and carried it back to the bedroom, and more or less pointed it at her husband. And then the gun went off. She says she loved him and didn't mean to kill him. I believe her.

Jorgé: How can you believe that? That is such crap. You can't believe that. You mean she is in a delirium when she goes to the closet to get the shotgun? When she takes it out of its case? When she loads it, because it probably was not kept loaded in the closet? That's the first thing you are supposed not to do. So she had to load it. Then she goes back to the room and has, even in her delirium, the good control to hit her husband's spine? You know, a shotgun jumps like hell when you fire it. That's what makes it hard to hit anything. But she has the good control to pop him right in the spine? Which is gonna kill him! This was obviously planned. She knew what she was doing. I bet she even practiced firing a shotgun. Besides that, she left him there on the floor to die. And she had a duty to act because he was her husband. That alone might be first-degree murder.

Hazel: You don't have any evidence that she actually planned it. All you have is *maybe* and *probably*. I don't think that is good enough to convict her of first-degree murder.

Cecily: Well, let's see what we do have. We know for certain that she fired the shot that killed him. She admits that. Do we have any hard evidence that she planned it? I don't think so.

Peter: How about the time? Doesn't that indicate that she planned it? She got up when the alarm rang. According to her own testimony, she went directly to the closet and got the gun. Like Jorgé said, she loaded it. Then she went to the bedroom, pointed the gun at her husband, and it went off. Guns do not go off by themselves. Somebody has to pull the trigger. She had to do it. Nobody else is there. Her actions are one, two, three, four. She had it all planned out. Everything she said she did once out of bed, everything leads directly to the shooting. Doesn't it make sense that if she was really in a delirium, she would not be so systematic? Wouldn't you expect her to do something that was not in line with a plan to kill her husband, maybe go to the toilet, or make tea for breakfast, or check on the girls, or sit on the bed in a daze for a few minutes?

Jorgé: Yeah, I agree completely. That's the case we make. If she was in a delirium, she would do something weird, something that has nothing to do with the shooting.

Nancy: But Hazel is right about the evidence for planning. All we have is our inference that it must have been planned because her actions seem systematic. It could be that she is so upset that she does all that because she needs to be released from the unbearable pressure that her husband puts her under. She can't take it another minute or another day. If we can't prove that she planned in advance, we can't get first degree. I think we should charge second degree. There is certainly intent to kill, and there is plenty to indicate that the husband abused her. The very fact that she showed the platform shoes and the wig is evidence of the sexual abuse. That would enrage me. [*To Cecily*] You can understand how she would be enraged?

Cecily: I can see it.

Peter: Wait. wait. Didn't we read about lying in wait to gain advantage over a victim? Yeah, here it is. I underlined that. That is evidence of premeditation.

Cecily: But Mary Winkler did not lie in wait.

Peter: No, but she did something like it. She got up when the alarm went off. She probably knew that her husband would not. So she had him at a disadvantage. He was asleep. That's a pretty big disadvantage. That looks to me very similar to lying in wait.

Jorgé: That's a really good point, Peter.

Hazel: I don't think it's anything the same. It's like Nancy said, she showed the evidence of abuse with the shoes and the wig. That would probably drive her crazy that she had to do that whenever he wanted. I can understand her need to kill him or her desire. It is second degree. In the reading [*see Appendix A*], it says "second-degree murder is the intent to kill without deliberation or premeditation." We are just guessing at premeditation. We have no real evidence.

Jorgé: Do we have to agree? Did he say we have to agree?

Nancy: He didn't say. I see no reason why we have to. You guys are too stubborn to be convinced that we are right, even though it is three against two.

Cecily: So why don't we do this. You two guys prepare your charge of first and the three of us will prepare second degree.

> *Jorgé:* I'll bet ten bucks we're right.
>
> *Nancy:* We're not allowed to gamble in school, Jorgé. Otherwise
> we'd just take your money because you're wrong.

Since several groups had split their decisions, we had a full-class discussion of the case; about one-third of the students argued for first-degree murder, and the remainder argued for second-degree charges. Arguments were similar to those in the group described previously; no significantly different perspectives surfaced. A few groups had considered voluntary manslaughter but rejected it.

Of course, the students wanted to know what really happened. I referred them to the TruTV website, from which I'd taken the facts of the case. The kids who checked it out came back to class shocked. Mary had been charged with voluntary manslaughter. The students couldn't believe that was possible. However, under Tennessee law, voluntary manslaughter is a crime of passion "produced by adequate provocation sufficient to lead a reasonable person to act in an irrational manner." We spent some time discussing how a jury might have come to that conclusion. Cecily pointed out that the jury was probably made up of fundamentalists and that they would have a different view of the abuse claimed by Mary Winkler than the students in our class might have. She said, "We may see Matthew's demand that she dress up slutty as a little bit kinky. But they might see it as the work of the devil. We might see it as harmless or perhaps a bit irritating. But they might see it as cause for damnation, for burning in the flames of hell."

I asked how such differences in perception might influence the interpretation of "provocation sufficient to lead a reasonable person to act in an irrational manner." The class agreed that our perspectives were probably far different from those of Tennessee fundamentalists. Most of us did not feel the abuse that Mary claimed was adequate provocation for a shotgun killing. But the class also agreed that others with different ideas about the abuse might see it as adequate provocation. Nancy pointed out that some would believe that it was someone's duty to kill Matthew Winkler. Cecily asked what the unnatural sexual acts were, and everyone laughed. Cecily protested that it was important. "I want to know if they think some kinds of sex acts are more sinful than others. Like is homosexuality more improper than sex out of wedlock? Maybe those unnatural acts are thought of as the worst kind of sinful act, you know, the greatest crime against the Lord."

Peter said, "It could be. You don't see the Catholic Church speaking out against girls who get pregnant much. But they denounce homosexuality all the time. I don't think the Catholic Church even recognizes it. Do they?" The class did not know for sure. Nor did I.

Nancy: But for sure, fundamentalist groups condemn homosexuality, especially male—they are always quoting that passage from the Bible that says in it's an abomination.

Jorgé: That's in Leviticus: "Thou shalt not lie with mankind, as with womankind: it's abomination."

Peter: How do you know that?

Jorgé: It came up in my Sunday school group. We was talking about homosexuality and did the Bible condemn it.

Peter: What did you decide?

Jorgé: We said no, not really, because it only comes up in a couple of places. Besides that, we don't see the Bible as the absolute word of God. It's a guide but not the law.

Teacher: Let's get back on the point. You were saying that some sexual acts are deemed to be more sinful than others. Or at least people regard some with greater disgust than others.

Nancy: I looked up Mary Winkler on the Net last night. She said that her husband wanted her to perform oral and anal sex. [*There are murmurs of disgust.*] I bet people would think that was worse than just sex outside of marriage. I think they might not like the platform shoes and the wig. But oral and anal sex would really be shocking.

Teacher: So what's your point?

Nancy: Well, if the people on the jury saw oral and anal sex as disgusting and really perverted, they might see it as adequate provocation, you know, uh, for, uh, you know, a reasonable person to go irrational and shoot the gun at him.

Teacher: What do the rest of you think?

Jorgé: Seems reasonable to me.

Cecily: Yeah. I think we settled this, for us, anyway.

Following our classroom discussion, I inform students that Mary Winkler had been found guilty of the voluntary manslaughter charge. In Tennessee, voluntary manslaughter carries a sentence of three to six years. The prosecution argued for the maximum, but the defense argued for probation, that is, that no time be spent in jail. The judge pronounced a sentence of 210 days, minus the 143 already served. Of the 67 days to be served, Mary could spend 60 in a mental health facility. Students were appalled.

We also talked about the jury, which had been made up of ten women and two men. The jury foreman said that the jury heavily favored Mary Winkler because there were "ten ladies" on it. The foreman claimed that after the first seven hours of deliberation, nine of the ten women appeared ready to acquit. He said, they "wanted her to just walk free." He told reporters that the verdict of voluntary manslaughter was a compromise. He said, "We had to settle on something." We talked briefly about the influence of the women on the jury. Basically, we simply reviewed our earlier ideas about what the women might see as adequate provocation.

Clarifying warrants and developing backing are central to the issues dealt with in this and other chapters of this book. What counts as a sacrifice? When is provocation adequate to let us believe that it would allow a reasonable person to act in a certain way? What characteristics must that provocation have? What are the conditions under which it is reasonable for police to use deadly force? These questions are among the most important ones we confront in making judgments about the way we should treat others and about the beliefs we cherish. These are the questions that make the difference between a just nation and a barbaric one. Their answers are never simple and should never be simplistic. They are complex and deserve our close attention and further questioning.

"This kind of debate is or should be the very heart and soul of what we do in English classes."

Some teachers are likely to see all of this as not even pertinent to the subject matter of English. I would argue that this kind of debate and consideration is what is most pertinent to the teaching of English. It focuses attention on the uses of language, on how different people with different values interpret events, on the necessity of using language purposively and thoughtfully, and the importance for critical thinking if we are ever to achieve a just society. This kind of debate is or should be the very heart and soul of what we do in English classes.

Tips on Selecting Problems for Discussion

If you want to find new problems for discussion involving the use of criteria, you can find them in the news, in magazines, in the literature that students will be reading, or you can invent your own. Here are some things to consider:

> » The best problems for discussion will involve relatively abstract ideas or terms, and will likely involve at least two (possibly opposing) points of view.
> » Be careful to select problems that are not so complex that there are no limits to what they might involve or so ambiguous that no criteria can be brought to bear.
> » Rather, try to find ideas that can be problematized. For example, our system of law problematizes the idea of murder by considering various *kinds* of murder and bringing criteria to bear to differentiate them.

Units of instruction nearly always benefit by problematizing the concepts with which they deal. Love, for example, is often chosen as the theme of a unit. But if it is not problematized, it will not be particularly interesting or productive to discuss. To problematize the concept of love, students might consider questions such as these:

> » What are the kinds of love in a relationship between two people or among many people?
> » How do those differ from the love a person bears an old friend? Or her country? Or his God?

As you begin to differentiate among closely related ideas, criteria will begin to emerge that will help discriminate among the ideas. If and when that happens, you may have found a good topic for instruction and discussion.

What Is Courage?

Developing and Supporting Criteria for Arguments of Judgment

GROWING UP, WE ACCEPT THE JUDGMENTS AND ASSUMPTIONS of others. Those views become our lenses for seeing and interpreting people, things, and ideas. All of us operate our lives on the basis of these views. As long as the views in our heads match the reality of our daily lives, we will be safe and do little harm to others. When they do not match that reality, they become the grounds for many of the most divisive and hurtful arguments in which we will ever engage.

Learned Judgments Shape Our Lives

If you had been born in the 1930s in Germany, you would have learned the supremacy of the fair-skinned, blond, blue-eyed, Aryan race. You would have learned that those of other racial and ethnic groups were inferior. You would have heard assertions that Jews, gypsies, and dark-skinned peoples should be removed from Aryan states; that homosexuals

"Growing up, we accept the judgments and assumptions of others. Those views become our lenses for seeing and interpreting people, things, and ideas. All of us operate our lives on the basis of these views."

and mentally defective people should be removed or sterilized; that Jews were active in a conspiracy to control the wealth and industry of the West by controlling banking; and that Jews were no better than vermin, to be destroyed by whatever means possible. You would have heard all these assertions and probably accepted them because adult authorities made them.

As a child, you would have learned what behavior was acceptable and what was not, and you would have learned to report people who engaged in unacceptable behavior, even including parents and siblings, to the Nazi authorities. You would have learned to defend the Reich at all costs, and if you were eleven, twelve, or thirteen, and male near the end of the war in late 1944 and 1945, you might have done so with other boy soldiers your age with no adult soldiers in sight. Thousands of German children did learn all these things, believed them to be true, and acted on their unwarranted beliefs, becoming the last line of defense against the advancing allied armies and losing their lives in the effort.

Without doubt, these children were following orders to step into the breech to stop the allied advance. The argument in their heads probably went something like this: *There is clear evidence that more soldiers are needed in the line of defense, and an officer has ordered us into the line. The inescapable conclusion is that I must step into the line. That is a warranted action because an officer has ordered it, and we have learned that following the orders of an officer is right (and good).*

A warrant like this is clearly a judgment. But what serves as backing for it? The mere fact that we say it is right to follow an order implies the opposite possibility. Under what circumstances is it not right? When is it appropriate to disobey? When we ask such questions, we question the *judgment* and the *criteria* by which the judgment was made. When we ask such questions, we are examining the *backing* of the warrants (rules).

Examining the Backing of Our Judgments

Everyone in each new generation learns the received wisdom and knowledge of the elder generation, in the form of principles and strongly held ideas—warrants that guide our conduct throughout our lives. Most of these warrants need to be examined and reexamined. But how?

Ordinarily, warrants in arguments of judgment cannot be supported by data or simply by piling up a set of examples. The backings for such warrants are *explications* and *analyses* of the *values* being applied to whatever is being judged.

To take a simple earlier example from Chapter Two, the warrant in the argument whether the "voluptuary" is fit to be king is essentially a *definition* of what a fit king is or does. We could do studies of what fit kings do and compile large data sets over many historical periods. But we would have to begin the study by presupposing which kings are fit. Or we could begin with sets of criteria to be applied to all kings in order to determine which are fit and which are not. In either case, we presuppose a definition of fitness, which makes our arguments circular. The warrants in arguments of judgment are conceptual and will be supported primarily by extended analysis and definition of the concepts involved.

Backing in *The Great Debaters*

Backing analysis is dramatized in the final debate of the movie *The Great Debaters*. A debate team from all-black Wiley College, in Texas, is invited to debate Harvard on the proposition, "Civil disobedience is a moral weapon in the fight for justice." In formal debates, one team is assigned the affirmative and the other the negative. Wiley is assigned the affirmative. James Farmer and Samantha Book are the Wylie debaters.

James Farmer begins by restating the proposition and asking, "But how can disobedience ever be moral? Well, I guess that depends on one's definition of the word," thereby focusing on whether civil disobedience is *moral* rather than on whether it can be considered a weapon in the fight for justice.

He provides the example of the British massacre of 379 men, women, and children who had gathered for an outlawed political meeting in Amritsar, India, in 1919. British General Dyer, who ordered his soldiers to fire on the crowd until they had expended their ammunition, said the massacre had taught a moral lesson.

Farmer explains that Gandhi had responded not with violence but "with an organized campaign of noncooperation. Government buildings were occupied. Streets were blocked with people who refused to rise even when beaten by police. Gandhi was arrested, but the British were soon forced to release him." Gandhi called this success a "moral victory." Farmer concludes his speech by saying, "The definition of moral, Dyer's lesson or Gandhi's victory? You choose." He has contrasted two uses of the term. In one, the term defends an action that must be regarded as totally without redeeming qualities; in the other, it is applied to an action that, though fraught with disobedience, is justified.

When the Harvard team takes up the question of what is moral, the speaker cites data about deaths in the First World War: 240 men died every hour for four years, for a total of 8,281,000 deaths. Is there anything moral about that? Nothing, except that it kept Germany from enslaving all of Europe. The Harvard debater continues, "Civil disobedience isn't moral because it's nonviolent. Fighting for your country with violence can be deeply moral, demanding the greatest sacrifice of all, life itself." If both violent action and civil disobedience are moral weapons in the fight for justice, then, Harvard argues, the true difference is that "nonviolence is the mask civil disobedience wears to conceal its true face, anarchy." If civil disobedience can be shown to bring about anarchy, it will be discredited.

> *"The warrant in the argument whether the "voluptuary" is fit to be king is essentially a definition of what a fit king is or does."*

The *Oxford English Dictionary* defines *anarchy* as "absence of government; a state of lawlessness due to the absence or inefficiency of the supreme power; political disorder." The implication of Harvard's point is that if one ignores the law for the purpose of civil disobedience, one enters a state of anarchy. This is a very common contention. Generally, our society accepts the idea that people cannot live together in a state of anarchy. They would heap indignities upon one another and even kill one another (*see* Hobbes 1958).

Samantha Book, debating for Wiley, denies that civil disobedience involves anarchy. She points out that Gandhi was influenced by Thoreau and that both he and Gandhi recognized that "lawbreakers must accept the legal consequences of their actions." She asks, "Does that sound like anarchy? Civil disobedience is not something for us to fear." Her point is that anarchy is not an appropriate characterization of civil disobedience.

> *"The warrants in arguments of judgment are conceptual and will be supported primarily by extended analysis and definition of the concepts involved."*

By bringing up Thoreau, however, Book provides Harvard with an opening. The Harvard debater says that Thoreau once said, "Any man more right than his neighbor constitutes a majority of one." He points out, "Thoreau, the idealist, could never know that Adolf Hitler would have agreed with his words. . . . The beauty and burden of democracy is this: no idea prevails without the support of the majority. The people decide the moral issues of the day, not a majority of one." Individuals, Gandhi, Thoreau, or any other, cannot decide which laws to obey and which to break.

Samantha Book responds for Wiley. "The majority does not decide what is right and what is wrong. Your conscience does. So why should a citizen surrender his conscience. . . . We must never, ever, kneel down before the tyranny of a majority."

A Harvard debater argues that we cannot decide which laws to obey and which to ignore. He gives an example of his father's best friend, a police officer, gunned down in the line of duty. Such action erodes the rule of law. The Harvard man concludes, "Nothing that erodes the rule of law can be moral no matter what name we give it."

James Farmer responds with the example of the lynching that he and his team witnessed earlier in the film. "In Texas they lynch Negroes," he says. "My teammates and I saw a man strung up by his neck and set on fire. . . . What was this Negro's crime that he should be hung in a dark forest filled with fog? Was he a thief, was he a killer, or just a Negro? Was he a sharecropper, a preacher? Were his children waiting up for him? And who were we to just lie there and do nothing? No matter what he did, the mob was the criminal. But the law did nothing, which left us wondering. Why? My opponent says, 'Nothing that erodes the rule of law can be moral.' But there is no rule of law in the Jim Crow south, not when Negroes are denied housing, turned away from schools, hospitals, and not when we are lynched. St. Augustine said that 'an unjust law is no law at all,' which means that I have the right, even a duty, to resist with violence or civil disobedience. You should pray that I choose the latter." That statement ends the debate, and Wylie wins.

Though this is just a movie, the content illustrates the development of backing necessary to support judgments used as warrants. As Farmer states at the beginning, it depends on how you define the word *moral*. The definition turns out to be an extended one.

Defining Concepts Through Contrasting Scenarios

Our students have to be taught to make a range of distinctions dealing with a concept and use those distinctions in making judgments. Making such distinctions, however, such as what it means—and does not mean—to be moral, is very complex and abstract and requires a kind of thinking that many students are completely unaccustomed to. For many students, a concept like courage brings to mind a mishmash of ideas including clichés and popular beliefs about whom we are supposed to assume are courageous people. Many adults and students cling ferociously to the notion that all firemen are courageous, for instance, and refuse to consider the circumstances in specific situations. In addition, many adults and students have difficulty in dealing with the abstract nature of the problems involved.

To facilitate more critical thinking, my Master of Arts in Teaching English (MAT) students and I began using contrasting scenarios, an approach prompted by our earlier attempts to make thematic units more meaningful. In the sixties, and even now, thematic units consisted of groups of literary works with common themes that teachers taught in a sequence they assumed would make them more readily understood. We decided to take an additional step and work with our students to define the underlying concepts—love or courage, for example—so our students could use those definitions to make inferences from the specific examples in the works they read (see Hillocks 1964). Our students developed definitions for these concepts sooner and more specifically when we presented contrasting scenarios.

The circumstances described in contrasting scenarios vary systematically. In scenarios focused on the nature of courageous action, for example, one might focus on a character facing great danger in robbing a bank; another, on a soldier attacking an enemy position in a rage and without thinking; another, on a person afraid to do anything in a dangerous situation; and so forth. Students get caught up deciding whether each of these characters' actions may be considered courageous, constructing criteria to clarify the differences among them, and finally developing extended definitions of the abstract concept of courage. We have used this process with several sets of scenarios, each in relation to a different concept, to help students learn how to develop their own definitions using criteria and examples with considerable success (see Hillocks, Kahn, and Johannessen 1983; Smagorinsky 1991).

These extended definitions amount to the *backing* that may be used to argue whether or not a character's actions are courageous. In other words, the thinking strategies involved in developing argument are very much the same as those in drawing and defending inferences about literature.

"For many students, a concept like courage brings to mind a mishmash of ideas including clichés and popular beliefs about whom we are supposed to assume are courageous people."

Learning to Define: Courage as a Complex Concept

Courage is a key value in our culture. Hardly an hour of news goes by without at least one mention of someone acting courageously: the runner who fights for a place on the Olympic team though he has lost both legs and runs on artificial ones, the young boy who grabs a toddler to keep him from falling into deep water, the firefighter who pulls the child from a burning building, the young woman with cancer who fights back.

The Nature of Courage

Aristotle, in the *Nichomachean Ethics*, identified courage as a foundational virtue because, without courage, justice, generosity, tolerance, even mercy would, in many cases, be impossible. Without courage, liars, cowards, and villains will have their way. Courage is arguably the most important virtue.

We all think we know what courage is when we see it. But what is courage really? Are there acts that appear to be courageous but are not? Are firefighters courageous at all times or only under some circumstances? Do people in the armed services qualify as courageous because they are in uniform, or do they qualify only under some circumstances? What are those circumstances? If we cannot draw such distinctions, then the quality of true courage loses its value. If we think every act is courageous, then no act is courageous.

We can speak of a person's courage in general terms, but it turns out to be a complex question: courage must be judged over many events and situations. Even a single act must meet several criteria to be judged courageous. In his *Nichomachean Ethics*, Aristotle defines courage or courageous action as the control of fear in the face of significant danger, which may be physical, moral, or psychological. That is, for an act to be labeled courageous, a person must face physical, moral, or psychological threats that have quite serious consequences for the person's well-being. A courageous act involves facing these dangers with equanimity and acting with resolve but with due regard to the safety of others despite the dangers. (Aristotle generally defines each virtue as a mean between two extremes of deficit on the one hand and excess on the other. Courage is the mean between the deficit represented in cowardice—having no control over fear—and the excess of foolhardiness—having no fear even in extreme danger.)

having no control over fear	← COURAGE →	having no fear even in extreme danger

He goes on to discuss several requirements that must be met without which an act cannot be considered courageous: For example, since courage is considered a virtue and, for the most part, we still believe it to be one, a courageous act must be noble, not evil or malicious. Thus, it is inappropriate to praise a robber as courageous regardless of the danger he or she must confront to commit the theft. (Students like to argue that Robin Hood's criminal acts are courageous because they are done for the good of the downtrodden people he supports. That is, his criminal acts have a noble purpose. Then we discuss how much of the loot he gives away and how much he keeps.)

Furthermore, for an act to be courageous, it must be deliberate, done with forethought and awareness of the dangers involved. It cannot be performed out of rage or insanity or from simple appetite. Nor can an act be considered courageous if it is performed out of fear of a greater danger. In that case, the act does not exhibit control of fear. It is done out of fear. And someone whose performance is enhanced by training or equipment may not be considered courageous, because special training or equipment reduces the level of danger.

Many of our students see things in absolute terms. Either something is dangerous or it is not. There are no degrees of danger for them. Such simplistic thinking blocks one's ability to make inferences.

In the *Art of Rhetoric*, Aristotle's summary of ethics is one source for propositions of probability. It is particularly relevant to arguments of praise or blame (epideictic arguments), for it is a deep understanding of courage that permits us to support a judgment of a person as courageous. That deep understanding provides, in Toulmin's terms, both warrants and the backing for them.

Why These Ideas Are Important for Students

Young people are particularly concerned about their own courage or at least how others view their courage. They want to seem courageous. They do not wish to appear wimps in the eyes of their peers. But they are often confused about the nature of courage.

"If we think every act is courageous, then no act is courageous."

"Many of our students see things in absolute terms. Either something is dangerous or it is not. There are no degrees of danger for them. Such simplistic thinking blocks one's ability to make inferences."

Each of us can recall situations in which we had a choice between joining with others in picking on the weak or trying to stop them from doing so. Perhaps we have had opportunities to act justly and failed to do so through lack of courage. Considerations like these can prompt writing of various kinds: personal narrative about taking (or not taking) true courageous action; extended definitions of courage that include contrasting examples that make clear the distinctions between true courage and seeming courage; and arguments claiming that a character's or person's action is or is not courageous.

Such arguments require the kinds of judgments we make when we interpret literature. Perhaps more importantly, they give rise to the kind of thinking necessary to examine our own behavior and the behavior of others.

When I was young, an afternoon I spent at Scout camp coming up with arguments based on scenarios the counselors presented changed my thinking for the rest of my life. I saw that I could, indeed, think through sticky problems. I learned that I liked thinking through such problems, and I am still doing it many decades later. I have had students confess to me that after this unit they were able to reevaluate their own courage in certain situations. Several no longer saw themselves as lacking in courage. Some found that acts they had regarded as courageous were not. By and large, most came to see courage in a different way. The important point is that our students become more able to deal with sticky problems in their own lives and in their thinking about problems in general.

Classroom Activity: What Is Courage?

When I began to work with students on the nature of courageous action, I knew that simply providing a definition and asking them to read what Aristotle said would be deadly. Instead I devised scenarios that illustrated both what courage *was* and what it was *not*. I have subsequently written, tested, and taught four sets of these scenarios. In the course of the activity, the students, in small groups, decide whether the action depicted in a given scenario is courageous or not. Then I ask them to devise one or more criteria for making that decision.

(1) **Introducing Students to Writing Criteria**

Because most middle and high school students have never written criteria before, I show them how to proceed with the help of the super-hero scenario in Figure 6.1.

FIGURE 6.1 **Superman, Lois, and the Rushing Freight Train**

One day while Superman is flying around the skies of Chicago, he lands atop the Sears Tower. Using his super-telescopic vision, he sees a woman tied to a railroad track in the distant south. Squinting, he sees that it is Lois Lane. Beyond her, perhaps only fifty yards away, is a rushing freight train, which, in seconds, will cut her fragile body to pieces. Superman leaps from the Sears Tower and flies toward the train with the speed of light. He screeches to a halt on the tracks facing the train. The train smashes into his outstretched arms, and Superman stops it dead. He turns to Lois and asks, "Gee, are you all right?"

After reading the paragraph aloud, I ask, "What do you think? Is Superman's stopping the train courageous?"

At least one student always says no. I ask why it isn't. There is usually one of two responses: "He doesn't have to be afraid" or "There is no danger for him." When I ask why not, the answer is some variation of, "He has superpowers."

"What difference does that make?" I ask.

A student always says something like, "If you are not afraid, it doesn't take courage." Eventually, students explain that courage means facing some danger when you are afraid.

Because I want students to develop criteria using more formal language, I need to show them how. I write on the board, "For an act to be courageous, it must. . . ."

"In light of this Superman example, let's try to complete this sentence. What must the act be?"

For an act to be courageous, it must. . . .

For an act to be courageous, it must involve danger for the actor.

Jane: It must be dangerous.

Jorgé: It gotta be dangerous for the person. And he has to know it's dangerous for him. This ain't dangerous for Superman, and he knows it.

Teacher: Is every act that is dangerous for the actor courageous?

Jane: Probably not. Let me think. I know what you're going to say. You want an example. Right?

Teacher: Right. Anyone have an example of an act that is dangerous but that would not be courageous?

Cecily: Well, it's dangerous to jump off high buildings, but doing that is suicide. It's not courageous.

Jorgé: Like if you light a cigarette while you're pumping gas, that's dangerous. But it's not courageous.

Teacher: And why is it not courageous?

Jorgé: Because it's stupid.

Teacher: Do you mean that the act has no intelligence?

Jorgé: No, no, no. It's stupid to *do* that.

Teacher: In what sense is it stupid?

Jorgé: It's like silly. There is no good reason to do it. You're just taking a big chance.

Cecily: There are a lot of dangerous things people do for no good reason. Most of them are just foolish.

Teacher: So, can we say, that for an act to be courageous, it must not be foolish—or another word for that is *foolhardy*. [*I write on the overhead, "For an act to be courageous, it must not be foolish or foolhardy."*] Okay, we have two criteria. For an act to be courageous, it must involve danger for the actor. And second, it must not be foolhardy. That is, as Jorgé says, it must be for a good reason. Now, given these two criteria, is Superman's act of stopping the train courageous?

Jane: Well, the act is not courageous because it does not hold any danger for Superman. On the other hand it is a good thing to do. He meets one criterion, but not the other. So he's not courageous in this act.

Teacher: Now I'm going to distribute a set of scenarios for you to examine. [*See Figure 6.2.*] In your groups I would like you to examine each one, decide if the act is courageous, and write a criterion as we have just done for the Superman scenario. I recommend that you begin each criterion with the words we have already used. "For an act to be courageous, it must. . . ."

I enjoy watching students get excited by rigorous thinking as they complete this activity. Many are caught up in clichés about courage from the popular media. Sometimes they are frustrated and upset because their favorite ideas about courage come under attack. (Even graduate students are not immune to this problem.)

As students work in small groups of four or five, I circulate from group to group. When group members lock horns, my job is to allow and encourage them to reason out their differences. If they cannot, they may submit multiple reports, but each faction must explain the reasons for their lack of agreement. Below are four examples of group talk about four different scenarios.

Group 1

Jorgé: "Thirteen-year-old James had been beaten many times by a group of boys in his neighborhood. He generally tried to avoid them. One day, they surrounded him on the street. He was so frightened he could not think clearly. In a panic, hardly knowing what he was doing, he ran as hard as he could at the boy nearest him, knocking him to the ground. Was James' attack courageous?" [*He looks at the group expectantly.*] Well?

Mel: I think he is courageous, because like we said before, it's a dangerous situation, and it has to be dangerous for him to be courageous. So when he attacks one of the boys, he is courageous because he could be beaten bad.

Cecily: But he hardly knows what he is doing, it says. That can't be courageous. It's like just doing it. If you are not aware of what you're doing, how can it be courageous?

FIGURE 6.2 **What Is Courage?**

OPINIONNAIRE: What Is Courage?

When people decide whether some thing or idea belongs in a certain category, they often use a set of rules to guide their thinking. Working with three or four of your classmates, do the following:

1. Read each of the following and check yes or no in answer to the question that ends the paragraph.

2. On the lines below each paragraph, write the criterion or rule by which you decided whether the action is or is not courageous.

3. Write at least one criterion for each scenario (begin your statement, "For an act to be courageous, it must . . .").

4. Some of your decisions will require more than one criterion. In those cases, write as many as necessary.

SCENARIOS

1. Near the end of his officer training, Roger volunteered to go on a mission that the captain said involved "real danger." The captain used this phrase to describe all missions, so Roger assumed that the mission was just another part of his training. When the plane carrying the men left the ground, Roger was surprised to hear the pilot say the men were part of an invasion of a small Caribbean island. Was Roger's willingness to volunteer for the mission courageous?

   Yes_____ No_____ Criterion:

   _____

   _____

   _____

FIGURE 6.2 **What Is Courage?** *(continued)*

2. Out of the corner of his eye, the Secret Service agent spotted a gun aimed at the president. Instantly, he threw himself in the line of fire, taking the bullet meant for the president. Was the agent's act of jumping in front of the president to protect him and take the bullet courageous?

Yes_____ No_____ Criterion:

_____

_____

_____

3. In the small town of Clinton, teenage boys liked to play "chicken" with their cars. Two boys raced their cars directly at each other. The first boy to swerve to avoid the crash lost. Were the boys courageous when they played "chicken"?

Yes_____ No_____ Criterion:

_____

_____

_____

4. Thirteen-year-old James had been beaten many times by a group of boys in his neighborhood. He generally tried to avoid them. One day, they surrounded him on the street. He was so frightened he could not think clearly. In a panic, hardly knowing what he was doing, he ran as hard as he could at the boy nearest him, knocking him to the ground. Was James' attack courageous?

Yes_____ No_____ Criterion:

_____

_____

_____

FIGURE 6.2 **What Is Courage?** *(continued)*

5. Joseph Wadsworth came from a family of military men. Both his father and grand-father had been soldiers. Joseph had no interest in being in the military, but he was afraid that his family would reject him if he did not join the military. He joined the service and volunteered to fight in Afghanistan. Was Joseph courageous when he joined the service and volunteered to fight?

Yes_____ No_____ Criterion:

_____

_____

_____

6. On Monday, a fire started on an oil derrick far out at sea. By Wednesday, the men working on the derrick had been rescued, but the fire was out of control. Red Granger and his men were called in to fight the dangerous fire. Red and his men had fought many oil fires. They had the training, equipment, and experience to put out the fire. Were Red and his men courageous when they fought the fire?

Yes_____ No_____ Criterion:

_____

_____

_____

7. On the oceanfront, Mr. Jones heard a swimmer shouting for help. He saw signs indi-cating that this part of the beach was extremely dangerous because of undertows. A lifeguard asked Jones to help him move a boat into the water to be used to help rescue the drowning man. Instead, Jones said, "Don't be silly!" He ran into the water to swim out to the drowning person. Was Jones' effort to save the swimmer courageous?

Yes_____ No_____ Criterion:

_____

_____

_____

FIGURE 6.2 **What Is Courage?** *(continued)*

8. Lesley was an accountant for a bank. Because she handled large sums of money, her work was carefully watched by security cameras and checked by computers. Despite the dangers, Lesley knew she was highly skilled and decided to transfer money from other accounts to her own. Was Lesley's theft of the money courageous?

Yes_____ No_____ Criterion:

_____

_____

_____

9. Arriving at school early, Mr. Grabowski assumed he was alone. Then he heard a hissing sound outside his classroom. He walked into the hall and interrupted two gang members who were painting their gang signs on the wall. Grabowski quietly returned to his room. He wouldn't tell; the gangs were too dangerous. Was Grabowski's decision not to inform on the gang members courageous?

Yes_____ No_____ Criterion:

_____

_____

_____

10. The expert tightrope walker had never had even a minor accident. For a special charity event, she decided to perform without a net. Was her performance without a net courageous?

Yes_____ No_____ Criterion:

_____

_____

_____

FIGURE 6.2 **What Is Courage?** *(continued)*

11. Harry learned that millions of dollars in gold would be moved from Washington, D.C., to Chicago. He knew it would be heavily guarded and protected by the very best alarm systems. The security guards were top-notch and heavily armed. Harry and his two companions were also heavily armed when they dropped from a bridge to the top of one of the train's boxcars. They immediately took fire from a guard stationed on the top of another car. They returned fire, killing the guard. Was their attempt to steal the gold courageous?

Yes_____ No_____ Criterion:

_____

_____

_____

12. Rose was trapped eight stories up in the burning building. Although rescue workers had attempted to reach her, they could not. With fire beginning to eat away at the floor behind her, she ran to the window. She looked back again and saw flames only about two feet away. Below she saw a large dumpster filled with paper and other debris. She climbed on the sill and jumped as far as she could to reach the dumpster. Was Rose's jump courageous?

Yes_____ No_____ Criterion:

_____

_____

_____

Linda: But he's surrounded by boys. They could just beat him up. I mean there's only him against a whole bunch. I think that's courageous.

Mel: Yeah. I think so, too, like I said.

Cecily: But when you don't know what you're doing, you don't even know it's a dangerous situation. If you don't know it's a dangerous situation, how can it be a courageous act? Like we said in number 1: "For an act to be courageous, the actor must be aware of the danger." That's what we said there.

Jorgé: Well, in number 1, the guy was guessing that it would not be dangerous. In this one, James knows it's dangerous because he has tried to get away from the boys before. But this time when he's surrounded, he still knows it's dangerous. But he panics and acts without thinking the way he usually does. So it's different. In the first one, the guy was acting, uh, what's that word?

Cecily: Rationally?

Jorgé: Yeah, the guy was acting rationally. But in this one, James panics and he ain't acting rationally no more. That's like a big difference.

Cecily: I like that. Yeah, it has to be a rational act. 'Cause if you're not aware of what you're doing, you won't be aware of what there is to fear. And courage is about dealing with fear, not about forgetting the fear.

Linda: So can we say, "For an act to be courageous, it must be rational"?

Mel: So James is not courageous even though he jumps one of the guys picking on him? That's bull.

Jorgé: No, remember what we said about Superman. He has to know something is dangerous for him. But here, it says he didn't know what he was doing.

Cecily: I don't think it's just knowing what you're doing. He has to act in spite of the danger he sees. But he has to choose the action, not just act in panic. Do you see what I'm trying to say? Like if he doesn't choose to act but just acts without being aware of what he is doing, it isn't courage. 'Cause he has to control the fear.

"The group nearly had this criterion worked out, but Mel's objection led them to work through it again and state it more explicitly."

Jorgé: That's what I said, sort of. He panics because he is very afraid. He ain't controlling fear. The fear is controlling him.

Linda: So what'll we say? How about this: "For an act to be courageous, the actor must choose the action and be in control of fear."

Jorgé: And not act because of fear.

The group nearly had this criterion early in the discussion, but Mel's objection led them to work through it again and state it more explicitly. This kind of reconsideration, though it may appear repetitious, usually clarifies things and helps all group members develop and understand more complex ideas.

Group 2

Peter: "In the small town of Clinton, teenage boys liked to play 'chicken' with their cars. Two boys raced their cars directly at each other. The first boy to swerve to avoid the crash lost."

Sam: That is real courage.

Nancy: You think so?

Sam: Yeah, it takes a lot of guts to drive at eighty or ninety miles an hour going straight toward another car going at the same speed. You got to be in control of your fear to do that. You've got all the ingredients. First, you got danger with a capital *D*. Second, you got fear. Third, you got control of the fear right up to the last millisecond. That has got to be courageous.

Hazel: It might have all that, but it's a stupid thing to do. It doesn't make sense.

Nancy: We said that foolhardy acts were not courageous because the people, the actors, don't pay attention to the danger when they should.

Sam: No, no. The guys in this game pay attention to the danger. They have to know when to pull out.

Hazel: But there is no good reason to do it in the first place.

Sam: There don't have to be a good reason. It's like I said: you got danger, fear, and control of fear. So this got to be courage.

Nancy: But I don't think that they have a real understanding that they could be killed. I mean, there was a story on the news a couple of weeks ago. Some boys in a town along the Rio Grande were doing this kind of game every week. The re-

"Sam's initial response is typical of many boys, who also want to argue that criminals are courageous, especially bank robbers. In my experience, girls are likely to argue the opposite in both cases, but not all do."

"Discussions like the one playing out here reinforce the need to consider more than the most salient criterion (i.e., danger and/or fear)."

porter said that one boy or both always pulled out on time to avoid a crash. Then, I guess, both drivers decided not to pull out. They crashed head-on and one car exploded. Both drivers were killed. I think the drivers think it is exciting but they don't think they are going to die. There is no good reason for it. They just do it for excitement. That is a perfect example of foolhardiness.

Sam: You guys don't think anything is courageous. You said no to everything so far. What do you think, Peter?

Peter: I agree with Nancy. When you do something that dangerous, without a good reason, it has to be foolhardy. You know, the risk isn't worth taking.

Sam: Well, I suppose the risk is pretty big, and there isn't a good reason to take it.

Hazel: Okay, so can we say that for an act to be courageous, it should not be foolhardy?

Sam: Yeah, and . . . and it has to be for a good reason.

Nancy: Then we have to define "good reason."

Peter: "We can do that later. Let's see if any others have that.

Sam's initial response is typical of many boys, who also want to argue that criminals are courageous, especially bank robbers. In my experience, girls are likely to argue the opposite in both cases, but not all do. Students have a tendency to fixate on one, two, or sometimes three criteria as Sam does at first. Discussions like the one above reinforce the need to consider more than the most salient criterion (i.e., danger and/or the fear).

Group 3

Marisol: "On the oceanfront, Mr. Jones heard a swimmer shouting for help. He saw signs indicating that this part of the beach was extremely dangerous because of undertows. A lifeguard asked Jones to help him move a boat into the water to be used to help rescue the drowning man. Instead, Jones said, "Don't be silly!" He ran into the water to swim out to the drowning person." So? What do you think? Is Mr. Jones courageous?

Francisco: This one is easy. In lifesaving class at the Y, we learned that the best approach to saving a person in the water is to use a boat, especially if the swimmer is fairly far out.

Glenda: Not only that, but it says the undertow is dangerous. That means it could pull you out into the ocean. It is just not smart to swim in that water. It's not safe. Jones is taking an unnecessary risk.

James: So this is taking an unnecessary risk and is really foolhardy.

Marisol: So what are we sayin'? Do you want to say no, because an act of courage cannot be foolhardy?

Francisco: Sounds good to me. Jones is acting stupid.

This group dispatches the scenario quickly, partly because Francisco already knows the protocols of rescue work. In groups without such experience, the discussion may be much longer. Some students insist Jones is courageous because he does not wait for the boat, which might take too long; others claim he isn't, because he may make the situation worse if he too becomes in need of rescue.

Group 4

Alysha: "Harry learned that millions of dollars in gold would be moved from Washington, D.C., to Chicago. He knew it would be heavily guarded and protected by the very best alarm systems. The guards security were top-notch and heavily armed. Harry and his two companions were also heavily armed when they dropped from a bridge to the top of one of the train's boxcars. They immediately took fire from a guard stationed on the top of another car. They returned fire, killing the guard. Was their attempt to steal the gold courageous?"

Tylor: This sounds like a movie.

Sharee: I think I saw it. [*Laughter.*] Didn't it have that guy, uh, Bruce Willis, or, uh, that other guy? I always get them mixed up.

Roberto: No. I don't think so. I don't think it's a movie.

Alysha: Well, but are they courageous?

Tylor: I think yes, but you guys are gonna say no. I mean there is real danger. They have to return fire right away. Anything could happen. They could easily be killed. But they go anyway. That seems to me to be courageous.

Alysha: Somebody said that courage is a virtue. If courage is virtu-ous, how can someone who is being a crook be courageous? Or doing anything immoral? I don't think it makes sense to say crooks are virtuous.

Tylor: I ain't saying they're virtuous. Just courageous. Like they face great danger. They know about the danger. They do not run away. I think they can be stealing money and still be coura-geous. There are a lot of movies where we want the bad guys to win. Usually that is because they are courageous.

Sharee: But usually the bad guys in movies lose. They get punished. Remember, we talked about that in our unit on heroes last year. I don't think they deserve to be called courageous. I think, like we said, that is a tribute. We don't praise bad peo-ple. That would be immoral.

Tylor: What do you think, Roberto? Come on. Help me out. Bad guys can be courageous. Of course they can.

Roberto: But if we believe courage is a virtue, then we should proba-bly not use it to describe bad guys.

Teacher: [*overhearing and stepping in*] What can you say about crooks who act in spite of fear?

Alysha: They overcome it. That doesn't say they are courageous. You could just say they act in spite of their fear.

Roberto: You could call them steadfast. Or even stubborn.

Tylor: Well. I still don't see anything wrong saying that robbers are courageous, if they are.

Alysha: Don't you see anything wrong with telling little kids that crooks are really courageous heroes? I mean, if you want kids to grow up to be good, why would you give them crooks as models to admire? When we say somebody coura-geous, that be praise. And we gotta keep praise for people who deserve it. Don't the Bible say that? I think it do.

Roberto: I don't know. But it makes sense to me that we should keep praise for people who deserve it and we shouldn't give kids bad models. You know, I never realized we had to pay so much attention to what we're saying.

"Developing criteria for courage that will exclude villains has been a problem (largely for males, less so for females) in every class in which I have taught this or similar material. Therefore, it's a good idea to make sure that small groups have both boys and girls."

> *Alysha:* So what are we saying about this? For an act to be coura-
> geous, it must not be something bad?
>
> *Sharee:* Or it must be something good, or for the good. Or virtuous.
>
> *Roberto:* Yeah. That's good. Maybe we should add that bad guys—
> what do you say—like villains can meet some of the criteria
> for courage but they don't meet all.
>
> *Tylor:* That's a good way to do it. I like that.

Developing criteria for courage that will exclude villains has been a problem (largely for males, less so for females) in every class in which I have taught this or similar material. Therefore, it's a good idea to make sure that small groups have both boys and girls.

③ Developing and Discussing a Class List of Criteria

After the small-group discussions, I usually have the groups report their criteria to the class, and we resolve any conflicts. Here are the criteria developed by the class comprising the groups discussed here:

For an act to be truly courageous . . .

» It must involve extraordinary danger for the actor—physical, moral, or social.
» The actor must be aware of the danger and experience fear.
» The actor must control his or her fear in the face of the danger.
» The actor must be acting in a noble or virtuous cause.
» The action must not be undertaken out of fear of a greater danger.
» The actor must not be undertaking a foolish action, one with no justification.
» The action must be chosen with a degree of deliberation.
» The danger cannot be diminished by experience, special equipment, special powers, and so on.

Once a list of criteria is developed, it is usually wise to review why failing to meet them excludes an action as courageous. Here's an example of such a discussion:

> *Teacher:* Why must the danger involved in a courageous act be ex-
> traordinary?

Jorgé: We said that it had to be extraordinary because nearly everything a person does has some danger to it. Like even going to the corner store, you could be attacked, and like most auto accidents occur near your home. So everything is dangerous to some extent.

Teacher: Anyone want to add to that?

Carolyn: Our group talked about the probability of harm coming to you. Like it might be dangerous to walk to the store, but the probability of harm affecting you is very low. The probability of having an accident driving to the store is low, but the probability of getting hurt if you are driving recklessly at ninety miles an hour is much higher.

Teacher: Everyone understand what Carolyn is saying? Let me give you another example. In our society, we tend to assume that anyone in the armed forces is courageous. What do you hear the politicians say about people in the military? What kind of language do they use?

Peter: They call them "our brave men and women who are defending our freedom." They always talk about them in glowing terms. They do that especially when they are talking about all the benefits the veterans deserve.

Teacher: There is a made-for-television documentary about World War II directed by Ken Burns. In the segment that focuses on March 1945 to December 1945, one of the soldiers comments that civilians back home saw all veterans in the same way. But he said there were enormous differences between those who had "pounded a typewriter" and those who had undergone combat, especially in places like Okinawa. In the fight for Okinawa, which is close to the home islands of Japan, some outfits of 235 men had lost all but twenty-four or twenty-five men, a 90 percent or higher casualty rate. Who do you think faced the higher probability of being killed or wounded in their assignments, those at a typewriter or those firing weapons on the field of battle?

Ralph: The ones on the field of battle.

Teacher: Yes. And the probability of injury or death was much higher in some combat situations than others. Some units going into Iwo Jima or Bastogne in the Battle of the Bulge or Okinawa were nearly wiped out. So the probability of injury or death becomes important in thinking about courage. Let me ask about another problem. Why do we think it is not courageous to undertake a dangerous action just because the actor is trying to avoid an even more dangerous act?

Francisco: Well, the main thing we said is, um, courage involves control of fear, not letting your fear control your actions. If you do something dangerous to get out of something you think is worse, you ain't controlling your fear. You're giving in to it. Like that guy Wadsworth. He joined the army because he was afraid of what his family would say more than he feared battle. That's what we thought.

Teacher: Anyone want to add to that? So could Wadsworth ever be courageous in war?

Cecily: Sure, sure, it can change. In a battle, he might not even think of his family. He could be very afraid while waiting to attack, but overcome his fear and lead his men in the attack to a place where he knows there is a high probability of being killed or wounded without, you know, without like being scared to death.

Teacher: So one act does not determine how he will act in the future or tell what the content of his character is?

Cecily: No. Absolutely not.

A review like this not only reinforces but also adds to what has already been learned. Students come to see what they have deduced from the scenarios in a more complete way. They add nuance to what they have learned and understand the relationships among their criteria more completely.

"A review like this not only reinforces but also adds to what has already been learned. Students come to see what they have deduced from the scenarios in a more complete way. They add nuance to what they have learned and understand the relationships among their criteria more completely."

(**4**) **Writing a Definition of *Courage* with the Class**

The next step is to write out a definition of *courage*. (The definition of *terrorism* at the end of Chapter Four can be used as model.) The definition should include the criteria, along with examples that *meet* and *do not meet* each criterion. Generally, I begin by helping the class develop an opening paragraph that lays out the general idea of what courageous action is.

"What do you think our first sentence might be?" I ask.

High school students typically have trouble with formal syntax and propose something beginning, "A courageous action is when a person. . . ." I ask them not to use *when* but to use a noun or pronoun after the linking verb *is*. We experiment with a couple of possibilities:

An act of courage is an act . . .

A courageous act is one . . .

Obviously such beginnings demand modifiers explaining the general characteristics of the act that qualify it as courageous, for it must be differentiated from all other acts. The class described earlier developed the following definition in fairly short order:

An act of courage is an act in which the actor confronts a danger, controls his or her fear, and benefits others despite the fear.

We then develop alternative openings that do not explicitly state the category. For example:

» Courageous action involves the control of fear in the face of grave danger.
» A courageous action involves acting despite great danger that is apparent to the actor.
» The primary characteristics of a courageous act include the control of fear in the face of grave danger to accomplish some noble end.

5 Students Write a Full Definition of Courage on Their Own

After we have developed four or five alternative openings as a class, I ask students to write a full definition using one of our openings or some other that they compose. They must fill out the definition by including at least four of the criteria we have discussed, along with positive and contrasting examples that clarify the criteria.

Cecily produced the following definition:

Basically, courageous action involves the control of fear in the face of grave danger. For an act to be truly courageous, it must meet several criteria.

First, because courage is considered to be a virtue, any courageous act must be a noble or virtuous act, such as saving a life or preventing harm to another person. Robbing a bank, no matter how dangerous and no matter how steadfast the actor, is not a noble or selfless act. Because it is not a virtuous act, it cannot be considered courageous.

Second, the danger must be grave for the actor. The action must have a high probability of harm for the actor. Driving a car holds some danger, but for a safe driver the probability of harm is low. My father drives to work each day, but even though some danger is involved, we would not award him a medal for courage on that account. Similarly, firefighters are trained to fight fires and have special equipment for doing so, thus reducing the danger for them. They do not receive citations for fighting fires that are ordinary. But if a fire is extraordinarily fierce, firefighters do receive citations for courageous action in rescuing people from such fires.

Third, for an act to be courageous, it must be deliberately chosen and not chosen out of panic and without thought. For example, a boy attacked by others might panic and strike out without thinking. Such an act is not courageous. But if, on the other hand, the boy makes a decision, even in a split second, that he must protect himself and stands up to his foes, his act might be considered courageous, if it meets the other criteria.

Fourth, it almost goes without saying that the actor must be aware of the present danger for the action to be considered courageous. If he or she is not aware of the danger, then there is no cause for fear and no fear to control. For example, a soldier might become lost and wander accidentally behind enemy lines. Such an act is not courageous because the soldier does not realize where he is and cannot be aware of the danger and cannot have cause for fear. On the other hand, a soldier who knowingly infiltrates enemy lines and is aware of the extreme danger will certainly be considered courageous if he meets all the other criteria.

Fifth, for an act to be courageous, it must not be chosen out of fear of a greater danger. For example at the invasion of Normandy in the Second World War, Germans placed captured Russian and Polish troops in the front lines with machine guns behind them. They were threatened with death if they did not fight against the opposing allied troops. Their action of fighting against the allies could not be considered courageous because they were fighting out of fear of being shot from behind. On the other hand, if they had turned on the Nazi troops, they might well have been considered courageous.

Sixth, for an act to be courageous it must not be foolhardy. That is, it must not be undertaken unnecessarily or foolishly, without a clear understanding of the dangers involved. For example, my father told me a story about two boys who, some years ago at an amusement park near Cleveland, dared each other to climb the tracks of a roller coaster in winter when there was snow and ice on the tracks. They had no other reason to climb other than the dare. The taunting involved in the dare was, "What? You chicken?" They climbed successfully to the top. I guess they thought they had proven they were not chicken.

"Students who have learned to think through the criteria for making judgments are less likely to jump to conclusions; they consider their ideas more carefully."

"Even the level of preparation described above does not mean students are necessarily able to write definitions of abstract concepts independently. They usually need to explore two more sets of scenarios relative to similar concepts before they are able to write definitions on their own."

Coming back down, one slipped on the ice and fell to his death. Even if both had climbed back down safely, their acts could not be considered courageous but foolhardy. On the other hand, had they climbed up to rescue some other foolish person who had climbed up and become trapped, they might have been considered courageous if they had met all the other criteria.

To summarize these criteria, for an act to be considered courageous, it must be a noble act but involve grave danger for the actor, who must be aware of the danger and must choose the action deliberately but not out of some fear of a greater danger. Finally, it may not be a foolish or foolhardy act. Many actions meet one, two, or three of these criteria but are not courageous. A truly courageous act meets all of them.

Reinforcing the Process: What Constitutes Freedom of Speech?

Students who have learned to think through the criteria for making judgments are less likely to jump to conclusions; they consider their ideas more carefully. Once these kinds of definitions have become a standard part of the curriculum, students can make and apply them to whatever they read, thereby reading more thoughtfully, with a better ability to interpret and understand (see Hillocks, Kahn, and Johannessen 1983).

But even the level of preparation described here does not mean students are necessarily able to write definitions of abstract concepts independently. They usually need to explore two more sets of scenarios relative to similar concepts (e.g., ostracism, good parenting, generosity, justice, honor, true love) before they are able to write definitions on their own. A set of scenarios related to freedom of speech (which produce great differences of opinion, some consternation, and considerable discussion) is provided in Figure 6.3. You can use these scenarios with students to develop and support and reinforce what they have learned.

FIGURE 6.3 **What Constitutes Freedom of Speech?**

The following scenarios all have to do with freedom of speech. Read through each one and answer, in writing, the following questions:

1. Should this use of speech be allowed?

2. Why or why not?

3. What criterion for defining the right to freedom of speech does this scenario suggest? Write out the criterion.

SCENARIOS

1. A student disgruntled with education at your school delivers a harangue on the steps of the main building, outlining what he believes to be faults in the teaching, the policies of the administration, and the general atmosphere of the school. He demands that these be corrected.

2. The Avowed Anarchists of America hold a political meeting open to the public at which the major speaker ridicules all forms of government, arguing the need for self-determination in all things.

3. The American Nazi Party holds a parade and rally in a predominantly Jewish community. The main speaker claims that a worldwide conspiracy of Jews has been at work in taking over all Western democracies. He uses as evidence what he calls "the disproportionate numbers of Jews in appointed positions of political power." He says Hitler had the right idea.

4. A group of college students, unable to obtain tickets for a big indoor rock concert, manage to enter the hall where the concert is about to begin. At a signal, they begin to shout "Fire!" as loudly as they can. Nothing happens.

5. The same facts as in 4, but a panic ensues and three people are trampled to death.

FIGURE 6.3 **What Constitutes Freedom of Speech?** *(continued)*

6. The *National Observer* publishes a story claiming that a famous politician, estranged from his wife, has been seen on several occasions with a beautiful model. The story claims that the politician entered the woman's Manhattan apartment at 2:00 A.M. and was not seen to leave until morning.

7. A large city paper charges that a local politician has been regularly cheating the city out of thousands of dollars by submitting fraudulent expense vouchers, taking his family on vacations at city expense, and receiving kickbacks from contractors who perform various services for the city's department of sanitation. When the politician brings a libel suit against the paper, lawyers for the paper prove that over a three-year period, the politician was overreimbursed by $900 for expenses and that he was entertained in expensive restaurants on seven occasions by contractors who performed services for the city, but they do not prove he cheated the city out of thousands of dollars.

8. An extreme left-wing political organization advocates the violent overthrow of the U.S. government. At a rally in Atlanta, the leader urges his listeners to buy high-powered rifles with telescopic sights and to begin ambushing police and government officials. If enough people are killing police, he says, the government will have no protection. The next step will simply be to march on city hall, take over, and let the reign of the people begin.

9. A group of students plan to dynamite a federal bank as a protest against American aid to right-wing governments in South America. They develop the plans in detail but never carry it out.

10. Orson Welles produced a radio dramatization of H. G. Wells' *War of the Worlds*, written as news flashes announcing an invasion of the United States by Martians. The program was so realistic that it caused panic on the East Coast, and highways were jammed for many miles as people tried to flee the area.

FIGURE 6.2 **What Is Constitutes Freedom of Speech?** *(continued)*

11. Paedeia Toys, a manufacturer of expensive educational toys, conducts a study showing that children whose parents buy Paedeia toys earn significantly higher grades and test scores than other children. The company runs a series of advertisements claiming that children whose parents care enough to buy the best educational toys will do better in school: "If you care enough to put your child at the head of the class, buy Paedeia Toys!"

12. A high school biology teacher instructs his students on the Darwinian theory of evolution—that the higher animals, including man, evolved from lower forms of life over millions of years. He explains that his students will be responsible for these concepts, including the sequence of development, on the final exam. When a student asks what he thinks of the Biblical creation story, he says, "That is an unscientific view of creation that some people believe." The parents of fifty of his students sign a petition objecting to his teaching of Darwin, the requirement for the exam, and his dismissal of the Biblical story. They claim he is forcing his ideas on a captive audience and demand that he be removed from his teaching post.

13. A woman going through security check at an airport jokes about hijacking her plane using the submachine gun and three grenades in her purse. Her purse is tiny. Nevertheless, she is immediately arrested.

Why This Matters

My MAT students and I believe that when our students have learned to think through the *criteria* for making judgments, they ordinarily do not make judgments in quite the same way as before the teaching of criteria. They create specific and elaborate criteria and defend them by using contrasting examples by way of explication. They are less likely to jump to conclusions about some matter of judgment and typically consider their ideas more carefully. All of that also shows up in their writing, as we have shown (Hillocks, Kahn, and Johannessen 1983).

The process of arriving at this greater thoughtfulness, as described above, has taken under three weeks of teaching and learning, usually about twelve classroom hours. We have used two sets of scenarios in the initial teaching and have required writing two definitions including the one on courage. As you will recall, clear definitions are crucial to judgments: warrants in arguments of judgment are conceptual and are supported primarily by extended analysis and definition of the concepts involved.

Once students have worked on defining two or three concepts, it becomes a fairly simple task to engage students in thinking about and applying what they have learned to other concepts as the curriculum moves along. In the kinds of conceptual units my colleagues developed in Euclid, Ohio, definition became a standard part of each unit and a standard part of the writing curriculum. With students, we defined concepts such as courage, justice, comedy, the outcast, the hero, tragedy, comedy, epic hero, social protest, science fiction, love, maturity, and so forth.

A major reason for working on such definitions is to apply them to works read. As discussed earlier, extended definitions amount to the *backing* that may be used to argue, for example, whether or not a character's actions are courageous. Such work engenders more thoughtful reading and interpretation and provides students with tools for understanding literary works beyond those read for class.

But just as important, the application of such definitions can reach far beyond the classroom, encouraging students to be more thoughtful human beings capable of making sound judgments.

"After students have learned to think through the criteria for making judgments, they are less likely to jump to conclusions about some matter of judgment and typically consider their ideas more carefully."

Argument and Interpretation

Teaching Students How to Make Literary Judgments

EVERY SECONDARY SCHOOL ENGLISH PROGRAM I HAVE EVER encountered, including those I have studied in detail (Hillocks 1972, 2002), has had a stated purpose of improving students' understanding and appreciation of literature. This goal commonly appears in state standards. Unfortunately, the people who write these documents do not tell us how the goal is to be achieved.

A common assumption is that merely assigning a great many works, contributing background information about the elements and structure of the works and the periods in which they were written, and then explaining what these works mean will somehow produce students who are active interpreters of literature themselves. But this approach only works for the very few students who are such good readers that they learn how to interpret on their own. Most students do not learn and reject English as not worth paying attention to. They believe, like this young man in Smith and Wilhelm's study (2006), that teachers do not teach; they just assign homework:

> My teachers will just give out thousands and thousands of pages of homework and expect that to teach you. [The teachers] don't teach. Its just like do chapters, questions 1 to 5. And they are going to assume you know it because you do the questions 1 to 5, and even if you talk with somebody you aren't going to know it. But if you actually get up there and teach it to people and ask questions, they are going to know it.

That's the problem in a nutshell. We tend not to teach our students *how* to interpret. The National Assessment of Educational Progress (NAEP) has shown that American students can read text at a literal level fairly well. However, when it comes to making inferences, they fail miserably (see NAEP 2002, 2005, 2007). The Common Core Standards ask students beginning in grade 6 to, "Cite textual evidence to support analysis of what the text says explicitly as well as inferences drawn from the text." So how do we *teach* students to do that?

Teaching Students to Make Inferences

In this chapter, I will demonstrate how the work I did with students in the previous chapter—developing and supporting criteria for arguments of judgment—lays essential groundwork for teaching students to make inferences. The interpretation of literature is all about the reader making judgments. The writer of any literature provides images, detail, narration, portraits of characters, but we, the readers, must construct the meanings for ourselves, making inferences and judgments in order to comprehend the work and determine its import.

Students who have learned to develop criteria to define a concept are able to bring that understanding, those criteria, to bear in the reading of a literary text and make inferences based on this understanding. In the particular instance detailed later in this chapter, I show how the students who defined *courage* are able to make inferences about a character's actions in the Stephen Crane story, "A Mystery of Heroism: A Detail of an American Battle" (1895). Is the main character a courageous man? To argue pro or con effectively requires an explicit definition of the *concept* of courage.

The concept we choose to teach will, of course, vary according to the literature we teach and the kinds of inferences we hope our students will make. For example, we probably hope our students will be able to infer a character's values, virtues, perhaps vices, heroism or villainy, use as a foil or symbol, and so forth. We hope they will make inferences about generic plot structures and the conjunction of character and plot in at least standard genres including the mythic, epic, tragic, comic, romantic, and perhaps picaresque. We hope they will make appropriate inferences when they encounter irony, exaggeration, understatement, symbolism, unreliable narrators, and other tools commonly used by writers. We may also hope they will make inferences about values inherent in a work of literature as a whole, both authorial and cultural, by attending to some critical theories. If these are our goals, we can then develop curricula that systematically provide students with the *knowledge* and *experience* to make these kinds of inferences.

Making inferences requires knowledge not presented in the text—knowledge about constructs or ideas that can be *brought to bear* on the text. To infer the reliability of a narrator, for example, one has to respond to the appropriate clues in the text. To know when a passage does not mean what it appears to mean on the surface, one has to know how irony works and how to recognize and interpret it. (Knowing the simple definition of verbal irony included in a glossary of literary elements doesn't do the trick.) In short, if we want to help students become strong inferential readers, we must provide the knowledge, experience, and practice that will allow them to do so. And that knowledge and experience must be developed incrementally, one unit at a time, concentrating on one or perhaps two or three related concepts.

Thinking Interpretively About Literature

To take a simple example, students in middle school (and even high school) usually find fables difficult to interpret, unless the fables are as familiar as "The Tortoise and the Hare." Typically, students are not able to provide a concise statement about what human frailties, vices, and virtues the animal characters represent. Though they understand that "slow and steady wins the race" captures the reason the turtle wins, they have difficulty applying the idea to the human condition. And when they encounter Thurber's "The Scotty Who Knew Too Much" or even Aesop's fable "The Fox and the Crow," they are usually unable to say what the Scotty or the crow represent. Younger

"Making inferences requires knowledge not presented in the text—knowledge about constructs or ideas that can be brought to bear on the text."

"In short, if we want
to help students
become strong
inferential readers,
we must provide
the knowledge,
experience, and
practice that will allow
them to do so. And
that knowledge and
experience must
be developed
incrementally, one
unit at a time."

students need to recognize that the animals in fables represent human qualities, some good, some not so good. And they need practice inferring which human qualities each animal represents: the crow, vanity; the fox, deceit; the tortoise, perseverance or steadfastness; the Scotty, arrogance. After doing this with a dozen or so fables, however, they are able to interpret *other* fables, new to them, with greater competence. The key question, therefore, becomes *how will a work interpreted today make students more astute interpreters of works to be read tomorrow?*

Systematic Planning of Instructional Units

One range of inferences has to do with the qualities that characters display or possess, such as courage—or a lack of it. These are the kinds of inferences I will focus on for the remainder of this chapter. As you will see, teaching this range of inferences will help students interpret the literature at hand, but it will *also* help them become more incisive interpreters of works they read in the future.

Throughout the history of English and American literature, indeed world literature, works have focused on characters' qualities—the whole range of virtues and vices, along with dozens of variations in human behavior that may have nothing to do with virtue or vice but simply with the ways in which people habitually respond to experience (open-mindedness, curiosity, fear, recalcitrance, eagerness, awe, pessimism, and so forth). There are plenty of possibilities to choose from. The problem for the teacher is deciding which will be the most productive and intriguing for her students.

"The key question,
therefore, becomes
how will a work
interpreted today
make students more
astute interpreters
of works to be
read tomorrow?"

In the following, I will show the steps I recommend for teachers who wish to plan a conceptual unit focusing on a human quality or characteristic. In step 1, you will also see my thinking in selecting *courage* as a concept or quality for study.

(1)   **Select a Concept to Examine**

The first step in developing an instructional unit is to select a concept to examine. When considering concepts, the following questions may be helpful.

» Does it have generative power?
» Can youngsters apply the concept to many reading and life experiences?
» Will students find the concept interesting?

Does it have generative power? As I considered teaching the concept of courage, the answer was clearly yes. It has generative power simply because courage is an important concern in so many works and because it is a foundational virtue. Without courage, many other virtues are not possible. Courage is required to act in a just way, to remain a good friend in certain circumstances, and often even to act in a generous and kind way. Furthermore, many other virtues share the same or similar criteria: acts of justice, generosity, friendship, loyalty, helpfulness—all must be enacted in a noble way without thoughts of personal (selfish) gain, with deliberation, and not out of fear or any negative motive.

Can youngsters apply the concept to many reading and life experiences? Will the concept or quality be useful to students as they read and interpret works beyond the literature we are studying today? Is it a concept they can readily connect to their own lives and experience? As noted above, courage is a central concern in many literary works. Aristotle believed that virtues are learned through practice. Whether we agree or not, we can examine the ways in which characters change with regard to virtues, how they learn to be generous or courageous or just. This study can also be the basis for considering when violence is required and when it is not, when it is appropriate to ask people to act courageously in the face of danger, a question that most certainly applies to real life. (The opening lines of the Declaration of Independence present one rationale.)

Will students find the concept interesting? I have already argued that courage is an idea students care about. They have many questions about their own courage and view courage as important in their own lives. Many of the boys and girls I have taught question their own courage and think they are not courageous, even though they are unlikely to say so in front of their peers. Part of the appeal of action movies is the courage shown by the characters. At any rate, the concept has always been a winner with seventh to tenth graders.

(2) **Define the Concept in Such a Way That It Can Be Differentiated From *Noninstances* and *Seeming Instances***

The second step is to define the concept in such a way that instances of it can be differentiated from noninstances and seeming instances. The preceding chapter indicates what those distinctions are for the idea of courageous action and gives examples of scenarios for discussion that will highlight those distinctions.

3 Select Works That Involve the Concept or Quality

The third (actually, ongoing) step is to select works that involve the concept or quality to some degree. A unit on courage or courageous action might include a wide range of works:

> » the chapter from Richard Wright's *Black Boy* about how he won the rights to the streets of Memphis
> » Leo Tolstoy's story "The Raid"
> » Stephen Crane's "A Mystery of Heroism: A Detail of an American Battle"
> » "A Test of Courage," a chapter from the novel *Parrot in the Oven*, by Victor Martinez
> » the one-act play *The Valiant*, by Hallworthy Hall and Robert Middlemass
> » Hemingway's "A Day's Wait"
> » numerous short works frequently included in school anthologies
> » poems addressing the ideas of courage directly or indirectly
> » novels that focus on courage to a greater or lesser extent, including
>> » *The Diary of Anne Frank*
>> » *Shane*
>> » *The Bridge over the River Kwai*
>> » *The Red Badge of Courage*
>> » *Warriors Don't Cry*

There is no shortage of material.

4 Build a Unit That Moves From Simple to More Complex Texts and That Provides for a Gradual Release of Teacher Responsibility

The unit should be built so that it moves from analyzing relatively simple texts to more and more complex texts: from short scenarios capturing basic aspects to short stories and poems to plays and novels or other longer works. At the beginning, the work will be guided by the teacher in whole-class discussions; then it should move quickly to small groups in which students assist one another in arriving at interpretations; finally, to independent work in which students make inferences and interpretations on their own. Writing about the inferences and judgments will also take place in stages and become more complex and independent as students refine their understandings.

Converting a Standard School Unit to a Conceptual Unit

For many years, *Romeo and Juliet* was a standard ninth-grade work in the Chicago public schools, and it is required reading in many ninth-grade English classrooms across the country. As in many schools, the board of education in Chicago did not care much what the teachers did with it, but it was required reading.

Although most English teachers recognize that their responsibilities include teaching inference, they may pay little attention to how making inferences in one work can be related to making inferences in another. When their students read *Romeo and Juliet*, for example, most teachers help students follow the plot and make a few inferences scene by scene, perhaps about Romeo's attraction to Juliet, Tybalt's hatred, the Capulets' willingness to marry their very young daughter to an older man, the role of the priest, and so forth. But all of these require different knowledge and different background information. Making an inference about any one of these problems will not contribute to making inferences about any other in the play. Nor will making any one of these inferences contribute much to making inferences when reading another work. Because there is no consistency in the inferential problems, teachers resort to asking leading questions until students make the necessary inference or until the teacher gives up and simply states the inference.

"Although most English teachers recognize that their responsibilities include teaching inference, they may pay little attention to how making inferences in one work can be related to making inferences in another."

A more effective way to organize the curriculum is to build a unit around sets of works that present comparable inferential problems, so that the inferences students make on one day with one work can be revisited on another day with a different work. A few years ago, I worked with a school faculty on developing a stronger English curriculum, and, after some discussion, our committee decided on a unit focused on two major themes of *Romeo and Juliet*, love and hate.

We believed the concepts love and hate were pertinent to the experience of ninth graders because they are beginning to think not only about boy-girl relationships but also about the hatred they see around them among groups who have no objective basis for that hatred.

Love

One teacher suggested that as part of the conceptual framework, we adopt four (of seven) stages of love suggested by the popular philosopher Deepak

Chopra in his book *The Path to Love* (1997)—attraction, infatuation, courtship, and intimacy.

Initial attraction comes through perception, through the recognition of some characteristic in another that a person finds attractive: physical appearance, mental ability, attitude, expression, and so forth.

Infatuation is the stage in which an individual manipulates perceptions in the privacy of the imagination. The resulting fantasies give the desired one a kind of status and power in the infatuated one's mind, but without any direct connection. Both these stages have considerable relevance to the lives of ninth graders.

Courtship goes beyond perception and imagination to contact with the loved one through dating, talking, and beginning to see how the person, who has until now been an ideal abstraction in the lover's mind, responds in a variety of social situations. Contact raises the possibility of conflict and a choice whether to continue the relationship or escape from it. At some point in this stage, infatuation confronts reality, and the lover may begin to see that the loved one may not be ideal after all. If the resulting issues are not examined and confronted, people can remain in the relationship but are likely to be insecure. If conflicts cannot be handled, intimacy is unlikely to develop.

In *intimacy*, lovers are mature, see each other's imperfections, and accept them. They are not threatened by other people, things, or interests, and so allow the other to develop without fear of loss or harm.

Understanding these processes would have great implications for students' own lives as well as for their interpretations of the works to be read in the unit.

Hate

Because the unit deals with hate as well as love, the committee asked themselves:

» What qualities result in attraction?
» What qualities result in repulsion?

At the basis of love is a consciousness of similarity, while difference, the sense of "otherness," is the basis of hatred. Some of our perceptions of qualities that we regard as attractive or repulsive appear to be culturally determined. Others may be the result of personal experience. However, in large part, we *learn* what and who are and are not appropriate to love or hate.

When we view the other as part of a group different from ours, we short-circuit our natural empathy with others and, in our minds at least, deny them their humanity. We often see the other as not quite human, not deserving of the empathy and sympathy that we reserve for those who are near and dear to us. The salient images of this phenomenon in our culture are the slave master, the Nazi, the mafioso, the gang member, who may feel deep empathy for those in their own families but cannot extend that to those outside the group. We see just such hatred in the family feud between the Montagues and the Capulets.

Applying Concepts of Love and Hate to *Romeo and Juliet*

Critical thinking and interpretation in the unit, then, entail questions such as these:

> » What kind of love does Romeo initially have for Juliet?
> » How can we explain his forgetting Rosaline so quickly?
> » To what extent or in what way is his love for Juliet different from his love for Rosaline?
> » What explains Tybalt's hatred for the Montagues?
> » Who and what conditions are culpable in the deaths of Romeo and Juliet? Why?
> » What evidence in the play supports these conclusions?
> » What advice concerning love would Shakespeare give Romeo and Juliet, their families, and the priest?

The answers to all these questions are debatable based on specific information in the text. However, the unit is not designed to elicit specific information but rather *to enable students to bring complex knowledge to bear on complex problems and to write thoughtfully and effectively about those problems.*

Teaching a Unit on Courage

After working with students to develop the concept of courage using the scenarios in the preceding chapter, my Master of Arts in Teaching English students and I moved on to a set of short stories, poems, and plays before concluding the unit with novels, as I described above.

A story we have used multiple times with great success is Stephen Crane's "A Mystery of Heroism: A Detail of an American Battle," about a

"At the basis of love is a consciousness of similarity, while difference, the sense of 'otherness,' is the basis of hatred."

soldier named Collins. (I present only part of the story here, although we use the entire story in class.) Older students can read the entire story before discussions begin. For younger students, we break the story into four parts and hold discussions at the end of each part:

1. when Collins goes to ask permission of the captain
2. after he pulls a bucket of water from the well
3. after he helps the dying officer drink from the bucket
4. after he reaches his regiment's lines

Here are the opening lines of the story:

The dark uniforms of the men were so coated with dust from the incessant wrestling of the two armies that the regiment almost seemed a part of the clay bank which shielded them from the shells. On the top of the hill a battery was arguing in tremendous roars with some other guns and, to the eye of the infantry, the artillerymen, the guns, the caissons, the horses, were distinctly outlined upon the blue sky. When a piece was fired a red streak as round as a log flashed low in the heavens, like a monstrous bolt of lightning. . . .

Fred Collins, of A Company, was saying: "Thunder, I wisht I had a drink. Ain't there any water round here?" Then somebody yelled: "There goes th' bugler!"

As the eyes of half the regiment swept in one machine-like movement, there was an instant's picture of a horse in a great convulsive leap of a death-wound and a rider leaning back with a crooked arm and spread fingers before his face. On the ground was the crimson terror of an exploding shell, with fibres of flame that seemed like lances. A glittering bugle swung clear of the rider's back as fell headlong the horse and the man. In the air was an odor as from a conflagration. . . .

A lieutenant of the battery rode down and passed them, holding his right arm carefully in his left hand. And it was as if this arm was not at all a part of him, but belonged to another man. His sober and reflective charger went slowly. The officer's face was grimy and perspiring and his uniform was tousled as if he had been in direct grapple with an enemy. He smiled grimly when the men stared at him. He turned his horse toward the meadow.

Collins, of A Company, said, "I wisht I had a drink. I bet there's water in that there ol' well yonder!"

"Yes; but how you goin' to git it?"

For the little meadow which intervened was now suffering a terrible onslaught of shells. Its green and beautiful calm had vanished utterly. Brown earth was being flung in monstrous handfuls. And there was a massacre of the young blades of grass. They were being torn, burned, obliterated. Some curious fortune of the battle had made this gentle little meadow the object of the red hate of the shells, and each one as it exploded seemed like an imprecation in the face of a maiden. . . . [*The story continues for several more paragraphs.*]

A private in one of the rear companies looked out over the meadow and then turned to a companion and said: "Look there, Jim." It was the wounded officer from the battery, who some time before had started to ride across the meadow, supporting his right arm carefully with his left hand. This man had encountered a shell apparently at a time when no one perceived him and he could now be seen lying face downward with a stirruped foot stretched across the body of his dead horse. A leg of the charger extended slantingly upward precisely as stiff as a stake. Around this motionless pair the shells still howled.

There was a quarrel in A Company. Collins was shaking his fist in the faces of some laughing comrades. "Dern yeh! I ain't afraid t'go. If yeh say much, I will go!"

"Of course, yeh will! Yeh'll run through that there medder, won't yeh?"

Collins said, in a terrible voice: "You see now!" At this ominous threat his comrades broke into renewed jeers.

Collins gave them a dark scowl and went to find his captain.

The class that discussed the scenarios in the preceding chapter had the following discussion at this point in the story:

> *Teacher:* What do you think at this point? Is Collins courageous to make this decision?
>
> *Hazel:* Not according to what we said before. It's really dangerous and he's like ignoring it.
>
> *Peter:* He's not even thinking about the decision. He's just doing it because the other guys are jeering at him. So there is no good reason to do it.
>
> *Jorgé:* Later on some guy says, "We ain't dyin' of thirst, are we? That's foolishness."
>
> *Teacher:* Okay, Jorgé is reading ahead. Someone does say that, but let's just consider what has happened so far.
>
> *Nancy:* He's going because he feels insulted by the other soldiers. He's acting like a little kid at this point. So I don't see how we could consider him courageous. He's a good example of foolhardiness.
>
> *Teacher:* Anyone have anything else to add? No? Let's continue reading.

[*The captain is amazed at Collins' request. But he gives his permission, suggesting only that Collins take some of the other soldiers' canteens with him. Collins' comrades surround him.*] They were very busy in preparing him for his ordeal. When they inspected him carefully, it was somewhat like the examination that grooms give a horse before a race; and they were amazed, staggered by the whole affair. Their astonishment found vent in strange repetitions.

"Are yeh sure a-goin'?" they demanded again and again.

"Certainly I am," cried Collins at last, furiously.

He strode sullenly away from them. He was swinging five or six canteens by their cords. It seemed that his cap would not remain firmly on his head, and often he reached and pulled it down over his brow.

There was a general movement in the compact column. The long animal-like thing moved slightly. Its four hundred eyes were turned upon the figure of Collins.

"Well, sir, if that ain't th' derndest thing. I never thought Fred Collins had the blood in him for that kind of business."

"What's he goin' to do, anyhow?"

"He's goin' to that well there after water."

"We ain't dyin' of thirst, are we? That's foolishness."

"Well, somebody put him up to it an' he's doin' it."

"Say, he must be a desperate cuss."

When Collins faced the meadow and walked away from the regiment he was vaguely conscious that a chasm, the deep valley of all prides, was suddenly between him and his comrades. It was provisional, but the provision was that he return as a victor. He had blindly been led by quaint emotions and laid himself under an obligation to walk squarely up to the face of death.

But he was not sure that he wished to make a retraction even if he could do so without shame. As a matter of truth he was sure of very little. He was mainly surprised.

It seemed to him supernaturally strange that he had allowed his mind to maneuver his body into such a situation. He understood that it might be called dramatically great.

However, he had no full appreciation of anything excepting that he was actually conscious of being dazed. He could feel his dulled mind groping after the form and color of this incident.

Too, he wondered why he did not feel some keen agony of fear cutting his sense like a knife. He wondered at this because human expression had said loudly for centuries that men should feel afraid of certain things and that all men who did not feel this fear were phenomena, heroes.

He was, then, a hero. He suffered that disappointment which we would all have if we discovered that we were ourselves capable of those deeds which we most admire in history and legend. This, then, was a hero. After all, heroes were not much.

No, it could not be true. He was not a hero. Heroes had no shames in their lives and, as for him, he remembered borrowing fifteen dollars from a friend and promising to pay it back the next day and then avoiding that friend for ten months. When at home his mother had aroused him for the early labor of his life on the farm, it had often been his fashion to be irritable, childish, diabolical, and his mother had died since he had come to the war.

He saw that in this matter of the well, the canteens, the shells, he was an intruder in the land of fine deeds.

He was now about thirty paces from his comrades. The regiment had just turned its many faces toward him.

From the forest of terrific noises there suddenly emerged a little uneven line of men. They fired fiercely and rapidly at distant foliage on which appeared little puffs of white smoke. The spatter of skirmish firing was added to the thunder of the guns on the hill. The little line of men ran forward. A color-sergeant fell flat with his flag as if he had slipped on ice. There was hoarse cheering from this distant field.

Collins suddenly felt that two demon fingers were pressed into his ears. He could see nothing but flying arrows, flaming red. He lurched from the shock of this explosion, but he made a mad rush for the house, which he viewed as a man submerged to the neck in a boiling surf might view the shore. In the air, little pieces of shell howled and the earthquake explosions drove him insane with the menace of their roar. As he ran the canteens knocked together with a rhythmical tinkling.

Teacher: Let's stop here. There are a number of lines and details to talk about. First of all, why do you think Collins felt that "he was an intruder in the land of fine deeds"? Anyone? No? Okay, let's go back to the paragraph beginning, "Too, he wondered why he did not feel some keen agony of fear." Everybody find that passage? Take a minute to read the two paragraphs beginning with that line. [*The students read.*] At this point, why is Collins thinking "heroes were not much"?

Cecily: He's thinking that if he is a hero, heroes are not much."

Peter: He sees himself as an ordinary guy, not a hero. You hear that kind of comment from soldiers who have just returned from Iraq. They think of themselves as ordinary guys, just doing a job.

Teacher: Why does he think of himself as ordinary or less than a hero? Reread the next paragraph. [*They do.*] Who can explain why he thinks of himself as ordinary?

Nancy: He thinks of himself as ordinary, but he thinks that heroes have nothing to be ashamed of in their lives. They don't have any weaknesses. But he does. So he can't be a hero.

Peter: Yeah, but his weaknesses are not very much. He borrowed fifteen bucks and didn't pay it back. And when his mother got him up to work on the farm he was sometimes lazy and crabby. But that doesn't detract from being a hero, does it? I mean why should it?

Hazel: No, it shouldn't.

Teacher: Then why does it?

Cecily: I think their thinking is a stereotype of a hero. You know, good in all respects, wears white hat, gets the bad guy, and all that.

Teacher: Actually, Cecily, you are agreeing with a study of ideas of courage and heroism in the South during the Civil War. People were reading the novels of Walter Scott then and derived their notions of the hero from those novels. Those heroes are romantic heroes with the characteristics you list. Now, I want you all to think about this line, "He had blindly been led by quaint emotions and laid himself under an obligation to walk squarely up to the face of death." This line tells us a bit about Collins' thinking. Do you think he sees things differently now than when he went to ask permission of the captain?

Sandra: I think so. He realizes what he has got himself into. But I don't get what he means by "quaint emotions."

Teacher: What do you guys think he means? What do you think *quaint* might mean? No? Well, what kind of things do you call quaint?

Nancy: There is this guy on 187th Street who puts up these wind chimes and little wooden windmills and birdhouses and little figures of elves in his front yard. My mother says it looks so quaint.

Peter: I know that house. My dad says it looks schlocky. You know, it looks cheap and too junked up.

Nancy: I don't think so. I think the stuff is cute. He adds a couple of new things each year. We always have fun looking to see what's new. My mom says that when she was young, lots of houses would have wooden windmills and birdhouses on their lawns. And more elaborate things as well. People used to enjoy making those things themselves and putting them on display. She says now it's a little old-fashioned to do that. But we still like that man's decorations.

Teacher: Okay, good. I looked up the word in the Oxford English Dictionary. The most current definition is this: "attractively or agreeably unusual in character or appearance; esp. pleasingly old-fashioned." The OED provides many more definitions but they are mostly rare or obsolete. So our question is what does *quaint* mean in this context, the context of *quaint emotions*?

Cecily: What we were saying before, old-fashioned ideas about heroes.

Jorgé: He allowed himself to be kind of taunted into going for the water, but he really didn't understand why. Like he didn't have an idea of what was going on. He was just caught up in it.

Teacher: Well, let's move along. In the next passage, think about these questions: Is Collins' running to the well to fetch water courageous? Is his drawing water from the well courageous?

As he neared the house each detail of the scene became vivid to him. He was aware of some bricks of the vanished chimney lying on the sod. There was a door which hung by one hinge.

Rifle bullets called forth by the insistent skirmishers came from the far-off bank of foliage. They mingled with the shells and the pieces of shells until the air was torn in all directions by hootings, yells, howls. The sky was full of fiends who directed all their wild rage at his head.

When he came to the well he flung himself face downward and peered into its darkness. There were furtive silver glintings some feet from the surface. He grabbed one of the canteens and, unfastening its cap, swung it down by the cord. The water flowed slowly in with an indolent gurgle.

And now as he lay with his face turned away, he was suddenly smitten with the terror. It came upon his heart like the grasp of claws. All the power faded from his muscles. For an instant he was no more than a dead man.

The canteen filled with a maddening slowness, in the manner of all bottles. Presently he recovered his strength and addressed a screaming oath to it. He leaned over until it seemed as if he intended to try to push water into it with his hands. His eyes as he gazed down into the well shone like two pieces of metal, and in their expression was a great appeal and a great curse. The stupid water derided him.

There was the blaring thunder of a shell. Crimson light shone through the swift boiling smoke and made a pink reflection on part of the wall of the well. Collins jerked out his arm and canteen with the same motion that a man would use in withdrawing his head from a furnace.

He scrambled erect and glared and hesitated. On the ground near him lay the old well bucket, with a length of rusty chain. He lowered it swiftly into the well. The bucket struck the water and then turning lazily over, sank. When, with hand reaching tremblingly over hand, he hauled it out, it knocked often against the walls of the well and spilled some of its contents.

In running with a filled bucket, a man can adopt but one kind of gait. So through this terrible field over which screamed practical angels of death Collins ran in the manner of a farmer chased out of a dairy by a bull.

His face went staring white with anticipation—anticipation of a blow that would whirl him around and down. He would fall as he had seen other men fall, the life knocked out of them so suddenly that their knees were no more quick to touch the ground than their heads. He saw the long blue line of the regiment, but his comrades were standing looking at him from the edge of an impossible star. He was aware of some deep wheel-ruts and hoof-prints in the sod beneath his feet.

Teacher: Okay, is Collins' running to the well to fetch water courageous?

Jorgé: I don't think he was courageous at the beginning. He is foolhardy, captured by "quaint emotions." I mean he just runs up kind of blind to what was happening around him. But then it changes. When he lies down and drops in the canteen and hears it gurgling, then he is really scared. It says, "He was suddenly smitten with the terror. It came upon his heart like the grasp of claws. All the power faded from his muscles. For an instant he was no more than a dead man." I think that means he was scared out of his skin. But, see, he didn't run away and try to be safe, because when he is so scared, he still tries to get the water. I think that means he is controlling his fear. And that is what we said that courage is, the control of fear. So I think he is courageous from that point.

Hazel: I don't agree. I think he is so frightened that he can't do anything else. It says he was like a "dead man." That means he was not feeling anything. So you can't say he was in control of his fear.

Cecily: But read the whole line. It says, "For an instant he was no more than a dead man." Then right away, when he realizes that the canteen will not fill quickly, he finds the old well bucket and uses the chain to drop that in. He's still in the grip of fear. But he controls it and does the work of retrieving water. I agree with Jorgé. At that point, he is courageous.

Peter: But going for the water in the first place was foolish. That isn't any less foolish now. He might be in control of fear, but that alone, according to what we said, is not enough. There has to be a noble cause. I don't see a noble cause. It's still a dumb thing to do.

Hazel: I don't think it is a deliberate action either. So it's not courageous unless it is deliberate.

Nancy: It certainly looks deliberate to me. He stands, looks around, sees the bucket and the chain, and then immediately takes the bucket and lowers it into the well. That is pretty deliberate. He was set on getting the water.

Thomas: I agree. It is deliberate, and also I think it is a noble cause. The men were thirsty. He's trying to bring back water.

Jorgé: Oh, come on. Jeez. He's just under the same stupid idea that he was to begin with. It is still foolhardy.

Cecily: No, no. We said that foolhardiness is a failure to recognize the danger. Collins, by this time, is really aware of the danger. I don't see how you can get around that.

After a bit more discussion, the class still disagrees about whether retrieving the water is less foolhardy now that Collins recognizes fully the danger. They read the next nine paragraphs.

The artillery officer who had fallen in this meadow had been making groans in the teeth of the tempest of sound. These futile cries, wrenched from him by his agony, were heard only by shells, bullets. When wild-eyed Collins came running, this officer raised himself. His face contorted and blanched from pain; he was about to utter some great beseeching cry. But suddenly his face straightened and he called: "Say, young man, give me a drink of water, will you?"

Collins had no room amid his emotions for surprise. He was mad from the threats of destruction.

"I can't," he screamed, and in this reply was a full description of his quaking apprehension. His cap was gone and his hair was riotous. His clothes made it appear that he had been dragged over the ground by the heels. He ran on.

The officer's head sank down and one elbow crooked. His foot in its brassbound stirrup still stretched over the body of his horse and the other leg was under the steed.

But Collins turned. He came dashing back. His face had now turned grey and in his eyes was all terror. "Here it is! Here it is!"

The officer was as a man gone in drink. His arm bent like a twig. His head drooped as if his neck was of willow. He was sinking to the ground, to lie face downward.

Collins grabbed him by the shoulder. "Here it is. Here's your drink. Turn over! Turn over, man, for God's sake!"

With Collins hauling at his shoulder, the officer twisted his body and fell with his face turned toward that region where lived the unspeakable noises of the swirling missiles. There was the faintest shadow of a smile on his lips as he looked at Collins. He gave a sigh, a little primitive breath like that from a child.

Collins tried to hold the bucket steadily, but his shaking hands caused the water to splash all over the face of the dying man. Then he jerked it away and ran on.

Teacher: In this episode of the story, what do you think about the courage of Collins?

Nancy: Well, when Collins ran past the officer, who was clearly dying because he had his arm shot off, and then he had been hit again and was trapped under his horse, and Collins just ran by, I thought he had lost his courage. But no, he came back and gave the officer a drink before running back to his lines. So I think he controlled his fear and did a good thing, giving the dying man drink.

Winnie: But he was rough with the officer, don't you think? He was not what you would call gentle. So I don't think it was such a good thing to do.

Peter: Oh, come on. You expect gentle in the middle of a great barrage? That's stupid. That doesn't have anything to do with it.

Mary Jane: Yeah. I mean the man is in great danger, but still he turns back to give the officer a drink. He has to return to him and then the officer can't sit up and Collins helps him up and holds the bucket for him. That's what we would call a noble reason for doing the act. So even if he wasn't courageous in the first place, but just foolhardy, he is now. He faced the fear, which was great, controlled it, and did a good deed in spite of the danger and his own fear. I don't see how anyone can say he is not courageous.

Teacher: You all agree? Can someone make an argument that Collins is not courageous?

Jorgé: Well, he ain't courageous at the beginning. He is just stupid—or I guess foolhardy. But after that he is courageous. I think there is no doubt, especially after he gives the officer a drink, even if he does splash the water a bit.

Teacher: Anyone want to add anything? No? Okay, now read on the end.

The regiment gave him a welcoming roar. The grimed faces were wrinkled in laughter.

His captain waved the bucket away. "Give it to the men!"

The two genial, skylarking young lieutenants were the first to gain possession of it. They played over it in their fashion.

When one tried to drink, the other teasingly knocked his elbow. "Don't, Billie! You'll make me spill it," said the one. The other laughed.

Suddenly there was an oath, the thud of wood on the ground, and a swift murmur of astonishment from the ranks. The two lieutenants glared at each other. The bucket lay on the ground empty.

Teacher: So what do you think about the ending of the story?

Jorgé: Somebody ought to shoot those turkeys. What a couple of ding-dongs!

Nancy: Jorgé, maybe they will be shot before long. Don't wish that on them. I agree they're jerks. But we don't want them killed because they're silly.

Thomas: I think they ought to be punished some way. I mean, think about it. All that effort that Collins put into getting the water, even though it may have been foolish. They got no reason to just spill it. I'd vote for shooting them.

Teacher: What do you think the men in the ranks thought about spilling the water?

Jorgé: They must have thought it was really stupid. They were pissed.

Teacher: Why do you say that?

Jorgé: Well look here, it says—

Cecily: It says, "a swift murmur of astonishment from the ranks." That implies that they were astonished that those jerks were so stupid as to spill the water. After what Collins did, they can't believe it.

Mary Jane: I know I would be astonished. Because they all saw what Collins did. I mean, even if they thought it was foolish to begin with, they must have recognized the danger. They must have seen him try with the canteen, then stand and get the bucket, run back, stop and return to the officer and give him a drink, then finally make it back with some water left in the bucket. They must have seen all that. And then they just play around and spill it. That is like a complete lack of respect for what Collins did.

Peter: Right on! Complete lack of respect.

Teacher: So why do you think Crane might have chosen to end the story with that final incident? [*No response.*] Think about it for a moment. The piece could have ended with the roar from the soldiers, couldn't it? So why the way it did?

Jorgé: Well, I'm not sure, but that incident about the lieutenants just contrasts with everything else in the story. I mean, even though we took everything very seriously, I mean, thinking about was he courageous or not, when they drop the bucket, it makes everything look stupid. Well, not everything, but you know what I mean?

Rick: I think it does contrast with everything else, especially if you read close, like we did. You know, Collins goes through all this terror and accomplishes the task he set, foolish or not. But these—what did you call them?—ding-dongs don't see it. They're just caught up in their own stuff. It's about how some people don't get it. I mean, this is about just a little incident, about a guy going for water. But it's really about a lot more. It's about how he changed in a few minutes time. *But the stupid lieutenants do not get it!*

Cecily: I think that's right. Look at the title, "An Incident." It's not the whole battle. It's just a short, tiny incident that probably didn't take longer to happen than it took us to read it. But Collins changes in it. And the ding-dongs do not get it. I think the story is about how war can change people in minutes, but because we may be concerned only about our own stupid things, we miss it. So I think it is about way more than an incident.

Teacher: [*as the bell rings*] That is a good place to stop. Tomorrow, we'll talk about writing your interpretations of this story.

Writing Interpretations Using Warrants and Backing

Helping students develop warrants and backing in order to interpret a character's actions and changes in attitude contributes to understanding the structure of the story: the *reasons* for the final incident. Without understanding the definition of courage and its possible warrants and backing, the students would not have been able to make the interpretations.

It also should be clear that students learn from one another in discussions like these. The last several student comments build on the preceding comments. If I had simply told them the definition, the students' concepts would not have been so apt; they would not have internalized the ideas as well. The members of this class are well on their way to being able to interpret the actions of characters independently.

More importantly, they are well on their way to becoming skillful in developing thoughtful arguments in which they can examine data, question them, develop ideas about them, make and support claims using evidence and warrants and even complex kinds of backing. They will reach what should be some of the most important goals of a high school education.

It is important to note that this development of thoughtful students takes place over many years of schooling. Argument should be part of the educational program at early stages. Learning to make a case we know can begin as early as the fifth grade as with our mascot arguments in Chapter Two. If schools were to adopt a policy of teaching through inquiry, making arguments would be taking place every day in every subject matter from language arts to mathematics. This would make learning more exciting—and much more meaningful.

"Without understanding the definition of courage and its possible warrants and backing, the students would not have been able to make the interpretations."

"If schools were to adopt a policy of teaching through inquiry, making arguments would be taking place every day in every subject matter from language arts to mathematics."

Definitions of Murder in the United States

Murder

Intent to Kill

The law generally defines murder as inexcusable or unjustifiable homicide with intent to kill. The problem, of course, lies in defining *intent to kill*. Murderers do not announce their intentions. Ordinarily, the intent to kill is inferred from the defendant's use of a deadly weapon—a gun, a knife, poison, among others. But even the use of a deadly weapon does not conclusively prove intent to kill. A defendant can try to convince a judge or jury that even though he used a deadly weapon, he did not intend to kill—for example, that he waved a loaded pistol in order to frighten someone and fired it accidentally.

Deadly Weapons

There is also the question, what is a deadly weapon? It is frequently defined as one with which almost anyone can kill. A better, more encompassing definition is *a weapon that, in the way it is used, is likely to produce death or serious bodily injury.* Obviously, guns, knives, and poisons are deadly weapons. But under the latter definition, automobiles, bricks, clubs, scissors, broken bottles, picture wire, and so forth may also be deadly weapons. Even pins and penknives, in the hands of someone who knows how to use them to cause grievous harm, may qualify as deadly weapons. Determining whether or not a weapon is deadly depends both on what it is and how it is used. Hands and feet used repeatedly by strong people on weaker victims can be deadly weapons. More subtle means have been used to kill and have been classified as deadly weapons: opening a cold draft on a helpless victim or shouting to frighten someone with a weak heart or someone standing in a precarious position.

Failure to Act

Intent to kill may also be established on the basis of a failure to act when there is a duty to act. For example, if a husband is having a heart attack and his wife fails to summon help, her failure to act can be classified as intent to kill, because she has a duty to act—to find help. The duty to act is based on special personal relationships, not simply on the moral obligation one human has to another. Husbands and wives have a duty to each other, as do parents to children, masters to servants, ship captains to crews, teachers to students, and so forth. Or the duty to act may be required by law (as in the case of police) or by civil contract. If one voluntarily assumes the care of an individual, one has the duty to continue the care. In one case, a grandmother who took over the care of her grandchild from the mother became drunk and let the infant smother. The court found that she had a duty to act to prevent the occurrence. Her drunkenness was no excuse, and she was found guilty of manslaughter. Similarly, if one creates peril for another individual, one has the duty to rescue the person from that peril. For example, a defendant had beaten a victim and left him lying unconscious on the road. Later, the victim was run over by an automobile and killed. The court found that the accused had a duty to save his victim from the peril he had created. However, a passerby who sees the victim in peril has no legal duty to act. In criminal homicide cases, it must be shown that the accused had a duty to act and that the failure to act caused death.

High Risk

The creation of a very high degree of risk is also interpreted as intent to kill if the risk results in death: shooting into a crowded area or a room likely to be occupied, driving at very high speeds on crowded streets, playing Russian roulette with another person, shooting at a point near but not at another person. A death resulting from actions like these is sometimes referred to as "depraved-heart murder." The most ambiguous aspect of this definition of murder lies in the phrase "very high degree of risk" (an ambiguity increased because laws concerning involuntary manslaughter involve a similar phrase). In addition, does one need to be aware of the risk one is creating? Drunkenness cannot excuse conduct that causes high risk, but what about other factors? Some cases have held that if a "reasonable person" would have recognized the risk as a very great one, then the accused is guilty, whether or not he himself recognized the risk.

Summary

To summarize, then, murder is criminal (unjustifiable) homicide with intent to kill. Intent to kill may be presumed from the use of a deadly weapon (defined as an instrument that from the manner used will cause death), from the omission to act when there is a duty to act, and from the creation of very high risk.

First-Degree Murder

All but twelve states provide two subcategories of murder: first and second degree. Ordinarily, first-degree murder includes two different situations:

1. intent to kill when that condition is accompanied by both premeditation and deliberation
2. murder accompanied by one or more felonies, especially robbery, arson, burglary, or rape

To be guilty of the first form of first-degree murder, the accused must be proved to have done all of the following:

» intended to kill
» deliberated about the crime
» premeditated doing it

Careful definitions of *deliberate* and *premeditated* are difficult to come by. One writer suggests that premeditation consists in asking a question such as, "Shall I kill him?" The intent to kill is the positive answer, "Yes, I will." Deliberation involves a question-answer sequence such as, "What about the consequences?" "I don't care. I'll do it anyway."

Premeditation and deliberation are both difficult to prove. One problem has to do with the time involved in premeditating and deliberating before an act of killing. Lawyers often argue that premeditating and deliberating take only a few seconds. However, as the time becomes less and less appreciable to the point of being instantaneous, the difference between first- and second-degree murder disappears. A second problem has to do with whether the accused was capable of cool reflection. Insanity, emotional rage, intoxication, or feeblemindedness might render an individual incapable of any premeditation or deliberation. And while he might still have intended to kill, he would then be guilty of second-degree murder.

It is not enough to prove that the accused had both the time and the capability for deliberation and premeditation. It is necessary to show that these actually took place. Unfortunately, criminals do not always announce to witnesses what they are thinking. Occasionally, they do; when they do not, premeditation and deliberation must be inferred from behavior before and at the time of killing. In some states, the manner of killing is taken to be evidence of premeditation. For example, the use of poison over time and lying in wait are evidence of premeditation. In several states, a homicide that takes place during the commission of certain felonies is automatically classified by law as first-degree "felony" murder.

Three categories of evidence are important in proving deliberation and premeditation:

1. facts about what the accused did before the killing that indicate he was planning the crime
2. facts about the accused's relationship to his victim that show he had a motive for the killing
3. facts demonstrating that the manner of the killing was so exacting and precise that the killer must have acted according to some plan thought out in advance

Second-Degree Murder

The major distinction between first- and second-degree murder is that *second-degree murder is intent to kill unaccompanied by deliberation and premeditation.*

> » Murder committed during the commission of a felony other than one automatically requiring a first-degree finding (usually rape, robbery, arson, burglary) is second degree.
> » If the law makes it a felony to remove "detour" or "danger" signs from roads being built or repaired and a motorist is killed as the result of the removal of such a sign, the perpetrator may be accused of both the felony of removing the sign and second-degree murder.
> » In addition, the creation of "very high risk" resulting in death is classified as second-degree murder.
> » If failure to act results in death (and it is not accompanied by deliberation and premeditation), it too is second-degree murder.

Voluntary Manslaughter

Legal thinkers often consider voluntary manslaughter not as a categorically separate crime, but as a crime, different in degree from murder at one extreme and from justifiable or excusable homicide at the other. That is, it is not bad enough to be classified as murder. But it is too bad to be no crime at all.

Ordinarily, voluntary manslaughter involves intent to kill or to do serious bodily injury short of death or extremely reckless conduct. As such, it often amounts to murder. However, if the defendant can demonstrate the presence of certain circumstances that make the commission of the crime more understandable, the crime can be reduced from murder to voluntary manslaughter. The chief of these circumstances is that the defendant, prior to the killing, had been provoked to such an extent that he killed in "the heat of passion." Usually the passion in question is extreme rage. Sometimes it's terror. The presence of such provocation does not excuse the crime. But it does render it more understandable and, therefore, less reprehensible than murder.

To have the crime reduced from murder to voluntary manslaughter, the defendant must show the following:

1. There was a "reasonable provocation."
2. He was in fact provoked.
3. A reasonable person would not have cooled down in the time between the provocation and the crime.
4. The defendant did not cool down during that time.

The two most important definitions in determining the nature of voluntary manslaughter, as opposed to murder, are those for "reasonable provocation" and "reasonable man."

A "reasonable provocation" is one that would normally cause a "reasonable man" to lose his self-control. The courts have presumed that such provocations include physical harm to the defendant himself or a close relative, unlawful arrest, and the discovery of a wife in the act of adultery. (Historically, however, a wife discovering her husband in the act of adultery might *not* have been able to claim "reasonable provocation.") Abusive language or trespassing on private property, though perhaps enraging, do not constitute "reasonable provocation." The assumption is that a reasonable man would not become enraged to the point of killing over mere words or mere trespassing.

The great problem is the same as with other "reasonable man" clauses. Who is to decide what a reasonable man is and what standard a reasonable man should be held to? Over the centuries catching the wife in an act of adultery has become established as reasonable provocation. But given the changing moral climate, with far looser sexual codes, can we still believe that a truly reasonable man or woman would be enraged to the point of killing? A judge or jury must decide what a reasonable man is and the standard to which he must be held given the peculiar circumstances of any given case.

Involuntary Manslaughter

Involuntary manslaughter has two subcategories: criminal negligence and unlawful act involuntary manslaughter. For the sake of brevity and because it involves such a high degree of ambiguity, unlawful act involuntary manslaughter will be excluded from consideration here.

Criminal Negligence

» To be found guilty of criminal negligence manslaughter, the defendant must have created a high and unreasonable degree of risk of death or serious bodily injury. And his negligence must have resulted in someone else's death.

» The defendant must know the circumstances and be aware that his conduct creates the risk.

As in other categories, however, intoxication is no excuse. The problem here arises in defining the phrase "a high and unreasonable degree of risk."

Generally, involuntary manslaughter of the criminal negligence type has to do with the negligent use of automobiles and firearms. For example, a person who drives a car on public highways, knowing full well that he is subject to attacks of vertigo, loss of consciousness, or epilepsy that would cause him to lose control of the automobile, may be found guilty of criminal negligence if his conduct results in the death of another person. Likewise, a hunter who fires when he sees movement although he knows that many other hunters are in the area may be criminally negligent if the shooting causes a death. The owner of a nightclub in Rhode Island was found guilty of criminal negligence manslaughter when 480 patrons lost their lives in a fire because he had not provided adequate fire exits and other safety provisions. A parent who fails to provide medical aid for a child at a time when aid might have saved the child and whose child dies as a result is criminally negligent.

All these cases reflect criteria used in defining the "high and unreasonable degree of risk" involved in involuntary manslaughter. The defendant's negligent conduct must have been the cause of death. If the defendant's conduct is not the cause of death, criminal negligence cannot be charged. For example, had the nightclub patrons mentioned above escaped the fire to stand about watching and had a wall collapsed on one of them, the nightclub owner would not be guilty of criminal negligence in such a death, even though the fire itself might have been attributed to the owner's negligence. The patrons' decision to stand and watch is an intervening event for which the owner cannot be held responsible. Similarly, a parent who decides to rely upon prayer for the cure of a sick child is guilty of criminal negligence only if the child dies as a result of the failure. If the child would have died anyway, there is no criminal negligence.

» Third, the victim must be a person or member of a class of persons foreseeably endangered.

The word *foreseeable* can be defined only in a general sense. As it is used in relation to criminally negligent manslaughter, it seems to mean "more than possible" but "less than probable." A foreseeable event is not highly or readily predictable, but it is more likely than merely possible. For example, if a person is subject to attacks of dizziness, the collision of his car with another is foreseeable. It is *possible* for a driver in generally good health to have a heart attack, lose control, and collide with another vehicle. But the event is not likely. At the other extreme, it is probable that a drunken driver driving at very high speeds through crowded streets would kill or do serious bodily injury to someone. The heart attack victim is likely to be guilty of no crime. But the drunk has created the very high degree of risk found in "depraved-heart murder." Criminal negligence manslaughter is concerned with what lies between—a foreseeable danger.

» The fourth requirement is that the victim be killed in a manner that is foreseeable.

Let us say that two men are hunting in the same half-acre area without knowing of each other's presence. Assume that hunter A fires his rifle at an animal target and that hunter B is badly frightened by the report of the rifle. As a result, hunter B suffers a heart attack and dies. The manner of death is not "foreseeable" and, therefore, hunter A is not liable to prosecution. On the other hand, assume hunter A fires at a movement in a thicket in an area he knows to be crawling with hunters and kills hunter B. Death is the foreseeable consequence of such conduct under such circumstances. Therefore, hunter A may be found guilty of manslaughter.

» Finally, the type and degree of harm to the victim must be foreseeable.

In the case of fire in a crowded nightclub with no fire exits, it is foreseeable that patrons will burn to death should there be a fire. If a driver loses consciousness, it is foreseeable that his car will collide with another, seriously maiming or killing passengers in his own or other cars. Such circumstances are likely to bring charges of manslaughter.

References

Alsup, Janet, Janet Emig, Gordon Pradl, Robert Tremmel, and Robert Yagelski with Lynn Alvine, Gina deBlase, Michael Moore, Robert Petrone, and Mary Sawyer. 2006. "The State of English Education and a Vision for Its Future: A Call to Arms." *English Education* 38 (4): 278–94.

Annin, Peter, Dante Chinni, John Leland, Annetta Miller, Tom Morganthau, Marc Peyser, and Pat Wingert. 1995. "Everyday Heroes: A Tribute to Americans Who Care." *Newsweek* (May 29).

Aristotle. 1947. *Nichomachean Ethics*. Translated by William Ross. Edited by Richard McKeon. *Introduction to Aristotle*, 308–543. New York: Random House.

———. 1991. *The Art of Rhetoric*. Translated by H. Lawson-Tancred. New York: Penguin.

———. 1994–2000. *Posterior Analytics*. Translated by G. R. G. Mure. Available at: http://classics.mit.edu/Aristotle/posterior.html.

———. 2007. *Prior Analytics*. Translated by A. J. Jenkinson. eBooks@Adelaide. Available at: http://ebooks.adelaide.edu.au/.

Beals, Melba. 1994. *Warriors Don't Cry: A Searing Memoir of the Battle to Integrate Little Rock's Central High*. New York: Pocket Books.

Booth, Wayne C. 1974. *A Rhetoric of Irony*. Chicago: University of Chicago Press.

———. 1983. "A New Strategy for Establishing a Truly Democratic Criticism." *Daedalus* 112 (1): 193–214.

Boulle, Pierre. 1954. *The Bridge over the River Kwai*. New York: Presidio Press.

Carroll, Lewis. *Through the Looking Glass*. www.sabian.org/Alice/lgchap06.htm.

Chopra, Deepak. 1997. *The Path to Love*. New York: Harmony Books.

Chua Seok Hong. 2008. Narrative and Argument in the Literature Essay: An Inquiry into Literary Competence in the Secondary Literature Curriculum in Singapore. Unpublished doctoral dissertation. Singapore: Nanyang Technological University.

Common Core Standards. 2010. www.corestandards.org/the-standards/english-language arts-standards/writing-6-12/grade-9-10.

Crane, Stephen. 1994 [1895]. "A Mystery of Heroism: A Detail of an American Battle." In *The Heath Anthology of American Literature*. Vol. 2. Edited by Paul Lauter, 709–714. Lexington, MA: D. C. Heath and Co.

———. 1956. *The Red Badge of Courage*. New York: Pocket Books.

Csikszentmihalyi, Mihaly. 1990. *Flow: The Psychology of Optimal Experience*. New York: Harper & Row.

Csikszentmihalyi, Mihaly, and Reed Larson. 1984. *Being Adolescent: Conflict and Growth in the Teenage Years*. New York: Basic Books.

Dewey, John. 1938. *Logic, the Theory of Inquiry*. New York: H. Holt and Company.

A Few Good Men. 1992. Produced by David Brown, Rob Reiner, and Andrew Scheinman. Directed by Rob Reiner. 138 minutes. Columbia Pictures and Castle Rock Entertainment. Videocassette.

Fish, Stanley. 1980. *Is There a Text in This Class? The Authority of Interpretive Communities*. Cambridge, MA: Harvard University Press.

———. 1983. "Short People Got No Reason to Live: Reading Irony." *Daedalus* 112 (1): 175–91.

Frank, Anne. 1967. *The Diary of Young Girl*. Garden City: Doubleday.

Frye, H. Northrop. 1957. *Anatomy of Criticism: Four Essays*. Princeton, NJ: Princeton University Press.

Fulkerson, Richard. 1996. *Teaching the Argument in Writing*. Urbana, IL: National Council of Teachers of English.

Goodlad, John. 1984. *A Place Called School: Prospects for the Future*. New York: McGraw-Hill.

Graham, Steve, and Dolores Perin. 2007. A Report to Carnegie Corporation of New York Writing: Next Effective Strategies to Improve Writing of Adolescents In Middle and High Schools. New York: Carnegie Corporation.

Graves, Donald. 1980. "Research Update: A New Look at Writing Research." *Language Arts* 57: 913–19.

The Great Debaters. 2007. Produced by Todd Black, Kate Forte, Oprah Winfrey, and Joe Roth. Directed by Denzel Washington. 124 minutes. The Weinstiein Company. Videocassette.

Hillocks, George, Jr. 1964. "The Theme Concept Unit in Literature." In *Patterns and Models for Teaching English*. Edited by Michael Shugrue and George Hillocks, Jr., 17–25. Champaign, IL: National Council of Teachers of English.

———. 1971. *An Evaluation of Project Apex: A Nongraded Phase-Elective English Program*. Trenton (Michigan) Public Schools [Study conducted and published under the auspices of USOE].

———. 1972. *Alternatives in English: A Critical Analysis of Elective Programs*. Urbana, IL: ERIC Clearinghouse on Reading and Communication Skills and National Council of Teachers of English.

———. 1984. "What Works in Teaching Composition: A Meta-Analysis of Experimental Treatment Studies." *American Journal of Education* (November): 133–70. Reprinted in Miller, Susan, ed. 2008. *The Norton Book of Composition Studies*. New York: W. W. Norton & Co.

———. 1989. "Literary Texts in Classrooms." In *From Socrates to Software: The Teacher as Text and the Text as Teacher. 88th Yearbook of the National Society for the Study of Education*. Edited by P. W. Jackson and S. Haroutunian-Gordon, 135–58. Chicago: The University of Chicago Press.

———. 1995. *Teaching Writing as Reflective Practice*. New York: Teachers College Press.

———. 1999. *Ways of Thinking, Ways of Teaching*. New York: Teachers College Press.

———. 2002. *The Testing Trap: How States Control Thinking*. New York: Teachers College Press.

———. 2007. *Narrative Writing: Learning a New Model for Teaching*. Portsmouth, NH: Heinemann.

Hillocks, George, Jr., Bernard J. McCabe, and James F. McCampbell. 1971. *The Dynamics of English Instruction.* New York: Random House.

Hillocks, George, Jr., Elizabeth Kahn, and Larry Johannessen. 1983. "Teaching Defining Strategies as a Mode of Inquiry: Some Effects on Student Writing." *Research in the Teaching of English* (October): 275–84.

Hobbes, Thomas. 1958. *The Leviathan, Parts I and II.* Indianapolis, IN: Bobbs-Merrill.

Holt, Rinehart, and Winston. 2009. Elements of Literature website. http://eolit.hrw.com/.

Illinois State Board of Education. 1994. *Write On, Illinois!* Available at: www.gower.k12.il.us/Staff/WRITEON/index.htm.

———. 2008. *Illinois Learning Standards.* Available at: www.isbe.net/ils/ela/standards.htm. Accessed June 30, 2008.

Kinneavy, James, and John E. Warriner. 1993. *Elements of Writing: Course 3.* New York: Harcourt School.

La Salle, Mick. 2007. "Review: '3:10 to Yuma' a Western classic with modern flourishes." http://www.sfgate.com/cgi-bin/article.cgi?f=/c/a/2007/09/06/DDBQRR59R.DTL#ixzz16ABUHEmg.

McCann, Thomas. 1995. Student Argumentative Writing in Three Grade Levels. Unpublished doctoral dissertation. Chicago, IL: University of Chicago.

McCann, Thomas, Larry R. Johannessen, Elizabeth Kahn, and Joseph M. Flanagan. 2006. *Talking in Class: Using Discussion to Enhance Teaching and Learning.* Urbana, IL: National Council of Teachers of English.

National Assessment of Educational Progress. 2002. *The Nation's Report Card: Reading.* Washington, D.C.: U. S. Department of Education, Institute of Education Sciences.

———. 2005. *The Nation's Report Card: 12th-Grade Reading and Mathematics.* Washington, D.C.: U. S. Department of Education, Institute of Education Sciences.

———. 2007. *The Nation's Report Card: Reading.* Washington, D.C.: U. S. Department of Education, Institute of Education Sciences.

National Governor's Association and State Education Chiefs. 2010. Common Core State Standards. www.corestandards.org/the-standards/english-language-arts-standards/writing-6-12/.

Nussbaum, Martha C. 1999. *Cultivating Humanity: A Classical Defense of Reform in Liberal Education.* Cambridge: Harvard University Press.

Nystrand, M., with Adam Gamoran, Robert Kachur, and Catherine Prendergast. 1997. *Opening Dialogue: Understanding the Dynamics of Language and Learning in the English Classroom.* New York: Teachers College Press.

Plato. 1999. *Euthyphro, Apology, Crito, and Phaedo.* Translated by H. N. Fowler. Loeb Classical Library. Cambridge, MA: Harvard University Press.

Powell, Colin. 2003. Speech before the Security Council of the United Nations. Available at: www.cnn.com/2003/US/02/05/sprj.irq.powell.transcript/.

RSCC online Writing Lab. Retrieved 2008. Available at: www.rscc.cc.tn.us/owl&writingcenter/OWL/ElementsLit.html.

Schaefer, Jack. 1994. *Shane.* Portsmouth, NH: Heinemann.

Scott v. Harris. The Oyez Project. Oral argument Monday, February 26, 2007. Case 05-1631. Available at: www.oyez.org/cases/2000-2009/2006/2006_05_1631/argument/.

Smagorinsky, Peter. 1991. "The Writer's Knowledge and the Composing Process: A Protocol Analysis." *Research in the Teaching of English* 25: 339–64.

Smagorinsky, Peter, and Michael W. Smith. 1992. "The Nature of Knowledge in Composition and Literary Understanding: The Question of Specificity." *Review of Educational Research* 65, 279–305.

Smith, Michael W. 1989. "Teaching the Interpretation of Irony in Poetry." *Research in the Teaching of English* 23: 254–72.

Smith, Michael W., and Jeffrey Wilhelm. 2006. *Going with the Flow.* Portsmouth, NH: Heinemann.

Snell, Marilyn. B. 2007. "Bulldozers and Blasphemy." *Sierra* (September/October). Available at: www.sierraclub.org/sierra/200709/bulldozers.asp.

Supreme Court of New Jersey. 1976. *In re Quinlan,* 70 N. J. 10, 366 A. 2d 647.

Tannen, Deborah. 1999. *The Argument Culture: Stopping America's War of Words.* New York: Ballantine.

Tennessee v. Garner. United States Supreme Court. 471 U.S. 1, 1985.

Texas Education Agency. 1993. *Exit Level 1993–1994 Writing Collection Scoring Guide for Persuasive Writing.* Austin, TX: Author.

Toulmin, Stephen E. 1958. *The Uses of Argument.* Cambridge: Cambridge University Press.

———. 2001. *Return to Reason.* Cambridge: Harvard University Press.

Treat, Lawrence. 1987. *The Clue Armchair Detective.* New York: Ballantine Books.

U.S. Government Printing Office. 1986. Public Report of the Vice-president's Task Force on Combating Terrorism. Washington, D.C.: U.S. Government Printing Office.

Vygotsky, Lev S. 1978. *Mind in Society: The Development of Higher Psychological Processes* (M. Cole, et al. Eds.). Cambridge: Harvard University Press.

The War. Episode Seven, A World Without War, March 1945–December 1945. 2007. Directed and produced by Ken Burns and Lynn Novick. 128 minutes. Florentine Films for Public Broadcasting Service.

Welles, Orson. 1938. *War of the Worlds.* www.archive.org/details/Orson WellesMrBruns.

Wells, Herbert George. 1898. *War of the Worlds.* London: William Heinemann.

Williams, Joseph M., and Gregory G. Colomb. 2007. *The Craft of Argument.* New York: Pearson Education.

Willman, Fred. 2005. *Why Mascots Have Tales: The Illinois High School Mascot Manual from Appleknockers to Zippers.* Addison, IL: Mascots Publishing.

Study Guide for
Teaching Argument Writing

Teaching Argument Writing, Grades 6–12: Supporting Claims with Relevant Evidence and Clear Reasoning focuses on helping teachers develop in their students the specific skills needed to write an effective argument and challenges us to deeply engage the students in our classrooms.

As Hillocks emphasizes throughout his book, critical and reflective practice is essential to good teaching. The best practices are honed in collaboration with colleagues through both discussion and practice. We hope you will consider forming interdisciplinary teams for this study group, as there are many points of entry for teachers of all core disciplines. The intersection of argument with forensic science, law, literature, and original research invites applications in a variety of courses.

Each chapter in this book has clear content objectives, but we are also interested in helping teachers hone their pedagogy in ways that can be applied more broadly. To that end, for each chapter we are providing discussion questions as well as suggestions for action. We hope you will experiment with these actions in your individual classrooms and then report back to your group to share results. It is this kind of collaboration and reflection that can lead to a lively and rewarding Professional Learning Community.

Guiding Questions for the Introduction

Hillocks uses Mihaly Csikszentmihalyi's concept of flow or optimal experience as a starting point for this book because he believes creating flow experiences for students it is the cornerstone of all effective pedagogy. Without it, meaningful learning will not take place. Read over Czikszentmihalyi's definition of flow on page 3.

Discuss and Reflect

» Think about a moment in your life, past or present, when you have had a "flow experience." Brainstorm a collective list of those experiences and what factors were necessary to create it. If you are meeting in a group, share some of those experiences.

» Discuss the findings documented by Csikszentmihaliyi and Larson (pages 3–5) about the disconnection between school and flow experience. Consider some tasks that students engage in in your classroom on a regular basis. How do you think your students would rate their levels of pleasure, confidence, and absorption in these tasks?

» Look at some sample objectives from a lesson from your classroom. How do they align with the criteria for creating a flow experience? Are there certain lessons or units which engage students more than others? Can you identify the characteristics of these units or lessons which help create a flow experience for students? How might you revise a less effective lesson to create the conditions that contribute to flow experience?

Things to Try

» Ask students to take a survey in which students rate their levels of pleasure, confidence, and absorption in certain tasks in your classroom. Bring the data back to your group and discuss.

» Bring a sample lesson or unit from your classroom that you would like to modify to align more closely with a flow experience. Using the criteria listed in the introduction, work with colleagues to create at least one task that could create a flow experience for students.

Chapter One: Solving Mysteries to Teach Simple Arguments of Fact

In this chapter, Hillocks has outlined ways to use mysteries and an inquiry-based approach to instruction to help students construct arguments of fact. This approach correlates directly with high levels of engagement and builds skills students need to craft an argument from existing data.

Discuss and Reflect

» Has anyone in your group used mysteries in the curriculum before? If so, with what goals?

» What were the strengths and weaknesses of your unit? What concepts did students grasp easily? With what concepts did they struggle? How would you rate the level of engagement?

» What are your concerns as you begin the teaching of this chapter?

Things to Try

» See the "Note on Pretesting" on page 39. Look at the list of criteria and try to agree on a shared list of objectives. Feel free to adopt this list in its entirety.

» Using the example on page 39, create a pretest scenario that will engage your students. As a group, implement this shared pretest and meet to discuss the collective data. What are your students' weaknesses? What skills might need extra scaffolding?

» Following the guidelines in this chapter, introduce the scenarios suggested. Schedule a weekly meeting to discuss successes and areas of concern, both in terms of pedagogy and student objectives.

Chapter Two: Teaching Simple Arguments of Judgment

This chapter focuses on the content of arguments of judgment. Although Hillocks walks you through the unit step by step, teachers often ask for more support around helping students succeed with small-group work. In order for this unit (and most teaching!) to be successful, we have to ensure the students have a clear understanding of the task as well as guidelines for working together. Before you begin this unit, consider the following questions.

Discuss and Reflect

» What has your experience been with small-group work and adolescents? What are the benefits to this work? The pitfalls?
» Brainstorm a list of specific strategies that have worked well, as well as areas of concern with small-group work.
» Read the "Tips on Using Small-Group Discussions" on page 65. Have you used these strategies before? Are there any new strategies which you would be willing to introduce?

Things to Try

» Focus on 2–3 specific strategies for success with small-group work and implement them during this unit. At the end of each day, make some quick notes in your planner on how the small-group work went. If you are teaching multiple classes, note the differences between each group. Share your findings and best practices with your colleagues.
» Observe one colleague's classroom during their small-group work. Act as a constructive friend, jotting down observations of the group work and the strategies used to optimize this class time. Debrief within the week and then share findings with larger group.

Chapter Three: Writing Simple Arguments of Policy

This chapter challenges teachers to encourage students to generate original data, rather than use secondary sources to drive their inquiry, research, and policy projects. Hillocks notes that the Common Core asks middle school students to "conduct short research projects to answer a question" and high school students to "conduct short as well as more sustained research projects to answer a question or solve a problem." What are your own research practices in your classroom and your school?

Discuss and Reflect

» What opportunities do students in your school have to generate and interpret data? Brainstorm a list of opportunities and lessons where students have had this experience.

» What kinds of research opportunities do students have in your current school curriculum? Would you consider these projects inquiry-based? How might you tweak these projects to reflect the kind of inquiry-based practice Hillocks offers in this chapter?

Things to Try

» Using Hillocks' outline as your guide, collaboratively plan an investigation with students. After each day of implementation, jot notes reflecting on the day and debrief with colleagues.

» Coauthoring a piece of writing is an effective tool for modeling thinking and writing habits. Hillocks offers tips on this process at the end of the chapter. Try this with your students, especially if this type of writing is a new genre for them. Use Hillocks' suggestions, balancing suggestions from a variety of students with your own input. Share this process and product with your colleagues.

Chapter Four: How Are Judgments Made in the Real World?

This chapter is a crucial one for those teachers, perhaps in the upper grades, who are interested in taking on the more complex nuances of argument in Chapters Seven, Eight, and Nine. Hillocks breaks down the kinds of judgments people make each day and demonstrates how this thinking forms the foundations of argument—and by extension the warrants and backing of arguments.

Discuss and Reflect

» Choose a court case (or a story that is mythic, an act of terrorism, or a satiric poem) and discuss a warrant that could apply. Then, brainstorm a list of criteria for this warrant and some examples that would meet each criterion.

» Discuss the necessary background knowledge you believe students will need for this kind of extended thinking. What evidence can you use to determine student readiness?

Chapter Five: Learning to Make Judgments Based on Criteria

In this chapter, Hillocks demonstrates how teachers can engage students with real-life problems to generate a set of criteria to defend. Through this work, students can connect with current events as well as apply a set of criteria to real-world issues.

Discuss and Reflect

> » Brainstorm a list of possible topics for which students could generate a list of criteria. See examples on page 131. Also, see Hillocks guidelines for choosing an appropriate problem on page 143.
> » Choose one from this list and brainstorm a list of criteria together in your group. After brainstorming, generate another list articulating the kinds of inferences students will have to make.

Things to Try

> » Using either one of the topics from the list you generated in your study group or the Giraffe Award used in the beginning of the chapter, take students through a specific case together. If you choose your own topic, see Figure 5.2 and create several other cases so students can test their criteria.
> » Use the sample case on page 128 and, using the small-group techniques from Chapter 2, conduct this lesson. As an extension, consider staging a courtroom case and assigning roles to each student. This incorporates the judgments generated from the criteria.

Chapter Six: Developing and Supporting Criteria for Arguments of Judgment

In this chapter, Hillocks broadens the task of making judgments and asks students to defend and extend their thinking. See Chapter Four for some background information, which will help facilitate the discussions in the activities outlined here.

Discuss and Reflect

» As a group, brainstorm the definition of courage. As Hillocks suggests, generate two or three scenarios that would be good examples for your students to discuss in order to help *them* define courage.

» After reading Chapter Six, discuss the kinds of judgments and assumptions you think are most prevalent in our society today. Which of these judgments do you see as the most dangerous? Why?

» Watch the final debate in the movie *The Great Debaters* referenced on pages 146–148. How does it help illustrate Hillocks' point in this section? How might this clip enhance students' understanding?

Things to Try

» Take students through the process of discussing the scenarios and generating a definition of courage. If you have written additional scenarios, consider using those as well. Compare the small-group discussions in your classroom with the transcriptions in this chapter. How are they similar? Different? Brainstorm with colleagues how to maximize this discussion time for students.

» Compare the definitions of courage in each of your classes and with other teachers' students. Are there similarities or differences? How might you reinforce or tweak the strengths or weaknesses next time?

» Discuss how you might use the methods Hillocks outlines in this chapter to guide students through the process of defining additional concepts or qualities that may be frequently referenced in media (e.g., heroism, patriotism). Consider collaborating to write scenarios for students to discuss for this additional classroom work.

Chapter Seven: Teaching Students How to Make Literary Judgments

In this last chapter, Hillocks challenges the status quo pedagogy in which teachers assign homework but do little to teach the higher-level skills needed to comprehend it or write about it effectively. Throughout the chapter, Hillocks demonstrates how the work described in his previous chapters connects with literature-based inquiry.

Discuss and Reflect

» Hillocks writes, "A common assumption is that merely assigning a great many works, contributing background information about the elements and structure of the works and the periods in which they were written, and then explaining what these works mean will somehow produce students who are active interpreters of literature themselves." (See page 177.) Have you ever made this assumption in your own teaching? Discuss together.

» If you have tried any of the activities in this book, have you seen evidence of growth in inferential thinking? Can you give evidence which may be helpful for your colleagues?

Things to Try

» Using Hillocks' guide and examples in this chapter, select a concept and a text to which you could apply it. Try to collaborate with at least one other teacher as you do this.

» Consider Hillocks' guiding philosophy: ". . . the unit is not designed to elicit specific information but rather to enable students to bring complex knowledge to bear on complex problems and to write thoughtfully and effectively about those problems" (185). Think about guiding questions that could help you enable your students to do this with the concept and text you have selected, above. Then, design an inquiry-based unit around the concept.

Index

Aesop ("Fox and the Crow, The"), 179–180
Analytic definitions, 110
Arguments
of judgment (*see* Judgment)
  of policy (*see* Policy)
  of probability, 19
  relevant evidence, 15–16
  sound, constructing and recognizing,
    108–109
  using mysteries to teach arguments of
    fact (*see* Mysteries)
Aristotle, 150–151
  Art of Rhetoric, The, 151
Art of Rhetoric, The (Aristotle), 151
Assessment
  clear feedback, providing, 9–11
  pretesting, 39–40
Assumptions, making unexamined,
    102–103
Augustine, St., 148

Backing analysis, 146–148
Beals, Melba Pattillo (*Warriors Don't
    Cry*), 182

Being Adolescent (Csikszentmihalyi and
    Larson), 3–4
Black Boy (Wright), 182
Blackburn, Chester A., 121
Blackburn, Mary Ruth, 121
Book, Samantha, 146–148
Boulle, Pierre (*Bridge over the River
    Kwai, The*), 182
Bridge over the River Kwai, The (Boulle),
    182
Bush, George H. W. (president, U.S.),
    110

Carroll, Lewis (*Through the Looking
    Glass*), 108, 109
"Case of the Dead Musician, The,"
    problem, 34–36
"Chewing Gum" project, 70–96
Chopra, Deepak (*Path to Love, The*),
    183–184
Clarity of goals and objectives, in
    planning for flow, 6–8
Clue Armchair Detective, The (Treat), 30
Coauthoring with students, 75–78

Collaboration while working on arguments of policy, 93
Common Core Standards, 15, 41, 69, 103, 178
Courage
    defining, 150–152, 168–172
    nature of, 150–151
    teaching unit on, 185–200
    value of, 151–152
    "What Is Courage?" activity (*see* "What Is Courage?" activity)
Crane, Stephen
    "Mystery of Heroism, A," 178, 182, 185–188
    Red Badge of Courage, The, 178
Criteria
    backing of judgments, examining, 145–148
    cases for discussion, 130–135
    defining concepts, 148–149
    developing and discussing a class list of, 166–168
    Giraffe Award activity (*see* Giraffe Award activity)
    Great Debaters, The, 146
    introducing specific cases, 128–130
    learned judgments, 144–145
    learning to use, 113–142
    murder judgments, 126–143
    small group discussions, 135–142
    topics for discussion, 143
    value of, 176
    "What Constitutes Freedom of Speech?" activity, 172–175
    "What Is Courage?" activity (*see* "What Is Courage?" activity)
Critical thinking
    approaches to teaching, 67–68
    defining concepts for, 148–149
Csikszentmihalyi, Mihaly
    Being Adolescent, 3–4
    Flow, 2–3
    on flow experiences, 6

Dadio, Beth, 119
"Day's Wait, A" (Hemingway), 182
Definitions
    analytic, 110
    extended, 110–112
    problem with devising, 109–112
Definitions of terms, 104
Diary of Anne Frank, The, 182
Distributive justice, 56–57
Duty to act, 129

Ebert, Roger, 103
Effective teaching, defining, 1–2
Evidence, reviewing, 25–28
Experts, asking students to be, 10
Extended definitions, 110–112

Farmer, James, 146–148
Feedback, providing clear, 9–11
Flow
    among adolescents, 3–4
    characteristics of, 4–5
    experiencing, 2–3
    planning for (*see* Planning for flow)
Flow (Csikszentmihalyi), 2–3
Forensic argument. *See* Mysteries
Foster, Jerry, 118
"Fox and the Crow, The" (Aesop), 179–180
Francis, David Sr., 116
Furigay, Marc, 34

Gandhi, Mohandas K., 146–148
George IV (king, England), 49
Gillray, John, 49
Giraffe Award activity, 113–126
    applying criteria to candidates, 114–126
    award worksheets, 116–122
    introducing, 114
Giraffe Project, 113, 115
Going with the Flow (Smith and Wilhelm), 177–178
Great Debaters, The, 146

Hall, Hallworthy (*Valiant, The*), 182
Harris, Victor, 104–108
Hate, converting standard school unit to conceptual unit for, 184–185
Hemingway, Ernest
    "Day's Wait, A," 182
    Old Man and the Sea, The, 10
Homeostatic experiences, 2–3

Inferences
    building units, 182
    converting standard school unit to conceptual unit, 183–185
    courage, teaching unit on, 185–200
    literature, thinking interpretively about, 179–180
    planning of instructional units, 180–182
    teaching students to make, 177–182
    writing interpretations using, 200
Interpreting. See Inferences

Jena Public High School (Louisiana), 103
Judgments
    backing of, examining, 145–148
    defined, 102
    importance of, 102
    by inferring details from portrait, teaching simple arguments of judgment, 49–65
    learned judgments, 144–145
    making unexamined, 102–103
    "Proper Mascot, The," activity, 42–49
    in real-world (*see* Real-world, judgments in)
    teaching simple arguments of, 41–65
    using criteria to make (*see* Criteria)

Karen Quinlin, case of, 104

Larson, Reed (*Being Adolescent*), 3–4
LaSalle, Mike, 103

Learned judgments, 144–145
Learning, characteristics of flow in, 4–5
Literature, thinking interpretively about, 179–180
Love, converting standard school unit to conceptual unit for, 183–184, 185
"Lunchroom Murder, The" problem, 8, 31–34

Martinez, Victor (*Parrot in the Oven*), 182
McCann, Thomas, 42
Middlemass, Robert (*Valiant, The*), 182
Murder
    cases for discussion, 130–135
    introducing specific cases, 128–130
    judgments, 126–143
    topics for discussion, 143
Mysteries
    "Case of the Dead Musician, The," problem, 34–36
    independence, moving students toward, 30–38
    "Lunchroom Murder, The," problem, 8, 31–34
    "Peacock's Poser," problem, 30–31
    problems, introducing the, 16–25
    report, writing a, 28–30
    reviewing evidence, 25–28
    "Slip or Trip?" problem, 16–17, 30
    teaching arguments of fact through, 15–40
    writing general rules, 25–28
"Mystery of Heroism, A" (Crane), 178, 182, 185–188

National Assessment of Educational Progress, 15, 178
Nicholas, Joseph, 116
Nicomachean Ethics, 150

Old Man and the Sea, The (Hemingway), 10

OPINIONNAIRE: What Is Courage?, 156–160

Optimal experience. *See* Flow

Oxford English Dictionary, 147

Oyez Project, The, 106, 108

Parrot in the Oven (Martinez), 182

Path to Love, The (Chopra), 183–184

"Peacock's Poser" problem, 30–31

Planning for flow, 5–11

  clear feedback, providing, 9–11

  competence and control by students, 5–6

  goals and objectives, clarity and specificity of, 6–8

  instructional units, 180–182

  task complexity, appropriate, 8–9

Policy

  in action, teaching argument of, 70–96

  "Chewing Gum" project, 70–96

  coauthoring with students, 75–78

  collaboration while working on arguments of, 93

  components of arguments of policy, 74–75

  conclusions and recommendations, writing, 75, 86–93

  findings in arguments of policy, 75

  identifying and clarifying problems, 70–71

  interpreting results, 75, 83–86

  introduction, writing the, 74–78

  investigation, conducting, 73–74

  planning investigations, 72–73

  presenting, explaining, and interpreting findings, 75, 78–82

  process, benefits of, 93–96

  researchable problems, 69

  research design and methods, writing about, 74–75, 82–83

  results, writing about, 75, 83–86

  simple arguments of, writing, 67–96

Pretesting, 39–40

Probability, arguments of, 19

Proffitt, Ray, 122

"Proper Mascot, The," activity, 42–49

Quinlan, Karen, 103

"Raid, The" (Tolstoy), 182

Reagan, Ronald (president, U.S.), 110

Real-world, judgments in, 101–112

  definitions, problem with devising, 109–112

  definitions as backing for warrants, 104–108

  importance of judgments, 102

  Karen Quinlin, case of, 104

  Scott v. Harris, case of, 104–108

  sound arguments, constructing and recognizing, 108–109

Reasonable force, 105

Red Badge of Courage, The (Crane), 178, 182

Report, writing, 28–30

Research

  approaches to teaching, 67–68

  coauthoring with students, 75–78

  conclusions and recommendations, writing, 75, 86–93

  design and methods, writing about, 74–75, 82–83

  presenting, explaining, and interpreting findings, 75, 78–82

  researchable problems, 69

Romeo and Juliet (Shakespeare), 183–185

Rules, writing general, 25–28

San Francisco Chronicle, 103

Savarin, Julian, 105

Scalia, Antonin, 105, 107, 108

Schaefer, Jack (*Shane*), 182

Scott, Timothy, 104–108

Scott v. Harris, case of, 104–108

"Scotty Who Knew Too Much, The" (Thurber), 179

Shakespeare, William (*Romeo and Juliet*), 183–185

Shane (Schaefer), 182

"Slip or Trip" problem, 16–17, 30

Small-group discussions
    planning and monitoring, 65–66
    writing criteria in, 155

Smith, Michael W. (*Going with the Flow*), 10, 177–178

Socrates, 103

Souter, David, 106

Specificity in goals and objectives, when planning for flow, 6–8

Stevens, John Paul, 105

Stoic philosophers, 103

"Superman, Lois, and the Rushing Freight Train," 153

Task repetition while working on arguments of policy, 93

Teaching, defining effective, 1–2

Tennessee v. Garner, 106–107

Terrorism, 109–112, 168–169

Thoreau, Henry David, 147, 148

Threat of bodily harm, 108

Through the Looking Glass (Carroll), 108, 109

Thurber, James ("Scotty Who Knew Too Much, The"), 179

Tolstoy ("Raid, The"), 182

Torres, Esteban, 120

"Tortoise and the Hare, The," 179

Toulmin, Stephen E., 151

Treat, Lawrence (*Clue Armchair Detective, The*), 30

Valiant, The (Hall and Middlemass), 182

Values, 146

"Voluptuary under horrors of Digestion, A," 49, 50, 60

Warrants, 24–25, 28
    definitions, problem with devising, 109–112
    explications and analyses in, 146, 147
    writing interpretations using, 200

Warriors Don't Cry (Beals), 182

Washington, Betty, 117

"What Constitutes Freedom of Speech?" activity, 172–175

"What Happened to Winston?", 30

"What Is Courage?" activity, 152–172
    courage, writing definition of, 168–172
    criteria, developing and discussing a class list of, 166–168
    introducing writing criteria, 152–154
    OPINIONNAIRE: What Is Courage?, 156–160
    small groups, writing criteria for, 155

Wilhelm, Jeffrey (*Going with the Flow*), 10, 177–178

Wright, Richard (*Black Boy*), 182

Writing criteria, introducing, 152–154

Zone of proximal development, 42